SCHUMPETER, SOCIAL SCIENTIST

SCHUMPETER

SOCIAL SCIENTIST

EDITED BY SEYMOUR E. HARRIS

HARVARD UNIVERSITY PRESS   CAMBRIDGE, MASSACHUSETTS

1951

PREFATORY NOTE

THIS volume is published under the auspices of the *Review of Economics and Statistics*. Of the twenty essays included in this volume, fifteen were published in the May 1951 issue of the *Review of Economics and Statistics*. Eighteen distinguished social scientists here have tried to evaluate the works of a great social scientist, Joseph Alois Schumpeter, and to give the highlights of his life.

Professors Haberler, Hansen, and Mason helped in the planning of this volume. Mrs. Joseph Schumpeter kindly provided the photographs. The responsibility for this volume, however, rests with the editor. Miss Dorothy Wescott, Mrs. Daniel Cheever, and Miss Lillian Buller helped greatly in various editorial and secretarial capacities. My wife helped with the manuscript and proofs.

SEYMOUR E. HARRIS

September 1, 1951

CONTENTS

Joseph Alois Schumpeter
1947

PROFESSOR JOSEPH A. SCHUMPETER

THE following minute was placed upon the records of the Faculty of Arts and Sciences, Harvard University, at the meeting of February 7, 1950:

Joseph Alois Schumpeter, who died on January 8, 1950, in Taconic, Connecticut, was one of the three or four leading economists of his generation and one of the great figures of this University. His erudition was immense and his interests and achievements were by no means limited to economics. The eighteen years he spent at Harvard were years of intense intellectual activity which have left a permanent impress on his colleagues, on hundreds of students, and on his chosen field of study.

Schumpeter was born in Triesch, Moravia, now part of Czechoslovakia, in 1883. His father died shortly after his birth and Schumpeter spent his boyhood in Vienna. He there attended the Theresianum, the famous preparatory school favored by the Austrian aristocracy, and went on to take his law degree in 1906 at the University of Vienna. In the closing years of the Hapsburg Empire, Vienna must have been one of the pleasantest places on earth, especially for those fortunate enough to have been properly born and properly endowed. Schumpeter was so born and so endowed and by all accounts he made the most of his opportunities. Although he became one of the most cosmopolitan of men, the experience of those early years in Vienna never really left him. He remained to the end the cultivated Austrian gentleman of the old school who had seen everything but who found in the succession of events from 1914 onward no very striking evidence of progress.

As is customary in continental universities, economics was taught in Vienna in the Faculty of Law. At the turn of the century, Vienna was, perhaps, the leading center in the world for the study of economics, and Schumpeter had as his teachers Menger and Böhm-Bawerk, two of the most eminent contemporary figures. Although he practised law in Cairo at the international Mixed Court of Egypt for two years after graduation, Schumpeter early indicated his choice of economics as his field of study by the publication in 1908 of his *Das Wesen und Hauptinhalt der theoretischen Nationalökonomie*. This book, appearing when he was barely twenty-five, immediately established his reputation as the ablest among the younger group of Austrian economists and led to his appointment as professor at the University of Czernowitz.

Czernowitz, in Bukovina — now Russian territory — was the easternmost of the universities of Austria-Hungary. Apparently Czernowitz was eastern, indeed, and Schumpeter's Harvard colleagues were later entertained by stories of extra-curricular activities that might well have come out of the Arabian Nights. In 1911, he was called to the University of Graz, where he spent the years of the first World War. His famous *Theorie der wirtschaftlichen Entwicklung* was published in 1912.

Schumpeter's earlier work had developed and refined economic analysis mainly on the basis of static assumptions. The Theory of Economic Development was a path-breaking study of the process of economic change. Later Schumpeter was frequently wont to observe that the whole of a man's intellectual work is usually foreshadowed by what he had done by the age of thirty; a somewhat dismal reflection for those of his colleagues less precocious than he. Schumpeter was twenty-nine when he published the Theory of Economic Development and much of his great work since that date represents an elaboration and development of ideas which he had by then already sketched out. His conception of the entrepreneur as the innovator, the agent of economic change, his brilliant but disputed theory of interest, his view of business cycles as the product of innovation and of the relation of innovation to the process of economic development, even his view of the rise and prospective decline of capitalism, are either stated or foreshadowed in his early work.

In 1913, Schumpeter made his first visit to the United States, as Austrian Exchange Professor at Columbia University, from which he received an honorary degree. He returned to his native country just before the outbreak of the first World War. During the war, though he took no active part in politics, Schumpeter's sentiments favored the minority anti-German group in the Austrian government and in circles around the imperial court. This was typical; throughout his life he was usually to be found in the minority, particularly on issues concerning which the majority view might be considered to be nationalistic or chauvinistic. In 1928, when one of the writers of this Minute visited Schumpeter in Bonn, he was surprised to hear him declare quite openly that the administration of Rhine cities by the French during their occupation was the best administration these cities had received within memory — an opinion which could hardly have been popular in that neighborhood. World War II again found him in the minority, this time with respect to the national policies of his adopted country. The years of the second World War must have been among the most somber and depressing of his life. Out of sympathy with the policies of this country and out of touch with many of his friends, Schumpeter buried himself in his professional work, unhappily watching the decline of much that he considered valuable in the western world.

Most of Schumpeter's life was wholly devoted to teaching and scholarship. But there had occurred immediately after World War I a short foray into politics, first as consultant to the Socialization Commission in Berlin and then as Minister of Finance in Austria's first Republican government. One has the impression that Schumpeter liked neither political life nor his political colleagues. Indeed, much later, in writing of Lord Keynes' political associates, he used the phrase "that intractable wild beast the politician." His incursion into politics was followed by an unhappy business venture during the period when currency inflation in Austria was destroying more than financial values.

Schumpeter was called back to academic life by his appointment in 1925 as Professor of Economics at Bonn on the Rhine. In 1927, he came to Harvard for a year as Visiting Professor, repeated his visit in 1931, and in 1932, became a permanent officer of this University. The time from the beginning of his professorship at Bonn until his death, a period covering twenty-five years, was his second period of incredible productivity. Every year a succession of articles flowed from his pen. He used the English language with a verve and pungency that few of his colleagues could equal. In 1939, there appeared his monumental two-volume work on *Business Cycles;* in 1942, his suggestive and influential *Capitalism, Socialism, and Democracy.* By the time of his death he had nearly completed a history of economic thought that his colleagues believe will for long be the outstanding work in this field. His wife, — Elizabeth Boody Schumpeter — an economist in her own right — who during the twelve years of their married life by her understanding and loving care has greatly contributed to his achievements in teaching and in scholarship, expects to rescue much more of Schumpeter's unpublished work.

His life at Harvard was that of a scholar of international fame whose views were sought by colleagues and students at home and abroad. He was one of the founders of the Econometric Society, its president from 1937 to 1941, and a powerful supporter of the use of exact methods in economics. In 1948 he became president of the American Economic Association, and, just before his death, he had been chosen as the first president of the newly formed International Economic Association.

Gifted with apparently boundless energy, Schumpeter expended it lavishly. He was always available for consultation by students and devoted a great amount of time to advising and guiding young scholars in all parts of the world. His intemperance in the giving of himself to others may well have contributed to his death. Returning to his country house in Connecticut from meetings of the Economic Association in New York, he was in the course of preparing a series of lectures to be given at the University of Chicago when he died peacefully in his sleep. But neither he nor his friends would have wished him to live differently. Vitality was part of him and the lavish expenditure of it his characteristic way of life.

G. Haberler
S. E. Harris
W. W. Leontief
E. S. Mason, *Chairman*

INTRODUCTORY REMARKS

Seymour E. Harris

ON January 8, 1950, a great economist died. Though the economists have a prior claim on him, historians and sociologists also can include him as one of their stars. In his departure, the country of his adoption, the social sciences, and Harvard University, all lost an outstanding scholar, teacher, and personality. As a social scientist, as a colleague in the Department of Economics, and as an editor of the *Review of Economics and Statistics* to whom we often turned for advice and help, Schumpeter richly earned the tribute we pay him in this volume. The contributors are present and former colleagues at Harvard, scholars both here and in Europe, and former students. I should perhaps not distinguish students from colleagues, for I doubt that Schumpeter's formal students learned as much from him as his colleagues.

In this introductory essay, I suggest very briefly the contents of this volume; and include a little biographical material.

II

Schumpeter was convinced that great abilities reside in the relatively few. His adherence to this theory of the elite explains in no small part Schumpeter's system. Thus, among his most important contributions was his analysis of the development process — the origins, growth, and decline of capitalism, the evaluation of the importance of the static and dynamic for the understanding of economic phenomenon. (Indeed, his static state was in some respects narrower than the models of others, since he excluded interest, profits, and in some respects monopoly, for example; and in some ways, broader since he allowed increases of population.[1])

Schumpeter's theory of economic development, which in its larger manifestation was a theory of the origins, functioning, and decline of capitalism, blossomed out into a theory of cycles and capitalism and socialism and largely colored his theory of money.[2]

Innovation is the catalyst in the whole system; innovation by the gifted few accounts for concentration and bunching of investments — not merely new discoveries but also new combinations of factors of production. In turn, this pressure upon limited resources and savings accounts for inflationary pressures and expansion in the supply of money. (Here is an ultra-modern theory of the inflation process introduced even before Robertson's great book, the *Banking Policy and the Price Level*.[3]) Soon the innovators are joined by the numerous imitators, with the resultant excess of investment and strains on the monetary system.[4]

In other aspects of the Schumpeterian system this emphasis on the gifted few also stands out. Monopoly gains are the result of the contributions of the innovators; and correct monopoly policy would not deny these monopolists an excess of price over short-run marginal costs, for this is a necessary cost of economic progress. In any case these gains, in a dynamic economy, cannot be long-lived, since the process of "creative destruction" continuously levels existing monopoly positions while creating new ones. The growth of a trustified society, by making innovation the automatic and largely impersonal contribution of a few large corporations, tends, as Mason emphasizes, to weaken the role assigned by Schumpeter to the capitalist elite. But such eclipse as the capitalist elite might suffer is only a prelude to the domination of society by another elite.

Schumpeter's support of the elite is also

[1] On his use of static and dynamic, see especially the essays by Machlup, Smithies, Chamberlin, and Stolper, below.

[2] A discussion of the origins and decline of capitalism will be found in Paul Sweezy's essay. For a discussion of the theory of money, see Marget's essay below.

[3] Cf. Marget and Haberler below on the monetary aspects of this problem.

[4] Cf., below, Hansen on the cyclical analysis of Schumpeter (and especially on the debts he owed to Wicksell, Spiethoff, Cassel, Tugan-Baranowsky), and Schneider, on his debts to J. B. Clark, Irving Fisher, and others.

evident in Wright's essay. Schumpeter's concept of democracy was a mechanistic, not an ethical, one; he had no penchant for theories of equality. As Smithies suggests, Schumpeter urged that the gains of business should not be jeopardized by high taxation, the welfare state, and the like; the masses would profit from the much larger output attainable if government did not put tax sands into the gears of the economic machine. Similarly, Schumpeter warned against anti-monopoly policies dictated by the politicians apparently favoring the masses against the few, for he was distrustful of the politicians. In his debate with Keynes, both oral and written, he emphasized the difference between the theory of full employment (associated with the scribbling of the intellectuals, hostile to business, and writing without responsibility) and the public policy likely to emerge. Even in his prognosis pointing toward socialism as the ultimate system, he hoped the way would be prepared by the training of the planners, managers, etc.; and he objected to the premature laboristic socialism currently in vogue.[5]

III

Schumpeter, like so many other great men, made his important contributions when he was young, in the "sacred fertile third decade," as he sometimes referred to the youthful twenties. In a moving tribute to Schumpeter, Paul and Alan Sweezy reveal what Schumpeter meant to those in their twenties.[6] Schumpeter had contributed importantly by the time he was 25, and had made his significant advances by the time he was around 30. From 1906, when he was 23, to 1917, when he was 34, he had, as Schneider demonstrates, developed his major contributions. In his *Business Cycles* and in his *Capitalism, Socialism and Democracy*, he built on his earlier works. As Hansen points out, the parallel of his early work on cycles, which presented brilliantly the broad outlines of his theory in summary form, and his massive two volumes on *Business Cycles*, replete with historical statements, sociological and institutional materials, is suggestive of Malthus'

early *Essay on Population* and his later voluminous work. It was not always clear (cf. Smithies) to what extent the masses of statistical and institutional materials used in the two-volume *Business Cycles* were mobilized to *prove* or to *test* Schumpeter's earlier cyclical theories.

Even more striking was his *Das Wesen und Hauptinhalt der theoretischen Nationalökonomie (Nature and Principal Content of Theoretical Economics)*, published in 1908 at the age of 25: "The book, nevertheless, touches on all the central problems of theory and foreshadows the approaches toward their solution which Schumpeter elaborated in his later works. Even the first outline contains nearly all the thoughts that only later came to full maturity. The concepts of statics and dynamics, the imputation problem, questions of price theory, the distribution theory, the principles of the theory of money, the method of variations, interest as a phenomenon in economic development — all these are found in this work." (Schneider)

Perhaps the most relevant tribute to Schumpeter's precociousness is a statement by his former colleague, Professor Spiethoff: "One scarcely knows which is the more amazing, that a man of 25 and 27 should shape the very foundations of his science, or that a man of 30 should write the history of that discipline." [7]

I am interested here in Schumpeter's precociousness in part because I believe it illuminates some of his weakness as well as strength. It is symptomatic that Schumpeter did not share or utilize effectively the most important advances of the last generation: Keynesian economics, the theory of monopolistic competition, and econometrics. (Samuelson's explanation below, that "he was too self-conscious an artist to let old age clutter up the aesthetic life-line laid down by the genius of youth," is suggestive and charitable but not adequate.) These developments all came substantially after Schumpeter had evolved his own system. (The reader should, however, compare the essays below by Marget and Stolper, who are more generous concerning Schumpeter's later absorptive qualities.)

---

[5] Cf. Smithies and Mason, below.
[6] See the essay by Paul Sweezy.

[7] Arthur Spiethoff, "Josef Schumpeter in Memoriam," *Kyklos*, III, No. 4 (1949).

To econometrics and monopolistic competition, he paid lip service. His attitude toward mathematical economics and econometrics puzzled his friends. In many statements, he insisted that mathematics and econometrics were the path of the future. Yet, though he worked on his mathematics, he never put it to use in his writings. Unlike his hopeful announcements about the contributions of mathematics in his first writings in 1906, in his latest he expressed doubts (cf. Machlup).

Professor Tinbergen, also puzzled by the differences between his avowals of faith and his practice, shows that Schumpeter was not only critical of econometrics but his treatment was even alien to it; and perhaps that he did not even understand the econometric models. His absorption with the exogenous approach (shock) to the trade cycle, his neglect of the endogenous approach, and his attack on the Kalecki models ("undeveloped mechanisms are like a *perpetuum mobile*" or "the starting impulse [in Kalecki's theory] might have been some trouble in the apple-growing industry at the time Adam and Eve dwelt in Paradise") — these suggest a de-emphasis of the endogenous approach which the econometricians tended to emphasize, for in their view the mechanism was subject to treatment whereas the shocks were not. Incidentally, Marget and Stolper, in their stimulating essays, seem to overlook Schumpeter's failure to incorporate econometrics into his system.

Chamberlin shows that, though Schumpeter paid lip service to monopolistic competition, he never incorporated it into his system: the fruitful marriage of the Schumpeterian system and monopolistic competition is still in the future. Schumpeter contended that the demand curve of the firm under conditions of product differentiation was essentially highly elastic; and he would not accept monopolistic competition as a permanent feature of the *static* model. Time and again he emphasized the importance of differentiation, selling costs, and the like, and yet his static system was essentially one of pure competition.

Schumpeter remained to the end *extremely* hostile to Keynesian economics — even though, as Marget well shows, he was one of the early contributors to the aggregative approach. His hostility to Keynes stemmed in part from a fear of short-run action, from a distrust of those who were to operate on the economy, from his awareness of the bridge between theory and its application, from the support given by the system to the intellectuals who seek policies not oriented to the interest of business, from the doubts raised against the most revered aspects of capitalism (e.g., thrift), and from the essentially static assumptions of Keynes.

The reader will find in Marget's essay an evaluation of Schumpeter relative to Keynes. In particular, the editor welcomes Marget's presentation of original contributions by Schumpeter in the field of money and income: the income approach, the segmentation of monetary flows and corresponding flows of goods and services — also essential parts of the Keynesian system. It is not my intention to enter this arena, for there is plenty of credit for both. Indeed, Marget is probably correct when he stresses Schumpeter's awareness of the continuity of thought (as Stolper and Usher also stress the importance of his historical approach, his building on Walras, Marx and others). That Schumpeter was more generous than Keynes in acknowledging his debt to his predecessors should not blind us to the great achievements of Keynes. Taussig used to say that to find earlier statements of a contribution was not difficult; what was especially germane was who put over the idea.

Schumpeter's distrust of Keynesian economics was costly. As Hansen and Smithies show, he could have improved his system had he been prepared to incorporate into it the advances in the analysis of interest, the consumption function, the multiplier, the marginal efficiency of capital.

In short, the world is greatly indebted to Schumpeter for his important contributions, primarily in his fruitful third decade. It was unfortunate that he had to a substantial degree frozen his system by the World War I period. A thawing out would have added to his stature. Undoubtedly the loss of eight potentially fruitful years in government and business, and the overwhelming ambition to fill out a program which would have frightened most, account in part for the failure to merge the newer economics with his own. In spite of his considerable knowledge of mathematics, unimpressed by the claims of the new monopolistic competition school, intolerant of Keynes and Keynesians, Schumpeter continued on his own course.

The reader should not conclude from this discussion that Schumpeter did not vigorously try to understand and absorb the newer economics. It is difficult to think of an economist, fifty years of age or over when the large advances began to be made in all three fields under discussion, who made a greater effort to understand and profit from these advances. Few, if any, economists of his age took the trouble that he did to discuss with students the issues raised in all these areas. Finally, the writer would mislead if the impressions obtained from this section were that Schumpeter stopped thinking, writing, and creating in (say) 1914. His contributions, both oral and written, after 1914 were of first-rate importance. But they were primarily super-structures based on foundations built in the years 1906 to 1917. They might have been more.

Although his great innovations stem from his youth, a series of incisive comments on the course of development continued to flow from his pen. His last great work was the *History of Economic Analysis*, close to completion at his death. Fortunately, Elizabeth Schumpeter is working heroically at the task of bringing out this book, which will reflect Schumpeter's striking command of the history of economic thought as well as his unusual capacity to relate it to relevant disciplines; and the book will also reflect Schumpeter's superior analytic powers. Social scientists owe a great debt to Mrs. Schumpeter for completing this work.

IV

Schumpeter's contributions were so numerous and varied that even a listing of them would occupy much space. The essays in this issue will aid the reader in evaluating the advances made by this remarkable man. Note in particular the advances in many fields (listed by Schneider), the integration of history and theory (Usher and Stolper), the unparalleled contribution in money, e.g., the income approach, income velocity, forced savings, etc. (Marget); the emphasis on dynamic economics; the study of the origin, functioning, and decline of capitalism (especially Sweezy [8] and Usher); the early recourse to interdisciplinary approaches,[9] with the expert use *inter alia* of history, sociology, statistics, economic theory (Schneider and Machlup); the dominant role given to the innovator (Usher); the insistence upon the importance of all methodologies (Machlup); the early integration of credit instability and cyclical indisposition (Marget and Hansen); the reinterpretation of modern economic history (Usher); the emphasis on the over-all functioning of the economic system in the appraisal of attacks on individual business units (Mason); the dynamic aspects of the rate of interest and profits (Haberler and Machlup); the emphasis on the delicate nature of the capitalist mechanism and its sensitiveness to short-run action of the politicians (Smithies).

V

As a friend and colleague of Schumpeter for almost twenty years, I have a few recollections to add.

A little volume published early in 1934 reminds me of several traits of Schumpeter, and particularly his loyalty to friends, expressed in part in a penchant for cooperative enterprises. This volume resulted from monthly meetings of a group known as the Schumpeter group (facetiously, as the eight wise men). For many years this group (D. V. Brown, Chamberlin, Haberler, Leontief, Mason, Opie, Schumpeter, O. H. Taylor, and the writer) met once a month for a Lucullan dinner, listened to a serious paper, and discussed it, not infrequently well past midnight. Out of these meetings grew, in 1934, the *Economics of the Recovery Program* by seven Harvard economists (Haberler had not yet joined us and Opie had left). This book was largely the product of Schumpeter's enthusiasm for cooperative ventures with his associates, as well as his general distrust of the embryonic New Deal Economics of 1933. Even then, as might be expected, he was distrustful

---

[8] To be included in the forthcoming volume; see footnote 2.

[9] Cf. von Beckerath, "Schumpeter as a Sociologist," *Weltwirtschaftliches Archiv*, 1950, and pages 110–118, below.

of the hybrid economic society — one that did not allow the capitalist system to function and yet would not tolerate socialism. I recall the many lively discussions of the book, and particularly Schumpeter's determination to argue out points of difference, as well as my reluctant yielding to his persuasive power.

The book was not a great success, and it was not a good book. Disgusted with its attack on the New Deal, the St. Louis *Post Dispatch* captioned the book "Harvard's Second Team Goes to Bat." An interesting sidelight of the book was Schumpeter's great concern over the inadequacies of his English style. Our assurances failed to reassure him; and he continued to fret. Perhaps he had some consolation when *his* essay was chosen for a book of readings on the use of English in the social sciences, as a model of writing. Anyone familiar with Schumpeter's writings knows that his style is pungent and any deficiencies are more than made up by the originality of ideas and phrasing.[10]

Schumpeter's loyalty to his friends and colleagues was evident not merely in his anxiety to work with his much younger colleagues at the expense of his more serious work to which he was devoted. He made it a point to be interested in every project in which any of us became involved. If you ever failed to tell him about your work, you were sure to be invited to lunch and to be asked to discuss with him your latest book. I always dreaded these lunches, though Schumpeter was always a most interesting and convivial companion. The point is that a luncheon with him was an exhausting experience. It would not be long before he knew more about the subject than the expositor, and soon he would begin sticking pins into the arguments, offering suggestions and debating every point with vigor. After one of these luncheons, I was of no use for the afternoon, though the net gain was large; but Schumpeter was almost certain to return to the classroom or spend arduous consultation hours with his students. In view of his generous criticisms of the work of his students and colleagues, I could never understand his failure to ask counsel from his friends. He never, to my knowledge, asked any one to read his manuscripts, though he sometimes would ask help on some particular problem.

His loyalty to his friends knew no bounds. He never entertained the petty hypocrisies that even close friends sometimes indulge in. His friends were always right, and it made no difference whether they were present or absent.

It is significant that economists of all shades of views and opinions — extreme 19th century liberals, semi-Keynesians, Keynesians, and Marxists — would join in an enthusiastic tribute to Schumpeter. From the appraisal of Schumpeter, it would be difficult to discover the extent of agreement or disagreement of the various writers with his work. Surely, no other great figure has received a similar tribute from economists of all schools. The explanation in part is that what mattered with Schumpeter was the quality of the man's work, and in part his insistence that the work of the scientist should not become an instrument of the policy maker. (As Mason suggests, it is not likely that Schumpeter's work can be used as a guide to the policy maker.)

Paul Sweezy has commented on one remarkable trait of Schumpeter's: he was essentially a conservative who disliked Keynesianism and New Dealism, which tinkered with the capitalist mechanism, and he had no love for communism or Marxism, which would supplant his system. (This did not prevent him from envisaging socialism as the successor to capitalism; and, unlike Keynes, he acknowledged the brilliance of Marx.) But differences in ideology did not affect his personal relations. He respected and liked Paul Sweezy, a Marxist; though he heartily disapproved of my penchant for Keynes and New Deal economics, this disapproval in no way affected our friendship. His appraisal of men was largely in terms of the quality of the job done, given the ideological presuppositions. In his personal relations he much preferred the bright Marxist or the Keynesian to the dull conservative. He once made this witticism: "When I see those who espouse my cause, I begin to wonder about the validity of my position."

[10] In fact, his English seems to be much better than his German — compare the sentence quoted by Paul Sweezy (page 123, below) as an example of an involved and almost incomprehensible sentence in the German.

VI

As Samuelson and Sweezy have pointed out, Schumpeter as a teacher was unusual. To understand Schumpeter as a teacher, one must also understand his views on the place of a university. He never quite understood the difference between a Continental and an American university. Nothing upset him more than the "nursing" of undergraduates in tutorial work at Harvard. The tutorial system to him meant an unforgivable waste of financial and human resources. Again, his worship of youth contributed to this position. That young scholars should have to give their best energies to wearing conferences with students, most of whom would not become important citizens, instead of to scientific work galled him. It never seemed clear to him that Harvard College was trying primarily to turn out good citizens and not scholars and that the vast funds of the College were made available largely for this purpose, or if aware of this, he did not approve. Nor did he seem to realize that graduate instruction, to which he was devoted, was financed in part by the funds made available by diversions of funds from Harvard College.

In view of Schumpeter's theory of education, it is a litle difficult to understand the vast energies he poured forth on his teaching. Given his remarkable abilities, it was a sheer waste of energies for him to teach three courses (and if he had his way, he would have taught almost every course), and devote endless hours to consultation. His consultation hours were sacred. Any student, undergraduate or graduate, or colleague could always consult with him as long as he or she wished. Although the brilliant students in particular flocked around him and often exploited him, he was accessible to all. And unlike many first-rate theorists, he was not intolerant of those who dealt with descriptive and institutional and statistical problems. Quite the reverse. He realized that all help was welcome and to each according to his ability. Schumpeter soon learned about the problems, scientific and personal, of a large number of students. It was not unusual for a casual passerby in the corridor outside Schumpeter's office in Littauer Center to hear him discuss with vigor and enthusiasm (say) A's thesis on the production function, B's honors thesis on the exogenous aspects of the trade cycle, C's book on *The Theory of Capitalist Development*. The strain of these conferences contributed to his untimely death. His friends time and again urged him to cut his hours, and gradually, under the pressure of lessened energies and advancing age, he reluctantly reduced them. Few scholars, if any, could match Schumpeter in the broad command of his subject matter and his acquaintance with the work of scholars everywhere.

Although these activities helped the students and scholars and also contributed toward Schumpeter's renown all over the world, they also diverted him from his main task. And I am sure that Schumpeter was indulging to some extent in the same mal-allocation of physical energies that aroused such resentment in him when the University *seemed* to put excessive burdens on young scholars. A typical example was a railroad trip after a fatiguing meeting. Either by accident or plan, a student of average ability was on that train. Schumpeter spent exactly seven hours going over the student's thesis outline with his characteristic vigor and enthusiasm (heard throughout the car). Generous? Yes. A wise use of his waning energy? No. Endearing? Yes.

In the University, Schumpeter's prestige was not what it should have been. This was in no small part his own fault and points up some of his weaknesses. As Smithies shows, his great success with the young and the old did not extend to his contemporaries. In the Department of Economics, there was a general awareness that Schumpeter was a great scholar, though this was not a universal appraisal. His occasional lack of tact, a tendency toward exhibitionism, a desire to be the center of attention, a low evaluation of some of his colleagues which he did not conceal too well, his popularity with students and young colleagues — all of these alienated some of his contemporaries and reduced his influence. The fact is that his influence in the Department was surprisingly small.

Relative to the issues under discussion, the reader may find the following of some interest.

In the first place, he certainly had a tendency in general conversation to *épater le bourgeois*. He liked to take an opposite point of view, in order to provoke discussion. He often pushed certain theories to a point of extravagance. Another failing may be mentioned in this connection. He cultivated the appearance of omniscience. He held forth on a great range of topics, on some of which he was thoroughly expert, but on others of which he may have derived his views from the few pages of a book at which he had happened to glance. The air of authority was the same in both cases.

The above is from Harrod's *Life of Keynes*; [11] but Schumpeter's friends might have guessed that this paragraph was from a biography of Schumpeter. Brilliant men often behave in this manner.

In the University, Schumpeter was not a leading figure. Many did not know him; and others, unaware of his large contributions to economics, history, and sociology, and irritated by his tendency to lecture rather than discuss, were inclined to consider him an arrogant and unimpressive fellow. Nor did courageous attacks on American foreign policy in the forties endear him to his colleagues. These pronouncements reflected a peculiar trait in Schumpeter: his unwillingness to stand with the majority, whether it be on matters of foreign policy or an appraisal of the merits of a dry martini. His high distinction as a social scientist was known to few outside the social sciences.

[11] R. F. Harrod, *The Life of John Maynard Keynes* (New York, 1951), p. 468.

In short, Schumpeter was a remarkable man, with energies far beyond those of the average scholar and yet dissatisfied with his inability to work more than 84 hours a week even at 60 and to make more progress with his work. Since he was anxious to finish his life's work, which at the age of 50 encompassed 17 books, including 2 novels, and since he fretted so over lack of progress, it was unfortunate that he did not make the best use of his unusual capacities. Yet this was a matter of conscious choice. Scholar, teacher, lawyer, finance minister, writer, banker — Schumpeter combined a passion for the advance of knowledge in his chosen field with a great zest for living. In this respect, at least, he reminds one of Keynes.

Few will insist that Schumpeter was a perfect man. He had many faults. Yet with all of this, Schumpeter was a great and a fine man. Below the superficialities, there was a man of the highest character, the most loyal and devoted of friends, a penetrating and creative mind, a great teacher, and an advisor to any member of the profession who needed his help.[12] No one can possibly fill the vacuum left by his departure. To many of us Harvard will never be the same. We are grateful indeed for the years we shared with him.

[12] Cf. von Beckerath, *op. cit.*

SOME PERSONAL REMINISCENCES ON A GREAT MAN[1]

Ragnar Frisch

THE reader must forgive me for striking a personal note when writing about my beloved friend Joseph Schumpeter. As judged by the frequency with which we actually met, I should perhaps not be entitled to the honor of calling him a personal friend. We lived, indeed, in different countries and saw each other only occasionally. However, on the occasions on which we did meet, I had an intense feeling that emotionally as well as in scientific matters we were very close. And I always knew that when I wanted his support and advice by correspondence he would give it fully and whole-heartedly. Therefore, I cannot think of him otherwise than as a beloved friend whose passing has deprived me of something that was vital and essential in my life.

My first contact with Schumpeter was in the 1920's, before the founding of the Econometric Society. He was one of those with whom I corresponded about the possibility of doing something of an organizational sort to promote econometric work, and he was one of those who contributed most constructively to the idea.

I did not meet him until much later — in Bonn and at Harvard. My first reaction was one of great surprise. How could it be that a man who had long ago produced such imposing scientific works as *Wesen und Hauptinhalt* . . . , etc., could be so *young?* Young by his ways of acting and thinking, full of vivacity, sparkling with intelligence and initiative. Of course, I learned that he was actually younger in years than I had thought, but he was even younger of mind. And he remained young until his last day. When I met him for the last time in February, 1947, at Harvard, I had exactly that feeling of talking to a man just as young as he had ever been. In the home of Alvin H. Hansen one evening he spoke of himself as "staggering towards his grave," but nobody talking with him that evening could believe that that was anything more than one of his usual jokes.

The human characteristics which impressed me most in Schumpeter were his *generosity* and *willingness to listen.* I have never met any person who was so eager to understand the other fellow's point of view and so willing to give credit for any valuable idea. Schumpeter was never satisfied until he had got to the bottom of the other fellow's thought and had succeeded in putting himself in his place. This cordiality of the atmosphere in which a conversation with Schumpeter always took place was even more to be remembered than his sparkling intelligence and great erudition.

We must appreciate this attitude all the more when we think of how far it is from that which we encounter most frequently amongst economists, statisticians, and mathematicians. I do not know whether these groups are any worse than other scientific groups, but it is a fact that in meetings and discussions we find too often an overcritical atmosphere. Too many of us are too preoccupied in expounding our own theories with little regard to those of others, always being on the alert to point out that what was said by the last speaker was only a special case of what we ourselves had published already on such and such an occasion. Schumpeter's attitude was the exact opposite of this. As Professor Haberler said in his excellent essay on Schumpeter in the August, 1950, issue of the *Quarterly Journal of Economics*: "By listening to Schumpeter's lectures and studying his reading assignments and suggestions, students could never have found out that he himself had ever written anything on those subjects."

These human qualities are just the ones we like to see in a person by whom we are to be reprimanded, in case it is needed. I well remember one of the — let us hope few — occasions on which I had written a critical article on a methodological question and had expressed myself in an unnecessarily strong and bad-tempered way. I shall never forget the sweetness and effectiveness with which Schumpeter put me right in a private conversation. Such

---

[1] This article is reprinted here with permission of the author, *Economie Appliquée*, and *Econometrica*.

things remain as memories for a lifetime and help more than anything else to build our character.

Like most great men, Schumpeter preserved the spontaneity and ability to *play* which is so characteristic of healthy children. I shall never forget one whole Sunday which he and I spent in the home of our mutual friend, Irving Fisher, on Prospect Street, New Haven. We were each of us brimful of things we wanted to talk over with the others. Fisher browsed around in his big office in the basement, which on weekdays was full of secretaries and research assistants, but which on that Sunday was completely quiet. Even though his secretaries were away, Fisher succeeded in producing from his huge files most of the charts and tables he wanted. Schumpeter and I had brought along our own "toys." And so we passed the whole day, having a meal hurriedly when strictly necessary, continually conversing, injecting ideas and receiving suggestions in the most cordial atmosphere. When we thought we had just begun, we found out that it was already late at night.

Schumpeter's system of classifying notes was something I have never been able to understand. In the course of a conversation he would constantly jot down remarks on small bits of paper which he stuck into his pocket in no apparent order. I have always wondered in what sort of receptacles he finally stored them, possibly in barrels. I imagine that the essential thing for him was to memorize the ideas by *writing* them. Whether he had thrown these bits of paper away immediately or had stored them in his barrel, it would probably have amounted to the same thing. The ideas themselves were already sorted and classified in his brain, which seemed to have a capacity without limit.

If I should characterize in a nutshell Schumpeter's position in our science, I might do it by quoting two things told me by one of my young Norwegian friends after he met Schumpeter. The first strong impression he had received was that Schumpeter stood out in our own time as a living representative of the Austrians and the neoclassics, these pioneers and founders. I quite understand his feelings. The younger generation at best read about the Austrians and the neoclassics in books and articles, but it is infinitely more impressive to meet a living person who actually has known many of the outstanding men of that epoch and by this fact can reflect the color of the problems they struggled with. No man was more admirably fitted than Schumpeter to bring down to us the inheritance of that epoch and to present it to us forcefully and in that particular kind of reformulation and with that originality which was necessary to meet the practical needs of our day.

The second impression that my young friend received was that Schumpeter was like a *Moses* who was called upon to lead his people to the land of promise — econometrics — and who should be allowed to *see* it but should not be allowed to enter into it himself. To my mind this interpretation of Schumpeter is very far from the truth.

It all depends on what is meant by econometrics. Econometrics, in the current definition — which was so wholeheartedly accepted by Schumpeter also — stands for a combination of economic theory, statistics, and mathematics. I for one will defend, as Schumpeter did, the position of mathematics in this tri-part combination as strongly as anybody. Mathematics — even the most refined form of mathematics — is a *necessary* tool, but it is only a *tool*. No amount of mathematical technicality, however refined, can ever replace *intuition*, this inexplicable function which takes place in the brain of a great intellect who at the same time understands mathematics and economic theory in a more orthodox sense and who has lived long enough (or, more correctly, intensely enough) to accumulate human experience and a sense of facts. This intuition is an *art*, the art of realistic model building, the art of making realistic abstractions, the art in which such men as Ricardo and Schumpeter excelled. This intellectual activity is and will always be the vital part of our science and *the true criterion of an econometrician*.

It is essentially the same intellectual activity as that we engage in when we discuss "tests of significance." In our economic and stochastic models we develop mathematical tests of significance. Sometimes we do it by very shrewd logical devices. And it is well that this is so. Mathematical tests of significance, confidence intervals, etc., are highly useful concepts. (If I had not thought so, I would not have spent most of my time during the last year lecturing on them.) All these concepts are, however, of *relative* merit only. They have a clearly defined meaning only within the narrow confines of the model in question. I wish it were more clearly and more commonly recognized by all model builders that all the shrewd mathematical tests are of this relative sort. As we dig into the foundation of any economic or stochastic model we will always find a line of demarcation which we cannot transgress unless we introduce another type of test of Significance (this time written with a capital *S*), a test of the *applicability* of the model itself. I well remember how Schumpeter again and again reverted to the question of how we could test the applicability of a model. Something of relevance for this question can, of course, be deduced from mathematical tests properly interpreted, but no such test can ever do anything more than just push the final question one step further back. The final, the highest level of test can never be formulated in mathematical terms.

To illustrate what I mean, let me quote a naïve "econometrician" well versed in the theory of linear regressions, including the formulae for the standard errors of the regression coefficients. With a view to developing an equation useful for economic policy-making in the period subsequent to World War II, he had thrown a number of economic variables — I do not recall which — into a linear regression analysis. Since he had only yearly data over some twenty-five years, he found to his great dismay that the standard errors of his regression coefficients were deplorably high. And hence his conclusion: "If I could only extend my yearly data twenty-five or fifty years further back and thus *increase my number of observations*, I should be able to get regression coefficients whose sig-

nificance would be increased to such and such a level."

Absurdities of this sort are unthinkable in Schumpeter's analysis. They are unthinkable because his wisdom and erudition and historical sense made him put the emphasis on the Significance (again written with a capital *S*), that is, on the applicability of the model itself to the problem at hand and to the nature of the data as they emerge in an ever changing world.

Schumpeter was able to understand and use mathematics for his purposes. He was remarkably able to *utilize* theorems developed by others who were more advanced in mathematical technicalities than he was himself. He knew mathematics not only to the point of understanding that it is a fundamental tool in our science. He knew it also to the point of understanding that it is only a tool and that it must be subordinated to the general intuitional and philosophical interpretation. The same applies to the utilization of data which the statisticians could put at his disposal. Therefore, in my mind, Schumpeter not only saw the land of promise from a distance, but in the best sense of the word he actually entered into it.

A high standing intellectually is not always combined with a high standing from the human viewpoint. In Joseph Schumpeter the two were combined into a personality never to be forgotten. He was one of those rare personalities who make us feel that this world is not only the world of hatred, lack of intelligence, and unwillingness to listen that manifests itself daily in important affairs all over the globe. He was one of those few who showed us that there also exist love, intelligence, and willingness to listen, and that, therefore, this world is bearable after all. This beam of light he gave us, and for that reason so much darkness was left behind him when he passed away.

MEMORIAL: JOSEPH ALOIS SCHUMPETER, 1883–1950[1]

Arthur Smithies

I. The First Three Decades 1883–1914

JOSEPH ALOIS SCHUMPETER was born at Triesch in Moravia on February 8, 1883. His father was a textile manufacturer and his mother, Joan Marguerite, the daughter of Julius Gruener, a physician in Wiener-Neustadt; he was their only child. Nothing more is known for certain about his forebears. His physical appearance, inherited from his father, suggests a mixed ancestry. He once toyed with the idea that the name Schumpeter came from Italy, but he could find no evidence to support it. As far as we know, the Schumpeter tree flowered luxuriantly only once; now it is extinct.

His father died when Schumpeter was four years old. The young widow, then only twenty-six, married Sigismund von Kéler, lieutenant-general in the Austro-Hungarian army, seven years later. Without doubt, his mother was the most important personal influence in Schumpeter's life. She was handsome, talented, and ambitious for her son. His devotion to her continued without diminution or disillusion not only to the end of her life but to the end of his.

Schumpeter seems to have regarded his stepfather as a distinguished and impressive figure — witness the frequency of military metaphors in his writing — but hardly as a father. Von Kéler was in command of all Austrian troops stationed in Vienna — a position of social as well as military eminence. From the age of ten, therefore, Schumpeter grew up in the aristocratic milieu of prewar Vienna. From 1893 to 1901 he attended the Theresianum, an exclusive school for sons of the aristocracy, that, like the corresponding English Public Schools, was distinguished for its classical education.

From 1901 to 1906, he attended the University of Vienna as a student of law and economics, and received the degree of doctor of law in 1906. Although he had an almost infinite capacity for work, he must have devoted most of his energies to economics, judging by what he accomplished. He attended the seminars of Inama-Sternegg, the medieval historian and statistician, of Wieser, a sociologist as well as an economist, and of Böhm-Bawerk, the single-minded economic theorist. He debated in seminars with Otto Bauer and Rudolf Hilferding, two of the most brilliant young Marxists of their day. He wrote papers on statistical method, and acquired an immense admiration for the general equilibrium system of Walras, whom he always regarded as the greatest of all theorists. At the end of his five years at the university, he was ready to launch himself as a theorist of great acumen and as a historian of wide learning. More important, the essentials of his "vision" of the social and economic process had already been formed.

In 1906 and 1907, Schumpeter spent several months in England. Many of the doors of English society were open to him. He lived as a fashionable young man in London, visited country houses, and intermingled his social life with occasional visits to Oxford and Cambridge. I have always felt that that year in England was the happiest in his life. He found English manners and English institutions completely congenial. Prewar England was to him the apotheosis of the civilization of capitalism. And only a few years ago he said in a letter: "I never really could understand anyone with the least chance to play some role at a measurable distance from Downing Street, doing anything else."

In 1907, he married an Englishwoman, Gladys Ricarde Seaver, who was twelve years his senior. The marriage very soon proved a

[1] Reprinted with permission of the author and *The American Economic Review*. Mrs. Schumpeter has published a complete bibliography of the author's work in the *Quarterly Journal of Economics* for August, 1950. I am also much indebted to her for allowing me to read Schumpeter's notes and diaries and to quote from them. I am also indebted to many friends and colleagues of Schumpeter's who read the manuscript of this article, especially Professor Haberler who saved me a great deal of labor by allowing me to take facts and dates from the manuscript of his article (pages 24–47, below). My greatest debt, of course, is to Schumpeter himself for his incomparable conversations during the last eighteen years.

failure, but was not formally dissolved until 1920, presumably because of legal difficulties and the fact that, at that time, Schumpeter belonged to the Catholic church. Thus from the age of twenty-four to the age of thirty-seven, he was precluded from the normal family life I am convinced he would have liked to have. As it was, he lived the life of a *fin de siècle* romantic with all his brilliance and intensity; he convinced his friends, and possibly himself for a time, that that was what he really wanted. His unsettled and inadequate personal life may have accounted in part for his prodigious scientific output. Judging by the comments he frequently made on the sedative effects of successful marriage on the formative years of a scientist's career, he may well have felt that the world had gained what he had lost.

In 1907, Schumpeter and his wife went to Egypt, where he practiced law and managed the financial affairs of an Egyptian princess. In the latter capacity, he performed the financial miracle of cutting rents on the princess's estates in half and doubling her income — by the simple device of appropriating to his own use no more than he was legally entitled to. While in Cairo, his first book *Wesen und Hauptinhalt der theoretischen Nationalökonomie* was published. In this book, he established his mastery of traditional theory and gave some promise of what was to come.

His career in Egypt was cut short by the onset of Malta fever. He returned to Vienna in 1909 and in the same year accepted a professorship in economics at the University of Czernowitz. Although he found the life of that city to his liking, he considered most of his academic colleagues dull and provincial — whatever their merits in their particular fields. He liked to shock them by appearing at faculty meetings in riding boots and aroused unfavorable comment by dressing for dinner when he and his wife were dining alone. But this type of amusement did not compensate him for the distance from Vienna.

In 1911, he was appointed to the University of Graz through the influence of Böhm-Bawerk with the Ministry of Education, despite a solid vote against him by a faculty that was reluctant to open its arms to the *enfant terrible* from Czernowitz. And it never did. Although he carried a heavy teaching load, he contrived to spend much of his time in the national capital — a practice he deplored among his Harvard colleagues — until his resignation from Graz in 1921. He spent the academic year 1913–1914 as visiting professor at Columbia and returned to Austria on the eve of the First World War.

By then the fateful third decade — the years of creative achievement, in his view — was over. *The Theory of Economic Development* was published in 1912 and presented his analysis of the economic aspects of capitalism in what turned out to be virtually its final form. In this work he achieved a directness of exposition and a cogency of argument that he was never again to attain. With *Economic Development*, Schumpeter became famous: the book has become a classic, yet, by his own exacting standards, he failed. He had set out to conquer the world of economics, but he got caught in a web of controversy with Böhm-Bawerk and the Austrian School. Before the world had a chance to consider its verdict, it was embroiled in the First World War. Not till more than thirty years later, so far as I can discern, did he consider trying again for the same kind of success. In 1946, he wrote: ". . . two months were real work and spelled progress in what I described to interested publishers as a book that should do from my standpoint what Keynes' *General Theory* did from his (which Washington agency now prosecutes dishonest advertising?). But then I had to break off to invest the remaining two months in my *History* which just won't go decently." What there is of this book probably exists only in his undecipherable Austrian shorthand; no manuscript has yet been found.

In 1914, he published his brief and brilliant *Dogmengeschichte* which laid the first foundations for his massive *History of Economic Analysis*, which was still unfinished at the time of his death. Although his basic ideas on sociology can be traced to this early period, they were slower in maturing than his purely economic analysis. His theory of imperialism appeared in 1919, his first major article on socialism in 1920, and his theory of social classes in 1927. And it was not till 1942 that he was willing to systematize his sociology in *Capitalism, Socialism and Democracy*. Although in some respects this is his greatest work, he never thought highly of it; and despite his brilliant performance in the field, and his insistence on its importance, he persisted in regarding sociology as the proper occupation for a tired or spent economist.

II. Interlude 1914–1925

The war years must have been unhappy ones for him. He was, and described himself as, a pacifist. Although he had no moral objection to war and admired military prowess, he was temperamentally utterly averse to violence and, above all, clearly saw the destruction that was being wrought to everything he valued. He took an active [2] part in the intrigues to negotiate a separate peace for Austria in 1916. In his *Crisis of the Tax State* (1918), he put forward his reconstruction proposals to achieve financial stability through a capital levy, a balanced budget, and foreign borrowing, and to rely for reconstruction on the liberated forces of private enterprise.

Late in 1918 he acted as consultant to the Socialization Commission in Berlin, apparently in a nonpolitical capacity. But in 1919, the incredible happened. He agreed to become finance minister, under socialist sponsorship, in the coalition government of the Austrian Republic. From the beginning the cards were stacked against him. Whatever their motives in appointing him, the socialists distrusted him because he was not a socialist; the right wing distrusted him because he had been the socialists' candidate; and the bureaucrats distrusted him because, from their point of view, he was an amateur. In his personal life he refused to compromise with bourgeois or proletarian standards of respectability; and he was touched, without justification, by the breath of political scandal.[3] But more important he differed basically from the socialists on Austria's external policy. Led by Otto Bauer, they supported union with Germany, while Schumpeter believed that Austria must rely on support from the West. Before he had the opportunity to present his financial proposals to the par-

liament, he was forced to resign, in the fall of 1919, and inflation ran its inevitable course. Schumpeter was always unwilling to discuss this episode, so one can only conjecture as to his motivation. His sense of history and his modesty would prevent him from believing that he alone could work miracles; his seriousness would prevent him from being merely amused by the ironies of the situation — although they doubtless did appeal to him. There were no compelling personal loyalties. But I suspect there was a strong vein of Quixotism in his nature that on this and other occasions led him to attempt the impossible.

He was then only thirty-seven, with the achievements and the experience of a lifetime behind him. In view of his opinion that all truly creative work is done before the age of thirty, he may well have felt that the time had come to cut loose from intellectual life and start another career — this time as a practitioner of capitalism rather than its diagnostician. In any event, he became president of the Biedermannbank, a private bank in Vienna, and for the time being his scientific work practically ceased. Partly because of economic conditions and partly because of the dishonesty of some of his associates, the bank failed in 1924. Schumpeter lost his personal fortune and went heavily into debt. Characteristically, rather than take advantage of the bankruptcy laws, he paid his creditors in full, partly by writing for the *Deutsche Volkswirt* and partly from his academic earnings over the next ten years. After the disaster he decided to return to the world of scholarship, and accepted a professorship at the University of Bonn in 1925. Again the world profited from his misfortune, and he assured his place in the history of economic thought.

III. The Years of Maturity 1925–1950

Shortly before he went to Bonn he married Annie Reisinger, the twenty-one-year-old daughter of the caretaker of the apartment house in which his mother lived in Vienna. He had known her for at least the past five years, and his mother and he sent her to schools in Paris and Switzerland to equip her to be his wife. She was his romantic escape from the barren romanticism of his past. When she died

[2] It is not known precisely what part he took or how active it was, but I do recall one conversation in which he said, "the last time we saw the Emperor."

[3] See Haberler's article regarding the "Alpine Montan Gesellschaft" affair (pages 34–35, below).

in childbirth within a year of their marriage, Schumpeter was heartbroken and mourned her for the rest of his life. In the same year his mother died at the age of sixty-five. These two great personal losses must have contributed greatly to his feeling that there was not much in store for him but his work, and probably had a good deal to do with his decision to remove himself far from the scenes of his sorrows and disappointments.

Although in ordinary circumstances, he probably would have found the atmosphere of Bonn entirely congenial, as it was he was unable to settle down there. He visited Harvard in 1927–1928 and again in the winter of 1930. He returned to Europe by way of Japan — the country that has probably extended him more esteem and admiration than any other. It is not surprising that, at that particular stage of its development, Japan should have greeted Schumpeter with such enthusiasm. His acclaim in Japan leads one to reflect on what might have happened in Europe had he written *Economic Development* at the same time as Marshall wrote his *Principles* rather than twenty years after. In 1932, he moved permanently to Harvard — in a mood of resignation rather than enthusiasm. In this I doubt that he was motivated by a desire to leave the sinking ship of Europe. Temperamentally, he was more inclined to go down with it.

For twenty-five years, from the time he went to Bonn till his death, he subjected himself to a ruthless program of incessant work: writing, teaching, lecturing, and encouraging his colleagues and students in countless informal ways. After he came to Harvard, he studiously avoided any attempt to exert a direct influence on practical affairs. His main purpose was to build on the foundation he had laid before the war, to test his earlier conclusions, and to modify them where necessary in the light of his historical and statistical research. And his last years, through his *History*, were devoted to a supreme effort to hasten the progress of economics towards scientific maturity. His years in Bonn were consumed largely with a work on money that never saw the light of day. I am told that, in 1930, he tore up one complete manuscript on the publication of Keynes' *Treatise on Money*; and, although he had completed another by 1935 he never published it. But apart from that, his stream of important articles, his second edition of *Economic Development* and his journalistic contribution to the *Volkswirt* were more than enough to absorb all the energy of any ordinary man.

During the first years at Harvard, his main preoccupation was *Business Cycles*, whose scope is more correctly indicated by its subtitle "A Theoretical, Historical and Statistical Analysis of the Capitalist Process." It was essentially an effort to clothe *Economic Development* with historical and statistical fact. Every one of its thousand pages clearly came from a single pen. It is certainly one of the great *tours de force* in the entire literature of economics. But it is, of course, far more than that. Apart from the light it sheds on the capitalistic process, both its merits and its shortcomings will provide an indispensable guide to research in the future. The book appeared in the fateful summer of 1939, and the chaotic years that followed have deprived it of all but a fraction of the attention it deserves. It is a sad irony that the success of *Economic Development* should have been marred by the First World War and that of *Business Cycles* by the second.

Capitalism, Socialism and Democracy appeared in 1942 and was an immediate success. He then commenced work on the *History*. When he began the book, he evidently expected it to be a short undertaking, possibly an expansion of *Dogmengeschichte*. He became immersed in it in 1943 because, as he said in a letter, "It is simply the subject, among all those at hand, that is furthest removed from current events." At that stage he had planned not only the *History*, but a treatise on money, a general theory, further sociological work, a theory of esthetics, and several novels to express those of his ideas that could not be fitted into a scientific mold. As it was, the *History* caught him in its toils. While I cannot help regretting the abandoned program, he did devote most of the last seven years of his life to the task that probably he alone, of all living economists, could perform.

The *History*, however, did not prevent him from continuing his brilliant series of biographical articles. His interest in biography had begun long ago with his articles on Walras and

Böhm-Bawerk. His more recent articles on Taussig, Keynes, Pareto, and Mitchell are written with an insight and sympathy that leave him with no modern rival except Keynes himself. And not the least reason for interest in these essays is that they could never have been written by a man who did not understand himself.

At Harvard, Schumpeter regularly taught courses in advanced theory, business cycles, history of economic thought, and socialism. He was profligate in the time he would spend with any student with the merest spark of an idea. His lectures were models of eloquence and wit. His apparently casual manner concealed a studied performance and painstaking preparation. But he lectured to those who had ears to hear; those who merely took notes left his classes with the sense of frustration he desired to produce in them. Those whose hearing was less than perfect frequently did not realize how wise he was till years afterwards. But there was an unforgivable omission: his students never heard one word of Schumpeterian economics. They were left to discover that for themselves, and appreciated it all the more when they did.

Throughout his life Schumpeter gave an inordinate amount of his time to the study of mathematics and to the encouragement of its study by others. His first publication was on the use of mathematics in economics, and while his interest remained, his hopes for it only began to wane during the last years of his life. One of the many ironies in his life is that his ardent support of mathematics in economics drove his students away from the fields of intellectual endeavor that made his own work so significant, and produced many results that he considered sterile. He always retained the forlorn hope that mathematics might produce the dynamic counterpart of the Walrasian system.

He was president of the Econometric Society from 1937 to 1941 and, belatedly, president of the American Economic Association in 1948. The painstaking attention to detail and the organizing skill he showed in arranging the program for that year effectively dissipated the impression of casualness and helplessness in practical matters that he strove so sedulously to cultivate.

During his first years in Cambridge, he lived under the paternal and benevolent care of the great Taussig at 2 Scott Street, but in 1937 he placed himself by marriage under the less rigorous but no less benevolent auspices of Elizabeth Boody. Without her companionship and single-minded devotion he might well have sunk into a state of intolerable melancholy and loneliness. In Cambridge, but especially at her beautiful place at Taconic, Connecticut, she provided him with what he had never really had before — a home.

The war years were unhappy and depressing ones for him. Not only was he overcome, as always, by the futility of war, and the destruction of his values that it would bring, but he alienated many of his friends by taking extreme positions when he felt that they were carried away by the emotions of the moment. Needless to say, his opinions in 1940 would have evoked a different response in 1950.

I close this section with an entry from his diary on February 8, 1945: "Good morning friend, how does it feel to be sixty-two — and definitely old and definitely to feel old? One thing to be recorded is my humble thanks to the United States. No repining, no sterile regrets, no sorrow about the state of things: acceptance rather and a feeling that it could be worse." I think that describes his state of mind until he died in his sleep at Taconic five years later.

IV. Personality and Vision

In his essay on Pareto, Schumpeter said: "Could we confine ourselves to Pareto's contributions to pure theory, there would be little need for glancing at the man and his social background and location. But into everything that was not a theorem in the pure logic of economics the whole man and all the forces that conditioned him entered so unmistakably that it is more necessary than it usually is in an appraisal of scientific performance to convey an idea of that man and of those forces." However true that is for Pareto, it is more true for Schumpeter, as he himself well knew. And the mere chronological record of his life does not seem to me to be enough. While it is a hazardous business, we must explore the deep pool of his personality, although, as he says of

Pareto, it can never be "drained so as to show what is at the bottom of it."

To explain his personality, I am convinced we have to go back to his earliest childhood and recall that he spent most of his first ten years as the only son of a young widowed mother. Of his devotion to his mother there is no question, but the important thing is that it seems to have had a profound effect on his relations with others. The facts that his first wife was twelve years older and his second, twenty-one years younger than he attest to this. Similarly with men, he was most at ease with those toward whom he had filial feelings—like Böhm-Bawerk or Taussig—or with those towards whom he felt paternal—like most of his close friends at Harvard. In these relationships he was superb, but he was not equally successful with his contemporaries. He found it difficult to persuade. He could win every point but fail to win the argument. He could fail in persuasion where others far less brilliant could succeed.

He was very sensitive about this, and the failure of *Economic Development* to be the sweeping success it might have been probably reinforced his sensitivity. In fact, time and again he seemed to stack the cards against himself so that he could be sure to lose with honor. As I have suggested, this may explain his political career; it may explain his refusal to submit his own doctrines to his students; and it may also explain the paradoxes in his later writing. *Capitalism, Socialism and Democracy* in particular is full of ironic twists that provide cold comfort for anyone who agrees with him. Capitalists, socialists, and intellectuals are all provided with strong emotional grounds for rejecting the argument.

The second point of decisive importance in the formation of his character is, I believe, the fact that while he was of middle-class origin and undistinguished lineage, he was brought up in a highly aristocratic environment. I am not alone in this opinion; it seems to have been widely held by those who knew him in Vienna. It is difficult for a young boy to be neutral to such a situation. He is either overwhelmed by it or sets out to master it. Schumpeter was of the latter sort. He adopted the manners, the habits, and the tastes of the aristocrat. I think

the Theresianum also had much to do with instilling in him the passion for perfection and the spirit of intellectual independence that were so prominent throughout his whole life.

But he must have realized that conspicuous success in the normal aristocratic pursuits — the diplomatic service or the army — was unlikely, and, besides, they would not afford him the intellectual life he demanded. To be anything less than first-class in his chosen line of endeavor would have been unthinkable to him. He therefore had to strike out on a line of his own.

He was neither aristocrat nor bourgeois, but he had no resentments, as did Marx. And he had a great intellect. In his essay on Marshall's *Principles* he writes: "I confess that few things are so irritating to me as is the preaching of mid-Victorian morality, seasoned by Benthamism, the preaching from a schema of middle class values that knows no glamor or passion." At the least, we have found fertile ground in which his vision of the innovating entrepreneur, who did have glamor and was not dominated by middle-class values, could grow. Such conjectures are of course not capable of proof; but no other economist had his vision and no other was exposed to environmental influences so favorable to it. There is a further cogent point. I have already referred to his admiration for England; in his opinion, the strength of the English system of government lay largely in the willingness of its aristocracy to recruit to itself the strongest elements of the bourgeoisie.

Although I feel confident in this analysis of Schumpeter's character, I would have hesitated to publish it had I not found among his papers notes for a novel entitled "Ships in the Fog." There are only a few paragraphs that are not in shorthand. They begin:

Now let me be quite pedantic about it. Or else you'll never take in what I'm going to paint. Now backgrounds, racial and social, are essential in order to understand what a man is.

Well he — let us call him Henry — was an Englishman by birth. But by race only on his mother's side. His father, before he acquired English citizenship called himself an Italian. But the matter is more complicated than that. The family belonged to the fringe end of the commercial and financial set of Trieste which racially was a mixture defying analysis. Greek, German, Serb, and Italian elements and presumably all of them contributed towards making our hero's paternal ancestry. His father had emigrated to England as a representative of Triestian shipping interests and married an English girl with a great pedigree and absolutely no money.

Their only child was four years old, when, well on the way to a considerable financial position, the father was killed on the hunting field. And the mother was henceforth the one great human factor in Henry's life. She was an excellent woman, strong and kind and amply provided with the delightful blinkers of English society. She did her duties in a way which can only be called manful, though it was truly womanly when I come to think of it. To make him an English gentleman was her one aim in life.

She had not much money . . . but she had connections which she resolutely exploited for her darling — that was among other reasons why to her dying day he belonged to one of the four or five best clubs though he hardly ever set foot in it and why he was seen on terms of equality in houses that rank much above what is referred to as the smart set, though, at the time of this story, he had ceased to frequent them and the corresponding country houses. But I want to make this quite clear — the social world was open to him from the beginning and shut only when he did not trouble to go and that meant much. No complexes. No faked contempt. No hidden wistfulness.

Disappointment was in store for her. Disappointment all the more bitter because realization was so near; all the more bitter, in a sense, precisely because in every other respect he gave her satisfaction and always not only felt but also manifested in every word and act his unconditioned attachment to her, his unbounded confidence in her. Confidence — not the right word. . .

That's it! . . . Where was he at home? Not really in England! Often he had thought so but ancestral past had asserted itself each time. But neither in France or Italy though he found himself drifting to both whenever he had a week or a month. Certainly not in Germany or what had been the Austro-Hungarian Empire.

But that was not the salient point. More important than country means class — but he did not with subconscious allegiance belong either to society or the business class or the professions or the trade union world all of which provided such comfortable homes for everyone he knew. Yes — his mother's corner of society had been his as long as she lived.

And for modern man his work is everything — all that is left in many cases. . . . Doing efficient work without aim, without hope. . .

No family.

No real friends.

No woman in whose womanhood to anchor.

It is hard to make out the plot of the novel except for its broad outlines. Henry's mother wanted him to enter politics. The way seemed clear but suddenly he found he could not go on with it. He spent some years in a state of indecision and revision, but then decided to go into business in America, not for the sake of making money but for the sake of the intellectual problems that business presented. One characteristically Schumpeterian incident: Henry instructed his secretary to buy up a controlling interest in the stock of the business he was interested in. The secretary objected that Henry did not think much of the directors. Henry replied: "How good must be a business that can stand such directors." All this occurred in 1932. Henry was approaching forty. How the venture turned out, how the heroine fitted in is stated, if at all, only in shorthand. But, fortunately, enough is written in English to throw a bright light on the personality of the author.

It is easy now to imagine how Schumpeter reacted to the intellectual influences to which he was exposed at the University of Vienna. The severe intellectual discipline of his education would naturally lead him to admire the logical structure of the Walrasian system, but it knew "no glamor or passion." Those very qualities in the Marxist doctrine obviously attracted him strongly, but with his personality and his passion for coherent logic he could never be a Marxist. If anything was anathema to him, it was a proletarian state. And furthermore, in the light of his personality and his circumstances, it seems to have been the most natural thing in the world for him to become an economist, and equally natural for him to refuse to be merely an economist.

Schumpeter himself studied the personalities of his biographical subjects in order to discover what he called their "ideological bias." While he recognized and insisted that "vision" was essential, as a prescientific stage, to any advancement of knowledge, he hoped that scientific research could eliminate the element of bias and reveal the element of objective truth. In this I think he was unfair not only to others but especially to himself. I think he should have recognized that there can be ideological insight as well as bias. In fact, can anyone who is thoroughly attuned to the society in which he lives take a comprehensive and critical view of it? Or if he does, is he not bound, almost as a matter of definition, to take an urbane and optimistic view of it? Is it not the province of exceptional men, exceptionally conditioned, like

Marx or Schumpeter, to perform a critical diagnosis of the body politic? Ideology there must be, but the baffling question is to decide whether, in particular cases, it results in bias or insight; and the task becomes even more difficult when we realize that the world is a different place because some exceptional men were able to put forward their ideologies in the guise of objective truth. But as Schumpeter insisted, the search for truth demands that the prescientific vision be identified.

V. The Schumpeterian System

I shall now give a summary, and therefore inadequate, account of Schumpeter's analysis of capitalism and capitalistic development. But before beginning, it is worth recording his own acknowledgement of the dominant intellectual influences in his life, Walras and Marx. In the preface to the Japanese edition of *Economic Development*, he states that in writing the book: "I was trying to construct a theoretic model of the process of economic change in time, or perhaps more clearly, to answer the question how the economic system generates the force which incessantly transforms it. . . . To Walras we owe a concept of the economic system and a theoretical apparatus which for the first time in the history of our science effectively embraced the pure logic of the interdependence between economic quantities. But when in my beginnings I studied the Walrasian conception and the Walrasian technique (I wish to emphasize that as an economist I owe more to it than to any other influence), I discovered not only that it is rigorously static in character . . . but also that it is applicable only to a stationary process. . . .

"It was not clear to me at the outset what to the reader will perhaps be obvious at once, namely, that this idea and this aim are exactly the same as the idea and the aim which underly the economic teaching of Karl Marx . . . I am not saying this in order to associate anything that I say in this book with his great name. Intention and results are much too different to give me a right to do so."

What this means, in my opinion, is that Walras provided the foundations for his edifice, but Marx suggested to him the method for building on that foundation a structure that reflected his own "vision." The essentials of that structure are:

1. Were it not for the forces making for "development," the capitalist system would settle down to a stationary condition of Walrasian equilibrium in which the whole national product was imputed to the services of labor and land. In comparison to development, the evolutionary effects of savings from the "circular flow" and population increase are of minor importance and can therefore be ignored. The assumption of perfect competition is modified in Schumpeter's later work, one of the great contributions of which is his discussion of monopoly and competition in the framework of capitalistic development. Consequently, his concept of equilibrium becomes less definite, but it retains a central position in his theory.

2. The capitalist system contains within it forces making for change and development. Since there is no possibility of profit in the circular flow, those who seek profits must introduce new products, contrive new methods of production, open new markets, discover new sources of supply or win new strategic positions in industry, that is, carry out "new combinations or innovations." The entire tendency towards equilibrium means resistance to change: the social environment reacts against novelty, the ordinary businessman is strongly inclined to continue on traditional lines, and change means a venture into the unknown. The exceptional ability of the exceptional man is therefore required to carry out innovations. And furthermore, in an industrialized economy the richest prizes are to be won through successful entrepreneurship — prizes that cannot be described in terms of hedonistic enjoyment but in terms of the "dream and the will to found a private kingdom," "the will to conquer; the impulse to fight, to prove oneself superior to others, to succeed for the sake, not of the fruits of success but of success itself" and finally "the joy of creating, of getting things done, or simply of exercising one's energy and ingenuity." Here is the central tower of Schumpeter's structure, and the rest of the building is designed to emphasize its impressiveness.

3. To carry out his designs, the entrepreneur must be able to raid the circular flow and divert labor and land to investment. Such savings as

are made from the circular flow are inadequate for the purpose. He must be provided with "credit" furnished to him and created by "capitalists." Capital, in Schumpeter's terminology, is, in fact, the means of payment available at any time to entrepreneurs; and the only credit that is essential to the capitalist system is the credit extended to them.

4. Since the process of imputation excludes the possibility of interest emerging from a circular flow economy, the only available source of it is entrepreneurial profit. If there were not profits for a sufficient period of time, interest would disappear. As it is, so long as there are prospects of profit, entrepreneurs are prepared to pay interest to capitalists for the use of their money. And once interest exists for this reason, it permeates the entire economy and appears to be a permanent revenue arising from the productive process. Schumpeter performed a great, though neglected, service to economics by his insistence that interest could be adequately explained only in the context of a monetary economy. But he involved himself in needless controversy and deflected attention from the most valuable part of his theory by defining his circular flow economy as one so devoid of uncertainty and change that interest could not occur in it. He could have accepted Böhm-Bawerk's theory of interest as a partial explanation without weakening his own position.

5. Development does not take place continuously, but innovations appear in "swarms," because the innovations undertaken by the most enterprising and venturesome create a favorable climate for others who are less venturesome to follow. This tendency is reinforced by the general conditions of prosperity produced by the creation and expenditure of new purchasing power. Schumpeter also recognizes that the low prices and unemployment resulting from a preceding depression help to explain the swarms of innovations, but he excludes this from his explanation since he considers it methodologically necessary to begin with an initial state of equilibrium. This is the basic element of the prosperity phase of the business cycle, but, in addition, rising prices and expanding purchasing power induce the secondary boom.

6. The boom itself generates conditions unfavorable to its continued progress. Rising prices deter investment; competition of new products with old causes business losses; and entrepreneurs use the proceeds of the sale of their new products to repay indebtedness, and hence start a period of deflation. These factors, rather than financial crises, are the basic causes of depression, which consists of the process of adaptation to innovation plus the phenomena of secondary deflation. Eventually, however, adaptation is complete, deflation comes to an end and equilibrium is restored.

7. The system so far described contains no obstacles to continued development. It is not haunted by the specter of diminishing returns and gives rise to no economic contradictions of the Marxian type. In fact, if left to itself, capitalism not only achieves spectacular increases in total real income, but is also a powerful engine for the redistribution of *real* income. Schumpeter's point that "the capitalist achievement does not typically consist in providing more silk stockings for queens but in bringing them within the reach of factory girls for steadily decreasing amounts of effort" has been consistently overlooked by economists and especially by statisticians who deflate all incomes by a single price index.

8. Schumpeter's belief in equilibrium as the central norm of his system precludes the possibility of the savings-investment dilemma in the absence of interference with its operation by the state. But that is precisely where contradictions do occur. The capitalist system itself generates the political and social attitudes that ultimately destroy it. The growth of big business places capitalism in a position particularly vulnerable to political attack and deprives the system of the vigorous individual entrepreneur who is most willing to defend it. The growth in political power of the bourgeoisie ousts from leadership the old aristocracies who knew better how to rule than the businessman. It is a typical Schumpeterian paradox that, as we noticed in the case of England, recruits from the bourgeoisie invigorate the aristocracy before bourgeois power eventually destroys it. Possibly most important, the rationalism of capitalist civilization produces critical attitudes that are necessarily directed towards the capitalist system itself. Thus anticapitalist policies, particularly modern tax systems and their expendi-

ture counterparts, prevent the system from functioning according to its logic. And the political ineptitude of the businessman leaves him defenseless. These are the areas in which we must look for the true explanations of vanishing investment opportunity and tendencies toward stagnation. In a way, Schumpeter is the most uncompromising stagnationist of them all.

9. He recognizes that the capitalist system can be kept alive by public income generation but he describes such a state as "capitalism in the oxygen tent — kept alive by artificial devices and paralyzed in all those functions that produced the successes of the past." [4] Up until very recently he held that the inevitable outcome of capitalist decay was socialism, but in his article on the English economists and in conversation he seemed to be veering to the view that what he called "laborism" might have a long, dull, and unimaginative future.

These paragraphs are confined to Schumpeter's analysis of the capitalistic process not only for reasons of space but because these are the central ideas that dominate his analysis in other fields such as socialism and imperialism. This summary is, of course, far too brief to do justice to the subject but brief enough to bring out the unity of the system and to show how it was built around his vision.

VI. The Advancement of Science

As we have already seen, virtually all of Schumpeter's system was worked out during the first thirty years of his life. I am sure that he was deeply aware of the extent to which he had depended on his own intuition for his theory and that *Economic Development* did not measure up to his scientific standards. Consequently, a major part of what I have called his years of maturity were devoted to testing his theory by statistical and historical research, and *Business Cycles* is the embodiment of his efforts. At the same time, his self-consciousness about his own work and his efforts to increase its scientific stature made him deeply conscious of the scientific inadequacy of economic doctrine as a

whole. His *History*, as well as his biographical essays, is essentially a work in the epistemology of economics.

The theory of *Economic Development*, in Schumpeter's judgment, emerged practically unscathed from its exposure to history and statistics in *Business Cycles*. In fact, the only significant change is that Schumpeter gave up the idea of a single cycle and adopted instead the complicated structure of Kondratieffs, Juglars, and Kitchins, all of which, however, arose from the process of capitalistic development. His researches compelled him to give greater weight than he had before to the effect of outside disturbances on the system and to recognize the existence of inventory cycles, cobweb cycles, and the like that originate from within the system. But he insisted that the fundamental explanation lay in his vision of the capitalistic process. As one reads the book, one finds it increasingly difficult to decide to what extent Schumpeter is writing history in terms of his theory and to what extent he is using the empirical information to test the theory. The change from the single cycle to the three cycle pattern is of course an example of the impact of the facts on the theory. But in general I believe the main effect of the book is to interpret the facts in the light of the theory.

My impression of his method is as follows. *Business Cycles* begins with an elaborate and cogently argued restatement of his theory. He then adduces historical evidence to show that innovation has in fact played a great part in development. Then in the light of the theory he infers that the process of development must have been of a cyclical character. The historical course of events is then recorded in terms of the theory, with some modifications of the theory in the process, but with no essential change in the grand design.

In *Business Cycles*, Schumpeter has, in my opinion, successfully demonstrated that his theory is not excluded by the empirical evidence, but he has not excluded other possibilities. Could not the evidence be used equally persuasively to support the thesis that, in the absence of disturbance, innovation would proceed continuously, but that business fluctuations do arise from the influence of external disturbances? But the importance of this book

---

[4] I have taken much of paragraphs (7), (8), and (9) from his article "Capitalism in the Post-war World." I thought it better to rely on Schumpeter's summary of his own views than to attempt to summarize the argument of *Capitalism, Socialism and Democracy.*

does not rest on the verification of a particular theory. As a study of history, its eminent stature is sure to grow. Whether or not the original theory is correct, history that is marshaled in terms of an explicit theory seems, at least to a nonhistorian, more suggestive and meaningful than history that purports to be theoretically neutral — provided it is written by a scholar of Schumpeter's integrity.

I recently asked a colleague how far *Business Cycles* had advanced economic knowledge. He replied: "Not at all; it will not do so until we have a historian who is Schumpeter's equal who can point out the flaws in it." It is hardly necessary to state that my appraisal of the book is a commentary on the state of economic knowledge and the difficulty of its subject matter. No other work combines theoretical, historical, and statistical research with greater mastery, and can any other theory make a better claim to validity? And has any other author subjected his own theory to such an exhaustive and conscientious process of appraisal?

Schumpeter must have realized that he had failed to establish a body of scientific knowledge that was independent of his ideology, and from that experience, he may well have concluded that it was impossible for anyone else to effect a complete divorce between science and ideology. Nevertheless, the scientist should continue to make unremitting efforts to do so. That is the purport of his Presidential Address to the American Economic Association.

Therefore, in his *History* and his later biographical essays, particularly those on Keynes and Pareto, he undertook the task of isolating ideological bias in the entire body of economic thought. But the further his studies carried him, the more ideologies seem to have loomed in importance. In fact, one of the chapter headings of the *History* is: "Is the History of Economic Thought a History of Ideologies?" Of course, one can argue that all that is irrelevant, that once a theory sees the light of day, it should stand on its own feet and be considered on its merits. That would be all right if we did possess techniques for testing economic theory, but it may turn out that the very nature of society prevents such techniques from ever being found.

As his awareness of the importance of ideol-ogies increased, Schumpeter became increasingly dissatisfied with the tools of scientific analysis. His high hopes for econometric work, on which he had placed such store in the 'thirties, waned visibly in the 'forties. His emphasis shifted steadily from theory to history. While he regarded history, statistics, and theory as indispensable for scientific progress, he states in the *History*: "I wish to state right now that if, starting my work in economics afresh, I were told that I could study only one of the three, but could have my choice, it would be history that I would choose."

It is impossible to convey, in advance of its publication, an adequate impression of his *History*, of the depth of his scholarship, of the breadth of his knowledge, and above all of the *élan*, the enthusiasm, and the confidence with which he immerses himself in every period of economic thought. He undertook a task that no other economist could have attempted and that perhaps even he could not have finished. It is not inappropriate that it will be published as an uncompleted work.

VII. Policies and Politics

Practical men have not been in the habit of consulting Schumpeter's work, and in his years in America he never made the slightest effort to persuade them to — partly because he studiously refrained from propounding "bold new programs" and partly because of his general reluctance to persuade. He felt, nevertheless, that the practical man was making a mistake. Several times his notebook of aphorisms contains the wistful entry: "Most tragic of all sights: a blind man who hits his seeing-eye dog." Let us look at a few examples of the practical wisdom on contemporary matters that he did dispense:

1. In his article on "Capitalism in the Post War World," in 1943, he states: "Everybody is afraid of a post-war slump. . . . Viewed as a purely economic problem the task (of reconstruction) might well turn out to be much easier than most people believe. . . . But in any case, the wants of impoverished households will be so urgent and so calculable that any post-war slump that may be avoidable would speedily give way to a reconstruction boom. Capitalist methods have been equal to much more difficult

tasks." But he felt that all this would be unlikely to come about because the strength of the bureaucracy and of labor would succeed in perpetuating the wartime system of economic controls. This country did get rid of its controls and did have the prosperity Schumpeter believed possible. Other countries that retained controls did not fare so well. While we cannot infer from those facts that Schumpeter's entire diagnosis was correct, at least it cannot be ignored.

2. In 1942, in *Capitalism, Socialism and Democracy*, he estimated that the American economy under capitalism was capable of doubling real output per head in the course of fifty years; and if that estimate is correct, he adds, "It is easy to see that all the desiderata that have so far been espoused by any social reformers — practically without exception, including even the greater part of the cranks — either would be fulfilled automatically or could be fulfilled *without significant interference with the capitalist process.*" The President's Council of Economic Advisers reached the same conclusion eight years later, and there is no telling how much earlier it was all perfectly clear to Schumpeter.

3. As a third example, consider Schumpeter's rejection of the stagnationist thesis as set out in the final chapter of the second edition of *Capitalism*. While it is impossible to accept as proved his contention that stagnation can only arise from anti-capitalist attitudes and policies, his warning that there may be dangerous contradictions in attempting to avert stagnation by adopting such policies and attitudes is heeded much more today than it was in the 'thirties.

This list could be readily expanded with economic and noneconomic examples. Recall that Austria did have to look to the West for help after the First World War and consider his views on Russia in the chapter just referred to. On the other hand, Schumpeter weakened his position in the contemporary scene by his refusal to discuss issues in terms of the Keynesian analysis which was a main preoccupation of most of his fellow economists. His aversion to Keynesian ideas of the baser sort is readily understandable, but his main objection was that, in his opinion, Keynes, next to Marx, cultivated the intellectual soil in which anticapitalist attitudes flourished. This basic objection prevented him from using Keynesian ideas to improve his own system. Surely monetary and fiscal policies that mitigated secondary booms and depressions would be entirely in accord with his diagnosis of the business cycle and have no anticapitalist undertones.

Apart from his writing, many of those who knew Schumpeter have frequently felt afterwards that they were carried away by the emotions or the events of the moment while he retained his Olympian calm, however much, from a purely personal point of view, he abhorred what was going on. All this does not mean that I believe Schumpeter could have been a good minister of finance or a successful chairman of the Council of Economic Advisers. But I do believe that Presidents and Prime Ministers should have consorted with him in those rare moments they could spare from being politicians. For Schumpeter was not a politician, and, for reasons that go deep into his personality was unable or unwilling to become one. But he clearly understood what was required for political success.

One of the main themes for his Walgreen lectures in Chicago was to be the relation between policies and politics. In the rough notes he had made for the lectures, he states: "Only in a very special sense can we speak of a nation's policy or policies. In general declared policies are nothing but verbalizations of group interests and attitudes that assert themselves in the struggle of parties for points in the political game, though every group exalts the policies that suit it into eternal principles of a 'common good' that is to be safeguarded by an imaginary kind of state. Nobody has attained political maturity who does not understand that policy is politics. Economists are particularly apt to overlook these truths."

VIII. Conclusions

I have not succeeded in bringing out many of the most admirable traits of Schumpeter's character. The liveliness of his wit and the elegance of his manner often concealed the simplicity and the sincerity in his nature. His successes in the lecture hall, the classroom, or the drawing room were no greater than his suc-

Joseph Schumpeter
1898

Joseph Schumpeter
1909

cesses in winning the affection of children. He could meet them on terms of complete equality and they blossomed under his influence. His warm and generous friendship once given was never withdrawn. It is not for his spectacular qualities that he will live in the hearts of his friends.

But most of his later life was that of the solitary and reflective, but impatient, scholar; and no one was invited to share it. His work was too much his own to be discussed. While he sometimes overloaded himself with equipment furnished by others, he made his intellectual journeys alone. His study was the workshop of the individual craftsman. By tearing pages out of periodicals, collecting reprints, and limiting himself to the books he really used, he was able to keep most of the tools he needed within easy reach. In addition, there were his own notes. Almost everything he thought, he wrote down. He went over his famous slips of yellow paper at the end of the day and transcribed what he thought worth while. And he was able to use what he had written years before; for part of his *History*, he relied on notes he had made in the British Museum in 1907. Thus he pursued his craft among the hills of Connecticut unimpeded by computing machines, research staffs, and other instruments of mass production.

He entered the more scintillating of his daily reflections in his book of aphorisms; I quote a few of them: "The best way to spoil a point of view is to make it a matter of principle." "Of all the reasons for the failure of able men the most important is inability to wait." "Sanguinary revolution is the sadism of the well behaved radical." "Strength wins not by being used but by being there." "The curious feeling when one is dying from another cause on a sinking ship." "Equality is the ideal of the sub-normal, but even the subnormals do not desire equality but only that there be nobody better." "There is a kind of humane tolerance that is nothing but lack of dignity."

His stern self-discipline required him to grade every day for his intellectual performance. The poorer days received a grade of zero and the best, one. And from the daily grades he built up to assessments of the weeks, the months and the years. His standards were such that he hardly ever satisfied himself. Here are some typical weekly comments: "full on the face of it, but God knows what good," "full but not very successful," "monotonous struggle," "getting into stride," "no history, seen many people," "ill in bed most of time, no math, no nothing," "no math, no Greek."

Towards the end of the summer of 1945, he made a still longer appraisal:

"Looking back on these months and on the weeks that are still left, and looking back on my life in the process, three things stand out.

"(1) Always the same mistakes committed and the same type of strength and weakness displayed.

"(2) The story might be written in terms of lost opportunities (though of course that stands out in retrospect); there were those that were seized and used promptly enough.

"(3) Yet there is no regret — if I had used every one of those opportunities I should not have done a better job of it all — perhaps even the contrary, for success up to the hilt with any one of them would have stuck me in the particular line and not only narrowed me but landed me in uncomfortable situations [and then some shorthand]. Ease me gently to my grave."

And the entry concludes:

"Never grudge the time

   (a) to think

   (b) for a bit of math."

JOSEPH ALOIS SCHUMPETER, 1883–1950 [1]

Gottfried Haberler

JOSEPH A. SCHUMPETER was one of the great economists of all time. His claim to that rare title — remember Keynes's famous dictum that "good economists are the rarest of birds" — rests as much on the fact that he was much more than an economist as on his achievements in the economic field itself. He himself used to say that an economist who is not also a mathematician, a statistician, and most of all a historian is not properly qualified for his profession. He was all these and more besides: he had an encyclopaedic knowledge not only of the history of economic doctrines, which was one of his special fields, but also of the history of economic facts and institutions and of general political and social history. He had not received professional training in mathematics, and the manipulation of numbers and of algebra did not come to him easily; but he acquired a great mathematical knowledge and could follow and effectively expound what even among mathematical economists is regarded as complicated mathematical analysis. He was not an expert statistical technician, but he had a profound understanding of the logic and limitations of statistical inference and kept abreast of new methods and of statistical source materials. All his life he was deeply interested in the theory of social relations and social philosophy and made important contributions to sociology and to social and political philosophy.

In some of these fields he had his superiors. There are in economics more refined and versatile mathematical theorists, there are more resourceful statisticians, and economic historians who know more about certain periods and certain subjects than he did. But as a master of all branches of economics and as a universal scholar, Schumpeter held a unique position among contemporary economists.

Schumpeter was not only a great scholar and original thinker, but he was also a strong, colorful, and exceedingly complex personality. A quite unusual capacity for understanding the minds and views of others, a strong touch of irony, which, at times, seemed to verge on cynicism, and a wonderful sense of humor were combined with deep moral convictions, absolute devotion to his friends, and intense likes and aversions. But his dislike of certain kinds of people was controlled by his kindheartedness and generosity. He was especially considerate to his students, and those who confided in him and sought his advice could always be sure of getting his help and counsel. Indeed, he spent a disproportionate amount of time tutoring and helping students — those of limited as well as of superior ability.

He was an effective and dramatic speaker, a master of the spoken as well as of the written word, and his lectures and addresses were always stimulating, had usually some new idea and striking formulation, and were never stale or dull. No wonder that he was a tremendously inspiring teacher.

Schumpeter died from a cerebral haemorrhage in his sleep on January 8, 1950, one month before his sixty-seventh birthday.

I. Childhood, 1883–1901

Jozsi (pronounced Yoshi), as he was called at home and by his friends, was born at Triesch in the Austrian province of Moravia (now Czechoslovakia) on February 8, 1883, the only child of the cloth manufacturer (*Tuchfabrikant*) Alois Schumpeter and his wife Johanna. Jozsi's mother was born at Wiener-Neustadt, an industrial town thirty miles south of Vienna, on June 9, 1861, the daughter of a physician, Dr. Julius Grüner, by his marriage with Julie Wydra. Little is known of the ancestry of

[1] Reprinted with permission of the author and the *Quarterly Journal of Economics*. I am grateful to a number of people for help and information, among them Professors A. Gerschenkron and E. H. Chamberlin, Mrs. T. Stolper, and Drs. F. Somary, H. Staehle, E. S. Mason, and Heinrich Höfflinger.

Schumpeter's parents; but so much is certain: that he was the product of a typically Austrian mixture of several of the many nationalities that lived in the Austro-Hungarian monarchy.[2]

Jozsi lost his father when he was four years of age, and the widow married at Kalksburg, near Vienna, on September 9, 1893, Sigismund von Kéler, Feldmarshalleutenant in the Austro-Hungarian army, a descendant of a German-Hungarian family. On July 3, 1906, her second marriage ended in divorce, but up to that time von Kéler had a considerable influence on Jozsi's education. The family lived in Vienna, and from 1893 to 1901 Schumpeter went as a day student to the Theresianum, the *Mittelschule* (approximately equivalent to the American high school plus the first two years of college) which was favored by the Austrian aristocracy. Already he gave evidence of his fine intellect and was graduated with high honors in 1901. At the Theresianum he received a thorough classical education including Latin and Greek, which was supplemented at home by a study of modern languages (French, English, Italian). Blessed with a retentive memory, he kept his knowledge of Latin and Greek throughout his life; in fact, in his Cambridge days he occasionally found time to read together with Greek students Greek classics in the original language.[3] The milieu at the Theresianum in conjunction with what must have been a highly cultured atmosphere in the home of his mother left a permanent imprint upon his personality. It was there that he acquired the agreeable, sometimes quaintly overpolite old-world manner, which, together with his natural charm, friendliness, and vitality, produced the man Schumpeter as we knew him.

II. University, 1901–1906

In 1901, Schumpeter registered as a student in the Faculty of Law at the University of Vienna, and in 1906 the degree of *Doctor utriusque juris* (doctor of law — literally: doc-

tor of each of the two laws, viz., of Roman law and canon law) was conferred upon him. In Vienna, as in most continental universities, economics was (and still is) taught in the Faculty of Law, and for the law degree, courses and a comprehensive examination in economics and political science were (and still are) required.[4] Schumpeter took his economics much more seriously than the average law student, but in passing it may be mentioned that he did not neglect his law. In fact, he practiced it for a short time during 1907–08 before the International Mixed Court of Egypt in Cairo. He liked and was impressed by the historical approach to the study of law and later during his years in the University of Bonn had occasion to support with considerable effect the retention of a large amount of Roman law in the curriculum of the law faculties in the Prussian universities.[5] He came, however, to the conclusion that the close connection between the study of law and economics as practiced in the continental European universities was a great mistake. "That the student cannot master jurisprudence and the social sciences at the same time seems to have been experimentally demonstrated: There is no use denying that the holder of a law degree (*Referendar*) knows nothing about economics, and the economist (*Diplomvolkswirt*) knows nothing about jurisprudence. No one who has himself experienced the fundamental difference of the two modes of thinking and the unmanageability of the combined material, can dispute the contention that this is not due primarily to accident or to avoidable mistakes." [6]

At the beginning of the century Vienna was a great center of economic learning. Menger had, however, withdrawn from active work in

---

[2] According to one theory, the name Schumpeter is of Italian origin, being a German corruption of Giampietro. Schumpeter's dark features, which he had inherited from his father, lend some support to this hypothesis. But I was unable to obtain reliable confirmation.

[3] One of the books found on the desk of the study in his Cambridge home was a small volume with favorite passages underlined — Homer's Odyssey in the original Greek.

[4] Since 1920, a special degree in political science, *Doctor rerum politicarum*, including economics, has been available. But it has not become very popular.

[5] "The essential mental training of the jurist, which only the University can give him and for which, in contradistinction to the mere knowledge of the content of the actual law, no amount of practice is an adequate substitute, consists of the sort of juridical thinking that can be taught only on the basis of Roman law and without which there would be no good judges and lawyers." Quoted in "Die Bedeutung des römischen Rechts für die juristische Ausbildung," by Professor E. F. Bruck (now at Harvard) in *Juristische Wochenschrift*, 1929, no. 26.

[6] "Die Wirtschaftslehre und die reformierte Referendarprüfung" in *Schmollers Jahrbuch*, Vol. LIII (1929), p. 644.

the University (including his celebrated seminar) before Schumpeter's time, although he did
not resign his chair until 1903 when Wieser
became his successor. Thus Schumpeter was
not a student of Menger, and according to reliable reports met him only once or twice.

His first serious work in economics seems to
have been done in what we would now call a
statistical research seminar conducted by the
eminent economic historian and statistician,
K. Th. v. Inama-Sternegg,[7] in conjunction with
Franz v. Juraschek.[8] Judging from the reports
which were regularly published in the *Statistische Monatsschrift*,[9] this seminar must have
been on a very high level. Three papers by
Schumpeter are there reported.[10] The first
(winter term 1903–04) is entitled "Die Methode
der standard population," and deals with the
methods of population statistics developed by
Körösi, Bortkiewicz, Westergaard, and others.
Its content is of no special interest, but it
already displays great knowledge of the literature in several languages. The title of the second paper read during the same term is "Die
Methode der Index-Zahlen." This paper is
characterized by an unusual interpenetration
of economic theory and statistics: it is thoroughly econometric. On page 193, the author
quotes (in English) with great approval a warning by Forsell "Beware of Statistical Averages"
— a theme which recurs frequently in Schumpeter's work throughout his life. The paper
shows complete mastery of a large body of
literature mainly in English. The third paper,
presented during the winter term 1904–05, is
entitled "Die Internationale Preisbildung," and
discusses in some detail the organization of the
markets of important world staples such as
wheat, cotton, coffee, and wool, as well as the
principal demand and supply factors determining their price.

Other seminars he attended were those of
F. v. Wieser and of E. v. Philippovich where
he seems to have reported on the beginnings

of his *Dogmengeschichte*. When Böhm-Bawerk
resigned as Minister of Finance in 1904, he returned to academic life as professor in the University of Vienna, and conducted in 1905 and
1906 a famous seminar, in which Schumpeter
was an active participant. Other prominent
members were Ludwig v. Mises and Felix Somary, his lifelong friend. It was made lively and
at times stormy by the participation of a
group of young Marxists who later became
theoretical and political leaders in the Austrian
and German Social Democratic parties. There
was Otto Bauer, the brilliant theorist, dialecti-
cian, and intellectual leader of the Austrian
socialists after 1918, who seems to have been
mainly responsible for Schumpeter's appointment as Minister of Finance of the Austrian
Republic in 1919. There was Rudolf Hilferding, the author of the famous book *Das Finanz-
kapital* and twice Minister of Finance of the
German Republic.[11] Another member was
Emil Lederer, later Professor in Heidelberg and
Berlin, who in 1934 became Alvin Johnson's
main collaborator in the foundation of the
Graduate Faculty at the New School for Social
Research in New York. Schumpeter and Lederer were friends throughout the latter's life,
and he seems to have been on good terms with
Hilferding.

Schumpeter's profound knowledge of Marxian theory and his intimate familiarity with
the continental socialist movement as well as
with the psychology of the socialist leaders,
which lent color and freshness to a long series
of articles culminating in his book, *Capitalism,
Socialism and Democracy* (see especially Part
V, "A Historical Sketch of Socialist Parties"),
originated in those seminar meetings.

A member of that seminar told the author
of the present essay that in the heated debates
between Böhm-Bawerk and the Marxists,
Schumpeter attracted general attention through
his cool, scientific detachment. The seemingly
playful manner in which he took part in the
discussion, an attitude which was strongly pronounced in his early writings (especially in his
first book, *Wesen und Hauptinhalt der theo-*

[7] See the biographical note on Inama-Sternegg by another eminent economic historian, Alfons Dopsch, in *En-
cyclopaedia of the Social Sciences*, Vol. VII.

[8] Inama was director of the Austrian Central Statistical
office and was succeeded by Juraschek.

[9] Ed. by the *Statistische Zentral Kommission* of Austria.
New Series, Vol. X *et seq.*, Vienna, 1905 and later years.

[10] *Op. cit.*, Vol. X, pp. 188–191, 191–197, and 923–928.

[11] See P. M. Sweezy's introduction to Rudolf Hilferding,
Böhm-Bawerk's Criticism of Marx (New York: A. M. Kel-
ley, 1949). This is Hilferding's reply to Böhm-Bawerk's
Karl Marx and the Close of His System.

retischen Nationalökonomie) and which never left him entirely, was evidently mistaken by many for a lack of seriousness or an artificial mannerism. Böhm-Bawerk, however, with whom Schumpeter had close personal connections, at once recognized his talents, and was instrumental in securing Schumpeter's *Habilitation* (i.e., granting the *venia legendi*, the right to lecture) in the University of Vienna in 1909 and his appointment to the chair of political economy in the University of Czernowitz in the same year. It must be mentioned, however, that the greatest Austrian economist of his generation never was offered a chair in his *Alma Mater Vindobonensis*, although there were many opportunities before he finally left his native country in 1925.

III. Early Academic Career, 1906–1918

After graduation in 1906, Schumpeter went to England for a stay of several months, mainly in London, but with occasional visits to Cambridge and Oxford, where he paid his respects to Marshall and Edgeworth. In 1907, he married Miss Gladys Ricarde Seaver, daughter of a high dignitary of the Church of England,[12] and in the same year the Schumpeters went to Egypt. The preface to his first book bears the date line "Kairo, March 2, 1908." Late in 1908 or early 1909, they returned to Vienna, and in the autumn he started his work as Professor in Czernowitz, the capital of Bukowina, the easternmost province of Austria, which was after 1918 included in Rumania, in 1939 annexed by Russia, in 1941 retransferred to Rumania, and is now a part of Russia.

Apparently Czernowitz was eastern indeed, and Schumpeter's Harvard colleagues were later entertained by stories of extracurricular activities that might well have come out of the Arabian Nights. The two years in Czernowitz seem to have been very happy ones, and the university, where the academic careers of many young Austrian scholars started, was by no means without intellectual stimulation. Eugen Ehrlich, the well-known founder of the sociological theory of jurisprudence, whose book, *Fundamental Principles of the Sociology of*

Law, was published in an English translation by the Harvard University Press, was Schumpeter's colleague. So was another eminent jurist, Georg Petschek, who in 1939 came as research associate to the Harvard Law School.

In 1911, Schumpeter was called to the University of Graz, the capital of the Austrian province of Styria, 150 miles south of Vienna. He was appointed by Imperial Rescript ("Zufolge Allerhöchster Entschliessung") against the vote of the faculty which had proposed some local nonentity. He was the youngest full professor in the faculty and, being the only economist in the university and having been put in charge of economic instruction at the *Technische Hochschule* as well, he had at first a very heavy teaching schedule ranging over the whole field of economics, including public finance. Despite all that, he managed to offer interesting special courses on such subjects as economic democracy and the problem of the social classes.

In the stuffy provincial atmosphere of Graz, which had none of the oriental lures of Czernowitz, he never felt happy and at home. But Graz was only a three hours' train ride from Vienna, and in later years he went there whenever possible. The academic year 1913–14 Schumpeter spent in New York at Columbia University, as Austrian exchange professor. He gave a course in theory, one in social classes, and a seminar. In March, 1914, he received the honorary degree of Litt.D. from Columbia,[13] and returned to Austria just before the outbreak of the war. He left Graz late in 1918, but remained a member of the faculty until 1921.

Schumpeter's scientific output during the years between his graduation from the University in 1906 and the end of the First World War was stupendous, especially if one considers that during that period he lived in five different places with as many different cultures, located in four countries on three continents, and that according to reports he made full use of the many opportunities to enjoy life which prewar Vienna and London, not to speak of Cairo and Czernowitz, offered in abundance.

In 1906 appeared his first major article "Über die mathematische Methode der theoretischen Ökonomie"; in 1908, when he was

[12] At the outbreak of the war in 1914, his wife was visiting in England. She did not return to Austria, and in 1920 the marriage was dissolved by mutual consent.

[13] He also received an honorary Doctor of Laws in 1939 from the University of Sofia, Bulgaria.

barely twenty-five years old, he published his first great book, *Wesen und Hauptinhalt der theoretischen Nationalökonomie*; and in 1912 his celebrated *Theorie der wirtschaftlichen Entwicklung*.[14] These two volumes immediately established his preeminence in the field of economic theory. "He never was a beginner" (Spiethoff in his beautiful obituary of Schumpeter in *Kyklos*, 1950). When he was thirty, he wrote a history of his science: *Epochen der Dogmen- und Methodengeschichte*[15] is a profound and mature piece of work which, however, only the expert can fully appreciate.

A sort of supplement to his *Dogmengeschichte* is the booklet, which discusses the past and future of the social sciences.[16] Having grown out of a lecture in Czernowitz in 1911, this essay is shorter and uses less heavy scholarly equipment than the *Dogmengeschichte*. It deals with economics and sociology in their relation to philosophy and history, but contains also interesting remarks on technical economic questions which foreshadow later developments. On page 125, for example, Schumpeter calls for empirical, "especially statistical," studies with a view to determining the shape of "demand curves." In addition to these books, every year there flowed from his pen a stream of important articles, some of them of considerable length, as well as innumerable book reviews.

An appraisal of Schumpeter's contribution to economics will be attempted later on in the present essay. At this point, only a few general remarks will be made. In his brilliant biography of Böhm-Bawerk,[17] Schumpeter remarked that Böhm-Bawerk's life illustrated and confirmed "the generalization which has been often surmised and has been more and more firmly established by biographical research (especially by Wilhelm Ostwald), namely that the roots of important original achievements, especially those of a theoretical nature, can almost always be found in the third decade of the lives of scholars, "that decade of sacred fertility." In later years Schumpeter was wont to repeat this observation. Surely his own scientific development is entirely in accord with that theory.

His business cycle theory was first fully expounded in the *Theory of Economic Development*, but the article on economic crises in 1910 already gave an outline of what was to come, and in the preface to the *Theory of Economic Development* Schumpeter stated that he had conceived the fundamental ideas as early as 1905. His famous theory of interest was clearly sketched in his first book, although fully developed in the second. The first book also contains interesting thoughts on the theory of saving, which recurred later in the book on *Business Cycles*. "Saving is not a function of income."[18] He holds that people quickly get used to higher income and do not really save more when their income rises.[19]

Schumpeter's basic sociological views, too, which were first published in 1927 in a lengthy paper[20] and were later elaborated in his *Capitalism, Socialism and Democracy*, seem to have crystallized at an early date. In a prefatory note to his 1927 article, he states that "the fundamental idea originated in 1910 and was first propounded in a series of popular lectures on 'State and Society' in Czernowitz during the winter 1910–11."[21] Similarly, many of his

---

[14] Translated into English by Redvers Opie under the title *The Theory of Economic Development* (Cambridge, Mass.: Harvard University Press, 1934). Hereafter the book will be referred to by its English title.

[15] In *Grundriss der Sozialökonomik*, Vol. I, Tübingen, 1914 (second impression, 1924), 106 large pages.

[16] *Vergangenheit und Zukunft der Sozialwissenschaften*, Munich, 1915, 140 small pages.

[17] "Das wissenschaftliche Lebenswerk Eugen von Böhm-Bawerks" in *Zeitschrift für Volkswirtschaft*, Vienna, 1914, pp. 454–528. A shorter article dealing more with Böhm-Bawerk's career as a statesman appeared in 1925 in the *Österreichische Biographie*. The remark which is referred to in the text is on p. 463 of the first, and p. 67 of the second, paper.

[18] *Wesen*, p. 308.

[19] He even maintains that more saving is done in lower and middle income brackets than in the very high ones (*ibid.*). Few will accept this statement, but it must be emphasized that he defines income *exclusive* of dynamic entrepreneurial profits. That is, I think, also the clue to his distinction between saving (out of income) and *not-spending*. This distinction which is made in *Business Cycles* (Vol. I, p. 75 ff) can already be found in his first book (*Wesen*, p. 309). The matter is a little obscure, but it seems that these dynamic profits are treated as capital gains and thus are not part of income. They are, at any rate, the almost exclusive source (apart from forced saving through inflation) of the financing of investment and of capital formation.

[20] "Die sozialen Klassen im ethnisch homogenen Milieu," *Archiv für Sozialwissenschaft*, Vol. LVII (1927), pp. 1–67.

[21] At Graz, Columbia, and later in Bonn he gave a course of lectures on social classes.

views on socialism, with which the Anglo-American public became first acquainted through his widely read book on socialism in 1942, found clear expression as early as 1918 in the brochure *Die Krise des Steuerstaats*, in 1919 in his brilliant essay *Zur Soziologie der Imperialismen*,[22] and in two exceedingly interesting and sparkling articles on socialism in England and in our country.[23]

Apart from the specific content, Schumpeter's very first publications display several features which are characteristic of all his work. There is, first, the great liking for the mathematical method in economics. It remained undiminished throughout his life, but it did not imply a neglect or underestimation of the importance of historical knowledge and research for the study of economics. On the contrary, he used to say that in case he had to give up either his historical or mathematical training, he would abandon the latter rather than the former.

His enthusiasm for the mathematical method was in contrast to the small use he made of it. In that respect, he was the exact opposite of Marshall: while Marshall had a mathematical bent of mind and mathematical training, and while his theoretical achievements would have been impossible without the use of mathematics, "he never gave full credit to the faithful ally" [mathematics] and "hid the tool that had done the work."[24] Schumpeter did not have an essentially mathematical mind but he extolled the use of mathematics, and his enthusiasm stimulated scores of students to utilize and to perfect mathematical methods of analysis in economics. But more important is that his earliest writings reveal two qualities which were so characteristic of the man and the scholar: his ideas and style of expression are highly original and supremely independent of his scientific environment.

By the time he left the university, he had read and studied a vast amount of economic literature, classical and modern, especially in English.[25] He was greatly impressed by, and highly admired, the work of Walras, the younger. In the preface to his first book, he said that Walras and Wieser, who was one of his professors, were the two economists to whom he felt closest. But while Wieser was hardly mentioned in his later work (although he wrote a beautiful though brief obituary),[26] he kept his high regard for Walras. In his appraisal of Marshall's *Principles* (1941), he calls Walras "the greatest of all theorists,"[27] and in his preface to the Japanese translation of the *Theory of Economic Development* (1937) he said that "as an economist" he owed more to Walras "than to any other influence."[28]

Schumpeter is usually regarded as a member of the Austrian school. The fact is, however, that as a man and as a scholar he was from the beginning a citizen of the world. He never liked to identify himself with any nationality, group, or school. What he said of Menger holds of Schumpeter himself: "He was nobody's pupil." This complete intellectual independence is already apparent in his earliest writings. Concretely, they show little specifically "Austrian" influence.[29] There is, it is true, a chapter on imputation in the *Wesen und Hauptinhalt* (and a long supplementary article on it appeared a year later), and his theory of cost may be termed "Austrian," but in most other respects his views were not those prevailing in Vienna at that time. Schumpeter refused to take sides in the *Methodenstreit* between Menger and Schmoller, although the skirmishing was still going on and the air was still full of the smoke of battle. The mathematical method was not very popular in Vienna.[30] Still less

[22] *Archiv für Sozialwissenschaft*, Vol. XLVI, pp. 1–39, 275–310 (also issued as a pamphlet).

[23] "Der Sozialismus in England und bei uns," *Der österreichische Volkswirt*, December 13 and 20, 1924.

[24] Schumpeter, "Marshall's Principles: Semi-Centennial Appraisal," *American Economic Review*, Vol. XXXI (June 1941), p. 240.

[25] See especially the article on the mathematical method in economics, 1906. His first book followed consciously the then current fashion (which he later gave up) of English and American books of dispensing with bibliographical footnotes almost entirely. But his great knowledge of the literature is clear from the text and other publications.

[26] *Economic Journal*, June 1927, pp. 328–330.

[27] *Loc. cit.*, p. 239.

[28] Page 2.

[29] It is entirely to the credit of the scientific milieu and a tribute to the great scholars who acted in it that it stimulated the growth of independent thinkers.

[30] Wieser especially did not like it. Böhm-Bawerk probably did not object, for he had a clear, mathematical mind himself, although unfortunately no mathematical training whatsoever. There were, of course, the two outsiders, Auspitz, and Lieben, whose *Untersuchungen über die Theorie des Preises* (Vienna, 1889) was an outstanding contribution

popular was the behavioristic attitude which he adopted in his first book and his rejection of the so-called "psychological method" and the use of "introspection." Wieser was especially critical of Schumpeter on that point.[31] It is worth noting that Schumpeter changed his views in this respect later on. In his theory classes at Harvard and in conversations he often argued on "psychological grounds," using introspection in favor of cardinal utility or, occasionally, even for the possibility of inter-individual comparison of utility.[32]

Schumpeter undoubtedly was influenced by Böhm-Bawerk's capital theory, and used the concept of roundabout methods of production in his theory of economic development. But he gave it a special dynamic slant and his interest theory is entirely different from the Böhm-Bawerkian.[33]

The great intellectual independence of environmental influences, the absolute refusal to be swayed by current fashions in science and politics, the complete freedom of mind, all this (paradoxically combined with a quite unusual capacity of understanding other people's views — witness his biographical essays) was strik-

ingly characteristic. People who did not know Schumpeter well frequently thought that this was nothing more than a passion to contradict, to take the opposite view, often intensified by an almost perverse pleasure in being unpopular and standing alone. It is true, he enjoyed *épater les bourgeois* and especially *épater les épateurs des bourgeois* (so he managed to shock and antagonize Philistines on the right and on the left at the same time), and he was quite capable occasionally of defending for argument's sake a position in which he did not believe. *L'art pour l'art* in discussions was by no means foreign to him. But he did not really relish being in a minority all the time. His independence was not a pose. One could truly say of him what Nietzsche said about Schopenhauer:

> "Seht ihn nur an —
> Niemandem war er untertan." [34]

IV. Foray into Statesmanship and Business, 1919–1924

Most of Schumpeter's life was wholly devoted to thinking, teaching, and writing, although he was never merely a bookish sort of person. He always took a lively interest in public and world affairs, felt intensely about, and never hesitated to express emphatic opinions on, current political issues. But it was only during the brief period from the end of the First World War to 1924 that he was actively engaged first in political life and then in business.

During the war he made no secret of his pacifist, pro-Western (especially pro-British)[35] and anti-German attitude. In the pamphlet on the crisis of the tax state,[36] instead of adopting the official phraseology and speaking of "the heroic fight for freedom and survival" or something like that, he referred to the war as that "bloody madness" which was "devastating

---

to mathematical economics. But there is no evidence that Schumpeter was especially influenced by them, although he was fully familiar with their work.

[31] See his review article "Das Wesen und der Hauptinhalt der theoretischen Nationalökonomie, Kritische Glossen," in *Jahrbuch für Gesetzgebung, Verwaltung und Volkswirtschaft im Deutschen Reich*, Vol. XXXV, Leipzig, 1911. Reprinted in F. v. Wieser, *Gesammelte Abhandlungen*, edited by F. A. Hayek (Tübingen, 1929).

[32] Lest anybody think this to be an obsolete and settled issue, I should like to quote from a recent work of one of the most eminent mathematicians and philosophers of our time: "Scientists would be wrong to ignore the fact that theoretical construction is not the only approach to the phenomena of life; another way, that of understanding from within (interpretation), is open to us. . . . Of myself, of my own acts of perception, thought, feeling and doing, I have a direct knowledge. . . . This inner awareness of myself is the basis for the understanding of my fellow-men whom I meet and acknowledge as beings of my own kind, with whom I communicate. . . ." Hermann Weyl, *Philosophy of Mathematics and the Natural Sciences* (English ed., Princeton, 1949), p. 283.

[33] See Böhm-Bawerk's long criticism, "Eine 'dynamische' Theorie des Kapitalzinses," *Zeitschrift für Volkswirtschaft, Sozialpolitik und Verwaltung*, Vol. XXII, 1913. In the same volume is a reply by Schumpeter and a rejoinder by Böhm-Bawerk. Böhm-Bawerk's article is reprinted in E. v. Böhm-Bawerk, *Kleinere Abhandlungen über Kapital und Zins* edited by F. X. Weiss (Vienna, 1926). The exchange with Böhm-Bawerk covers 120 pages and is one of the great controversies in our science.

[34] Friedrich Nietzsche, *Werke*, Vol. V (Leipzig: Alfred Kröner, Verlag 1930), p. 501.

[35] This attitude is most clearly revealed in his "Soziologie der Imperialismen" which appeared in 1919 but must have been written during the war.

[36] *Die Krise des Steuerstaats*. An enlarged version of a lecture, Graz, 1918. *Steuerstaat* is a state that relies on taxes for its revenue in contrast to the state in a socialist society which receives the bulk of its revenue from the income of nationalized industries. Thus the *Steuerstaat* is the fiscal complement to the free enterprise, capitalist economy.

Europe." Having good connections with the high aristocracy from his college days in the Theresianum, he seems to have been involved in the abortive attempt on the part of Emperor Karl and the court circle to arrange for a separate peace between Austria and the Western powers.

After the armistice the German socialist government set up a socialization commission in Berlin with the purpose of studying and preparing for the nationalization of industries. The head of the commission was Karl Kautsky, and Hilferding and Lederer, Schumpeter's acquaintances from university days, were prominent members. He received a call to join the commission, and spent two or three months late in 1918 and early in 1919 in Berlin. The work seems to have consisted in holding something like seminar discussions on the subject of socialization and other economic problems.

Schumpeter's membership in the *Sozialisierungskommission* has often been taken as proof of his socialist convictions. This is incorrect. The *Sozialisierungskommission* was not entirely composed of socialists, as the following passage from F. W. Bruck [37] shows: "So the '*Sozialisierungskommission*' was established in 1918 to which politicians and economists of various shades belonged. Among them were . . . some outspoken socialist theoreticians such as Kautsky, Lederer and Hilferding, and people of liberal standards like Franke and Vogelstein. This committee sometimes co-opted other men of high reputation as thinkers and practical men; in this way Professor Schumpeter joined the commission. . . ."

Schumpeter's attitude was revealed by his answer to the question, put to him by a young economist, of how he, who had extolled the role of the entrepreneur and the efficiency of the private enterprise system,[38] could be connected with the socialization commission: "If somebody wants to commit suicide, it is a good thing if a doctor is present."

On February 16, 1919, the first republican parliament was elected in Austria. The strictly Marxist socialists (official title: Social Democrats) emerged as the largest party and a coali-

tion government of the socialists and the so-called Christian Social party (a Catholic conservative party) was formed with Dr. Karl Renner, a right wing socialist, as head.[39] Neither of the two political parties was eager to take responsibility for the almost insoluble and politically unrewarding task of grappling with Austria's finances. So they agreed to let a nonpolitical expert try his hand at that hopeless and unpopular job. (In this respect, too, history repeated itself after World War II.) Otto Bauer, who was Secretary for Foreign Affairs in the Renner government, proposed Schumpeter for the position of *Staatssekretär für Finanzen*. On March 15, Schumpeter moved to the magnificent baroque palace built by Eugène of Savoy, one of Austria's greatest statesmen, where his teacher Böhm-Bawerk had held the same office under more favorable circumstances; he resigned from the Ministry of Finance on October 17, 1919.[40]

Schumpeter could not be called a successful Finance Minister by any conventional standard, but it is more than doubtful whether anybody could have been successful during that turbulent period. Politically and economically the situation was indeed chaotic. The war was lost, the old monarchy had collapsed and disintegrated, new states, new frontiers, and barriers to trade had arisen to the north, east, and south of Vienna. The supply of raw materials, fuel, and food from the customary sources outside the new state was interrupted, domestic production was far below the prewar level, food rations were extremely low, and from one week to the next the government did not know how to keep the population from starving and freezing to death. The political situation, too, was very precarious. Soviet regimes had sprung up in Hungary to the east and Bavaria to the west. Both were later suppressed in sanguinary

---

[37] *Social and Economic History of Germany from William II to Hitler* (Oxford University Press, 1938), p. 155.

[38] In *Die Krise des Steuerstaats*.

[39] The same coalition has again been in power since 1945, the only difference being that the Catholic party has changed its name to People's party, and the Social Democrats to Socialist party. In 1946 Dr. Renner became president of the second Austrian Republic.

[40] It was traditional for theoretical economists in Austria to take part in practical affairs. Menger took a lively interest in public issues and was highly influential in bringing about the Austrian currency reform in the 1890's which culminated in the adoption of the gold standard; Böhm-Bawerk was senior official in the Treasury and three times Minister of Finance; Wieser was Minister of Commerce.

counterrevolutions. The Austrian socialist leaders had great difficulty in restraining their radical followers, who were tempted to follow the Hungarian and Bavarian example, and one or two attempts to proclaim a *Rätediktatur* (Soviet dictatorship) in Austria had to be suppressed by force of arms.

No wonder that in such a milieu it was impossible to avoid inflation. The financial difficulties were tremendously complicated by the problems arising out of the dissolution of the Austro-Hungarian Empire. The new Austria was saddled with a disproportionate share of the debt of the old state, and had to take over a much larger number of the civil servants (and army officers) of the old Empire than were needed.

Apart from the insurmountable difficulties of his task, Schumpeter seems to have run into personal friction and suspicion right from the beginning. Many conservatives distrusted him, because they suspected him of being a socialist or, at least, of being too friendly with the socialists, having been "discovered" by Otto Bauer, the leader of the radical wing of the socialists. This was especially true of the powerful, highly competent, and efficient, but somewhat unimaginative, permanent officials at the Treasury who were deeply distrustful of the outsider — a colorful young man, a brilliant theorist, and eloquent speaker who had, however, never gone through the bureaucratic mill, but had been thrust upon them by the new rulers.

Moreover, he soon had really serious trouble with his socialist colleagues, and that caused his eventual downfall. Disagreements with the socialists were unavoidable, because his views and financial policies were essentially conservative and irreconcilable with the radical financial and economic policies advocated by the socialist party. It has often been said that Schumpeter, at the time he became Minister of Finance, favored socialization and radical financial policies. The record of his writings and his actions as a member of the government completely refute this contention.

The pamphlet *Die Krise des Steuerstaats*, mentioned above, contained an outline of the financial and economic policy that the author favored for the postwar period. When he was put in charge of the Austrian finances, he was,

of course, forced by events and practical political expediencies to modify and elaborate his program. But the basic ideas of his outline still can be found in the financial plans that he submitted to Parliament, especially the last one which he had ready when he was forced to resign.

In the first half of the pamphlet the author traces the historical evolution of modern taxation from the feudal state at the end of the Middle Ages to the present time. This historical analysis displays, as usual, tremendous erudition and the complete mastery of a vast material. He then discusses the limits to which various taxes can be raised without running into decreasing returns, thus killing the goose which lays the golden eggs. The second half of the pamphlet is concerned with the question whether the tax state and its complement, the free enterprise economy, i.e., capitalism, would be able to cope with the problems of financial and economic reconstruction after the war. The answer was an emphatic and unqualified "yes."

According to the author, there are two ways of solving the fiscal problem. The first is to let inflation take its course and so wipe out the war debt. The second is to eliminate the war debt by a capital levy. "I confess that at one time I favored the second method and I still believe that it is, in principle, the correct one. If I have become doubtful about its success, the reasons have nothing to do with the economics of the matter. But only a strong government with the broadest political basis, which impresses the people with real strength and with the personal prestige of its members, could dare to tackle the task of overcoming all obstacles, especially of preventing the capital levy from falling upon too small a segment of the economy, crushing it under its weight. Real political and financial ability is needed by the man who is to undertake that task — and in addition he needs a strong will and brilliant eloquence, which the people trust" (p. 45). When Schumpeter entered the government a year or so later, he thought he was that man; he tried and failed. He tried although he realized that "the fiscal policy up to now has made it nearly impossible to adopt the correct solution of the problem" (*loc. cit.*).

On the question as to whether it was more

advisable to rely on planning and governmental guidance than on the market mechanism and free enterprise for the transition from war to peace production, his answer was equally emphatic. The best thing the government could do was to refrain from interfering and to "release the tremendous reserves of energy which in Austria are wasted by the incessant battle against the shackles by which foolish legislation, administration, and politics restrain every economic move, and which deflect the entrepreneur from his organizational, technical, and commercial tasks, leaving him as the only way to success the back stairs to political and administrative bureaus" (p. 56). He favored free enterprise, also, in the field of foreign trade. "Every good bank has more credit abroad than the government." And a free system "will provide imports quickly and cheaply, if the bureaucracy does not hinder it by putting a mountain of paper and red tape between us and the needed raw materials" (p. 57).

But he concludes by saying that his proposal was meant "only for the concrete historical situation of the moment. I do not want to extoll the free enterprise economy as the last word of wisdom. Nor am I an uncritical admirer of the *bourgeoisie*. But what needs to be done now, is exactly what it can do best . . . Marx himself if he should appear today could not have another opinion and he would have a grim laugh for those of his followers who see in bureaucratic planning ('Verwaltungswirtschaft') . . . the dawn of socialism. . . . The hour of socialism will come, but it has not yet arrived. The war has postponed its arrival. . . . The hour that is, belongs to free enterprise. Only at the price of heavy sacrifice even for the working classes could the free enterprise system be given up at this time" (pp. 58–59).

As Secretary of Finance, Schumpeter never had a real chance to carry out his plan. As he had said himself, only a strong and united government could have done that. But the government was neither strong nor united. True, the socialists liked the idea of a capital levy, but they wanted it for the purpose of furthering the nationalization of industry by procuring for the state shares in industrial property. This was entirely incompatible with his ideas.

On the other hand, it soon must have become clear to Schumpeter that even under the most favorable circumstances a capital levy alone could not have restored financial stability and prevented further inflation; for elimination of the war debt, which he wished to achieve by means of the capital levy, would have been insufficient for the restoration of monetary equilibrium. He realized that the foremost requirement for financial and economic reconstruction was a foreign loan. On this assumption he based the grand financial plan which he worked out during the summer of 1919. This plan was never submitted to parliament. But it was discussed in the cabinet and was submitted to the Christian Social party which approved it. Its publication was expected with great impatience by everybody, for it was hoped that it would put an end to the progressive depreciation of the Austrian currency. But before the plan was officially revealed, Schumpeter was forced to resign.

The main content of the plan was as follows: [41] The guiding principle was that the budget must be balanced at all cost. "No bank notes or government paper money should be issued which serve directly or indirectly to satisfy the needs of the government." Governmental and private capital requirements for reconstruction must be financed by foreign loans. But the state has no chance of getting credit from abroad. The only basis for foreign loans can be private wealth. The property and credit of wealthy individuals must be used to secure foreign loans for the government. The inducement for private capitalists was to be provided through certain privileges in connection with the payment of the proposed capital levy. A capital levy rising progressively to 65 per cent of the net worth of the taxpayer was to be imposed, but those individuals, who agreed to provide through their private connections and personal guarantees foreign credit for the government amounting to at least 40 per cent of their net wealth, would have the privilege of paying their capital levy in 30 annual instalments instead of all at once. Additional

[41] *Grundlinien der Finanzpolitik für jetzt und die nächsten drei Jahre*, October 1919, 27 pages. Printed by the Government Printing Office. The pamphlet was, I believe, never published but copies were distributed to a number of people.

privileges were proposed in order to induce private capitalists to provide the foreign loans at the most favorable terms obtainable. The plan laid down the rule that the domestic currency proceeds of the capital levy were to be used exclusively for the purpose of reducing the war debt. Other provisions dealt with the establishment of a new bank of issue which was to be entirely independent of the government, with the early abolition of exchange controls, and with assorted revenue measures.

As mentioned above, Schumpeter was forced to resign before his plan was submitted to parliament. After his resignation inflation continued at an accelerated rate. It reached its peak and was stopped in 1922, but not before the Western powers had agreed to grant Austria a large international stabilization loan which was launched and administered under the supervision of the League of Nations.

It is not known exactly what led to his sudden resignation. But it was clear that his relations with the socialists had become very strained. Passive resistance of the powerful bureaucracy certainly contributed to his downfall, and it is a safe guess that there was not much enthusiasm in influential financial and industrial circles over the burdensome task which Schumpeter's reconstruction plan placed upon the wealthy classes.

His conflict with the socialists had various sources apart from the basic ideological differences. They objected to his "western orientation." The socialists, especially the Secretary for Foreign Affairs, Otto Bauer, were at that time staunch supporters of Austria's *Anschluss* to Germany, while the Western powers were for them the incarnation of capitalism. (Western, especially French, pressure caused Otto Bauer's resignation from the Foreign Office in the spring of 1919.) Schumpeter had excellent connections with the French and British missions in Vienna, and was accused, not only by the socialists but also by the highly respected periodical, *Der österreichische Volkswirt*, of intriguing against the *Anschluss* policy of the government. It is obvious, however, that apart from idealistic and ideological considerations, his policy of looking for help from the West was the only realistic one as subsequent events amply demonstrated, because only the West

could give the financial support that was urgently needed. Even twelve years later (1931), France was still strong enough to block the proposed Austro-German Customs Union on the ground that it was the first step towards a political union.

Another point of strong friction with the socialists was provided by the famous affair of the Alpine Montan-Gesellschaft, the largest iron and steel producer, and owner of the most important source of iron ore, in Austria. The socialists wanted to nationalize certain industries and, naturally, the iron and steel industry was at the top of their list. In June and July, 1919, there was a great boom on the stock exchange, especially in shares of the Alpine Montan-Gesellschaft, and it became known that a Viennese banking house had started to buy up the shares for an Italian group. The socialists were furious, or pretended to be, because they knew that they could not nationalize an industry in which there existed a strong foreign interest. They accused Schumpeter of having permitted, if not instigated that deal in order to make nationalization impossible. Otto Bauer charged Schumpeter with disloyalty to the government, and *Der österreichische Volkswirt* scolded him for making his own foreign policy at variance with that of the cabinet.

Schumpeter himself always denied that he or his ministry had anything to do with the transactions. Charles Gulick, in his book *Austria from Habsburg to Hitler*,[42] discusses the episode. He reprints two letters from Schumpeter in which it is pointed out that the authorities had no legal means of preventing the deal. The following passage (quoted by Gulick, *loc. cit.*, p. 141) makes the situation quite clear:

"1. I have never authorized, sanctioned, or suggested, anyone's purchase of stock in the Alpine Montan or any other corporation.

2. The idea of my doing so is absurd on the face of it, since no such authorization, sanction, or suggestion was required or would have induced anyone to carry out any such transaction.

3. I do not say that because I consider that such an authorization, sanction, or suggestion would have been wrong. On the contrary, I consider that, had I prevented a measure that could have only increased the difficulties of a difficult situation, this would have been a service to the country, the government and, above all, to the Social

[42] Berkeley, California, 1948, Vol. I, pp. 139–141.

Democratic party. I say the above because it is the truth." [43]

What really happened was that the socialists found it difficult for a variety of reasons to carry out their program of nationalization and were glad to find a scapegoat on whom they could blame their failure to keep their election promises to nationalize basic industries.

Even in a brief account of Schumpeter's life, mention must be made of a famous statement which he is supposed to have made either in Parliament or at a press conference — a statement which is remembered to this day by almost every Austrian whose family lost its savings through inflation. The statement was "Krone ist Krone" (a Crown is a Crown), meaning that any debt or obligation incurred under the old state could be discharged crown for crown with new money irrespective of the shrunken purchasing power of the monetary unit. For an economist there is, of course, nothing extraordinary about that. There has never been an inflation anywhere in the world where that rule did not hold; after all, a dollar is a dollar so far as the discharge of debts is concerned, even though prices have doubled. Nevertheless, it is a fact that the quoted statement made Schumpeter's name very unpopular with thousands of people who knew nothing else about him.

Looking back at the whole seven-month period, it seems obvious that Schumpeter could not have succeeded in stabilizing the Austrian currency. His financial plan was doomed to failure for the reasons he himself had foreseen so clearly. Under the then prevailing conditions, any Austrian Minister of Finance would have had to be regarded as expendable.[44] Inflation simply had to run its course. It required imminent and complete economic collapse to rouse the country to a supreme effort and to persuade the West that something decisive had to be done. The time for that did not come until two and a half years later.

There is no evidence that Schumpeter took his misfortune in statesmanship as a great tragedy. He had foreseen it in his 1918 pamphlet, where he had written: "It could be objected [to the fiscal program he recommended] that for such an effort the moral energy was lacking in Austria. This may be so, but that would be Austria's failure and not that of the *Steuerstaat*," i.e., of his program.[45]

Attacks on Schumpeter by the socialist press and in Parliament were rude and bitter, and he was rather brusquely forced to resign.[46] The treatment he received from the socialists must have been galling at the time, especially for a man like Schumpeter, who was extremely sensitive to any kind of vulgarity; but later he did not show any resentment. For example, his two articles "Der Sozialismus in England und bei uns" in 1924 (p. 23 above) contain a good-natured, occasionally slightly ironical, but at the same time sympathetic, criticism of the strategy and tactics of the continental and especially the Austrian socialist party, against the background of the British socialist movement. He there analyzes dispassionately but brilliantly and understandingly the enormous superiority of the British system, with its dignified, well mannered, evolutionary way of doing things, as compared with the revolutionary, dogmatic methods of continental socialism, always marred by bad manners and demagoguery. There is, however, no trace of annoyance or vindictiveness. This was typical of the man.

About two years after he left the government, Schumpeter became president of the Biedermann Bank, a small but old and highly respected private banking house. The bank did not long survive the stabilization crisis. It went

[43] *Der österreichische Volkswirt*, which was very critical on the whole, had to admit that the government had no legal basis to forbid the sale of shares to foreign interests. All they could do was to impound the foreign exchange proceeds resulting from such sales. That they actually did (August 23, 1919, p. 890).

[44] In a recent article, "There is Still Time to Stop Inflation," *Nation's Business*, June 1948, Schumpeter commented on the Austrian and German inflations after the First World War as follows: "But it was the absence (however understandable) of political stamina, not any *economic* impossibility of stabilization or any lack of knowledge as to what remedies would have been effective, that caused the ultimate catastrophe" (p. 33). He pointed out that the danger to the United States at present was attributable to the reluctance of political leaders to take action, because effective measures are unpopular with so many groups. This same theme was repeated in "The March into Socialism," his address before the American Economic Association in New York, December 1949.

[45] *Die Krise des Steuerstaats*, p. 43.

[46] The newspaper *Neue Freie Presse* reported on October 18, 1919, that the Christian Social party demanded that Schumpeter should "receive satisfaction for the brusque treatment he had received during the last days."

bankrupt in 1924, and since it was one of the first banks to fail and many people lost money — during the following years Austrians had to get used to bank failures, in fact hardly a single bank escaped that fate — the collapse of the Biedermann Bank came as a great shock and put its president in a difficult position. Unlike most other bankers, he did not save any part of his personal fortune in the crash and even managed in subsequent years to repay his personal debts out of his earnings.

He decided to return to academic life and accepted an invitation to be a guest professor in Japan. But when, soon after, he received an invitation from the Prussian Ministry of Education to a chair at the University of Bonn, which had become vacant by the retirement of Heinrich Dietzel, the eminent liberal economist, he went there instead. In his later years he never forgot that it had been a Japanese and a German university that offered him the opportunity to resume the quiet life of a scholar. His sentimental attachment to both countries and his sharp reaction to chauvinistic wholesale condemnation of the German and Japanese peoples and their culture during the Second World War had one of its roots in that experience.

Before he left Vienna, he married a charming and beautiful Viennese girl, Annie Reisinger, of humble origin, to whose schooling he had contributed for several years. This marriage was entirely happy, but very brief. His wife died in 1926 in childbirth in Bonn. Her death and that of his mother (also in 1926), to whom he had been greatly devoted, came as a terrible shock, and after that time a streak of resignation and pessimism was unmistakable in his character.

V. Academic Life in Bonn and Harvard, 1925–1950

Schumpeter's last twenty-five years were devoted entirely to scholarship and teaching. It was his second period of enormous productivity and also a period of tremendous academic success as measured by influence on students and recognition by the economic profession at large. He was one of the founders of the Econometric Society and its president from 1937 to 1941. In 1948 he became president of the American Economic Association, and when in 1949 plans

were laid for the founding of an International Economic Association, there was unanimous agreement that he was to be the first president of the new society. (In this connection, he planned to visit Europe in September 1950 for the first time in fifteen years.)

The move to Bonn constituted a complete break with his past life in more than one respect. As a typical member of the old Austrian (pre-1914) society, Schumpeter had never been a friend and admirer of Germany. In spite of that he soon felt at home in the scholarly and cultured atmosphere of the old university town on the Rhine. He formed a new set of lasting and intimate friendships. That does not mean that he forgot his old friends. But he never went back to his native country again except for a very short visit, *incognito*, on the occasion of the death of his beloved mother. I do not think the motive was resentment or wounded pride. It was rather the logical consequence of his resolve to give up all ambition to play a role in politics and business and to devote himself entirely to scholarship.

The change from Bonn to Harvard was less abrupt. He taught in Harvard during the academic year 1927–28, and again during the autumn term of 1930. But after he resigned from Bonn and went to Harvard permanently in 1932, he never revisited Germany although he spent the next three summers (until 1935) in Europe.

The chair Schumpeter held in Bonn was that of public finance. Economic theory and business cycles were taught by Arthur Spiethoff. But the course in public finance gave him plenty of opportunity to discuss theory, and during the last year before his departure from Bonn he gave a full course on economic theory, which was a great event. There was also the famous Schumpeter seminar which was concerned largely with theory, including the theory of money and especially, as befitted a German university, with epistemology. In respect to the last subject, Schumpeter saw his main function, I am sure, in debunking the application of particular philosophical systems to economics (which was so popular in Germany) and in disabusing his students of the philosophic preconceptions with which many were heavily overloaded. During the few years in Bonn,

Schumpeter exerted a strong and lasting influence on German economics through his teaching as well as his writing. The revival of economic theory in Germany was due to a large extent to the fact that he put his full prestige behind it. The many dissertations, articles, and books that dealt with his theories provide documentary proof of that contention.

While at Bonn, Schumpeter published a thoroughly revised edition of his *Theory of Economic Development* and an incredibly large number of very important articles of which only a few can be mentioned. In 1926 appeared a long and searching appraisal of the work of Schmoller, whose so-called "realistic" approach to economics was compared with the work of American institutionalists and especially with that of W. C. Mitchell. In 1927 appeared three brilliant articles on the work of Wicksell, Cassel, and Sombart as well as a long and penetrating essay of thirty large pages on the state of economic theory in Germany and Austria in the four-volume book, *Die Wirtschaftstheorie der Gegenwart*.[47] In the same year he published an essay of almost book length on the theory of social classes. In addition to all that, he found time for many book reviews and a large number of articles on current economic questions, especially problems of public finance. Most of these articles appeared in *Der deutsche Volkswirt* (1926–32) with whose editor and fellow Austrian, Gustav Stolper (member of the German Reichstag and formerly editor of *Der österrreichische Volkswirt*), Schumpeter was connected by the bonds of a lifelong close friendship. An incomplete but comprehensive monograph on money on which he had been working seems to have been discontinued in 1934 when he started writing his book on Business Cycles. The voluminous manuscript and extensive notes which he went on collecting are in Mrs. Schumpeter's possession, and it is to be hoped that its content will be conveyed in some form to the interested public.

In 1931, after a term in Harvard, Schumpeter returned to Germany by way of the Pacific and the Far East. He spent several months lecturing in Japan. His teaching and writing had a profound influence on Japanese econo-

mists among whom he has many devoted disciples. Most of his books are translated into Japanese; he was mourned there at the time of his death and even the daily newspapers published full length obituaries.

The outward course of his life during the eighteen years at Harvard (1932–50) is quickly traced. Apart from three brief summer vacations in Western Europe, a short lecture trip to Mexico (winter, 1948) and another one to neighboring Montreal, he did not leave the country.

These were years of most intense work. He spent his whole time the four seasons round at work — vacation periods, Sundays, and holidays included — in his home in Cambridge or in his country house in Taconic, Connecticut, or lecturing, or consulting with students and visiting scholars. The only interruptions from work were gatherings with friends, most of them professional, an occasional concert, a trip to the annual meeting of the American Economic Association, or a lecture trip to some university city.

He always had a most ambitious writing program and as time went on he tried more and more to economize his time. All his life he kept a short diary in which each day would get a high or low mark according to whether he thought he had accomplished much or little. But despite a feeling of increasing pressure to gather the harvest of a fertile mind and a full life's learning, reading, observing, and reflecting, he never refused to take time out for conversations with students and colleagues on their problems, reading their manuscripts, writing letters of recommendation, and the like.

The first years at Harvard he lived with F. W. Taussig. In 1937 he married Elizabeth Boody, a descendant of an old New England family and an economist in her own right. As time went on, he leaned more and more on her devotion and wise counsel in all practical matters. Without her loving and understanding care, he could not have achieved as much as he did.

During the years of the gathering storm and of the Second World War, Schumpeter found himself again in the minority because of his political views and convictions. While during the First World War he had been pro-

---

[47] Edited by H. Mayer (Vienna, 1927), Vol. I, pp. 1–30.

British and anti-German (of course only in a political sense), during the Second World War he gave the impression of being pro-German. Needless to say he had no sympathies with the Nazi regime. He knew and said repeatedly, that if he had remained in Germany he would have been one of the first candidates for the concentration camp.[48] But most of his friends thought that he underestimated the dangers, the aggressive power, and intentions of Hitlerism. He felt that Germany had genuine grievances, that she had been treated badly after World War I, and that excessive nationalism was the unfortunate reaction thereto.[49] But he hoped that if left alone she would eventually calm down. War was for him such a terrible calamity that to avoid it almost no price seemed too high. And he foresaw clearly the rise of communism in the wake of the war and all it meant for Western civilization.[50] At any rate he reacted strongly against anti-German (as distinguished from anti-Nazi) propaganda and policies. Thus the war years must have been among the most somber and depressing of his life. Out of sympathy with the policies of his adopted country and out of touch with many of his friends, Schumpeter buried himself in his scientific work, unhappily watching the decline of much that he considered valuable in the Western world.

The scholarly achievements of his Harvard years are most impressive indeed. There is first the great two volume work *Business Cycles* (1939), which is better described by its subtitle, "A Theoretical, Historical, and Statistical Analysis of the Capitalist Process." It is a monument to theoretical acumen, truly encyclopaedic erudition, painstaking scholarship, and perseverance. The main ideas, which are those of his *Theory of Economic Development*, as well as the general scope of the work, are well known and need not be indicated here. But what is not generally known, and perhaps sounds improbable, is that, apart from some clerical assistance, he wrote the book singlehanded. The fact is that, although he was a very sociable man and appreciated the necessity and usefulness of scientific teamwork, Schumpeter was always a lone wolf in his scientific work. Everything he published he wrote out in longhand, and for a long time, having no secretary, he had even to write his letters in his own hand.

But he always had the rare and priceless talent — Böhm-Bawerk called it a "gift of God,"[51] adding that it could be a dangerous gift — of easy and quick expression. He could read and absorb new ideas and facts with amazing speed, and he never found it difficult in writing or speaking to find the right word or phrase from a tremendous vocabulary in both German and English. In fact, he used the English language with a verve and pungency that few could equal. However, in the short run the reception of the business cycle book was disappointing. The reasons are not hard to understand. The book is not well arranged and is not easy to read. It is written in a heavy and often involved style with no concessions to the reader or to current fads. It appeared at the beginning of the war at a time when the wave of Keynesianism and depression economics was at its very height. But apart from these unfavorable external circumstances, it is the kind of book which takes considerable time to exert its full influence.

The next book, *Capitalism, Socialism and Democracy*, was (for a serious book, not a textbook) a great popular success. It has appeared in several editions,[52] and was translated into at

---

[48] He has been violently attacked by National Socialist economic writers on the ground that his economic theories were not German in spirit.

[49] His views on the reparations problem, Franco-German *rapprochement*, and related problems he stated in the special issue of *Lloyds Bank Monthly Review* (London, March 1932) on "World Depression and Franco-German Economic Relations: A German View by J. Schumpeter." He there expressed doubts on whether "reparations *per se*" had much to do with the economic plight of Germany, although he stressed their indirect, political importance. He attributed much more importance to "unsound fiscal policies." This article earned him sharp attacks in the nationalist German press.

[50] See chapter XXVIII, "The Consequences of the Second World War," added to the second edition of his *Capitalism, Socialism and Democracy* (1947), where he speaks his mind without restraint.

[51] See his criticism of Schumpeter's theory of interest in *Zeitschrift für Volkswirtschaft* (Vienna, 1913), Vol. XXII, p. 61.

[52] New York: Harper and Bros. first ed., 1942; second revised ed., 1947; third enlarged ed. with a new chapter, 1950. There have also been three editions in England (London, Allen & Unwin).

least five foreign languages. It was written within a year or two and the author regarded it as nothing more than a parergon.

During the last years Schumpeter had been working on a great history of economic analysis. The manuscript is almost finished and will be published by Mrs. Schumpeter in two volumes under the title *History of Economic Analysis*.

Apart from these books, he wrote many articles, among them the historical and biographical masterpieces on Taussig, Marshall, Keynes, Fisher, Pareto, and Mitchell (in that order). These essays, together with earlier ones on Walras, Menger, and Böhm-Bawerk and the essay on Marx in Part I of *Capitalism, Socialism and Democracy*, were published in May 1951 under the title *Ten Great Economists: From Marx to Keynes*, by the Oxford University Press.

During all his Harvard years (excepting two sabbatical terms which he spent working in his home in Taconic), Schumpeter carried a full teaching load, and, especially during the earlier part of the period, organized and attended all sorts of special discussion groups and seminars. He always felt that the official minimum teaching assignment in the university was too heavy to permit professors adequate time for research and writing, and strongly urged its reduction. But he himself usually taught much more than the official minimum. That again was typical: he preached wine for others but drank water himself.

Schumpeter was the most cooperative and considerate colleague anyone could imagine. He was always ready to offer his help, to serve on a committee, or to substitute for an indisposed colleague in a lecture or seminar, and was most reluctant and apologetic in asking for similar favors. His standards concerning the dignity and social status of university professors and scholars were of the highest order, and he often complained that, in most American universities and in American society at large, scholars did not enjoy the social status they ought to have and were overburdened with administrative duties. He nevertheless did his full part, along with the youngest instructors, in performing menial chores, such as foreign language examinations. He never behaved like a prima

donna, although he was often regarded as one, especially by outsiders.

His teaching program consisted of a full course in advanced theory which he offered every year. Every other year or so he would offer a half course in business cycles and one in the history of economic doctrines, and now and then a half course in money and banking. In recent years he gave regularly a half course in socialism and social movements. The content of all these courses would be varied from year to year, but they all suffered from one defect: by listening to Schumpeter's lectures and studying his reading assignments and suggestions, students could have never found out that he himself had ever written anything on those subjects.

Schumpeter kept working to the very end, which came with merciful suddenness without serious illness or pain, though not without premonitions. He attended the annual meeting of the American Economic Association in New York from December 26 to 30, 1949, where he faithfully took part in all the meetings of the executive committee and performed with his usual verve and brilliance. There he presented his last paper, entitled "The March into Socialism." [53] Characteristically he spoke from notes and not from a prepared paper. He returned, very tired, to Taconic and started to write out this paper for the Proceedings and to put the finishing touches to a series of six lectures which he was to give in the University of Chicago under the title *American Institutions and Economic Progress*. During the night of January 7–8 he passed away peacefully in his sleep.

VI. Schumpeter's Contribution to Economics

The time for a complete and detailed appraisal of Schumpeter's scientific achievements and of his place in the history of economics has not yet arrived. Full appreciation of a work of such magnitude and complexity requires greater time distance for proper perspective, especially inasmuch as his last great book, the *History of Economic Analysis*, which promises to be in itself a major event in the history

[53] Reprinted in third edition of *Capitalism, Socialism and Democracy*, 1950.

of economic thought, is not yet available. The following remarks are therefore nothing more than a preliminary sketch.

In the opening pages of his revealing biography of Böhm-Bawerk,[54] he points out that Böhm-Bawerk's entire scientific work is one thoroughly integrated whole. Practically everything Böhm-Bawerk wrote was directed towards the well-defined goal of working out his model of the capitalist economy. Also his numerous and endless controversies were devoted to the sole purpose of clarifying and supporting Böhm-Bawerk's own theoretical structure.[55] "He knew exactly what he wanted in science and in life, which one can say of but few men, and therefore it is easy to review his work."[56]

Schumpeter's own work is much more difficult to describe, and his place in modern economics not easy to define. There are several reasons for this. It is true that Schumpeter, like Böhm-Bawerk and most great social scientists (Edgeworth might perhaps be regarded as an exception), had a broad over-all picture of the socio-economic process, a "vision" as Schumpeter used to call it which, like the plot in a good drama, gives unity to his work. His "grand design," the contours of which can already be discerned in his first book (*Wesen und Hauptinhalt*, 1908), found its full expression in his *Theory of Economic Development* (1912) and was lavishly, sometimes laboriously worked out, illustrated, and tested in his *Business Cycles* and further elaborated in his *Capitalism, Socialism and Democracy*. It is much more complex than that of Böhm-Bawerk and other neoclassical economists.

In the first place, while Böhm-Bawerk's model (also that of Walras but not that of Marshall) is essentially static,[57] Schumpeter's model is dynamic in nature. It is not dynamic in the sense of modern sequence analysis; it is not "micro-dynamics," the word "micro" being here used not in the sense of dealing with the behavior of the smallest economic units (household and firm) as contrasted with aggregate quantities (national income, consumption, investment). In this latter sense, Schumpeter *is* a "micro-theorist," at least as far as his methodological credo is concerned. He was always suspicious of aggregates and averages — "beware of averages," he said, in his very first paper (see page 20, above) — and he often urged that economic analysis should be based on the theory of household and firm. But in his "theoretical practice," he was, it seems to me, like other economists who hold similar views, unable to avoid the use of aggregates and averages. The word "micro" is here used in the sense of being concerned with minor, unimportant fluctuations. Schumpeter's theory was not micro-dynamics as exemplified by modern post-Keynesian multiplier-acceleration models, and the like. He was quite familiar with those models. He highly appreciated the mathematical ingenuity which goes into their construction, discussed them in considerable detail in his classes,[58] and was willing to make limited use of them for the explanation of minor oscillations around the great waves of economic development,[59] but he felt that they are just as incapable of explaining the great economic rhythm as the ripples caused by high winds

---

[54] "Das wissenschaftliche Lebenswerk Eugen von Böhm-Bawerks," *Zeitschrift für Volkswirtschaft, Verwaltung und Sozialpolitik*, Vol. XXIII (1914), Vienna. The title of this lengthy essay (73 pages) does not do justice to the content. It is not confied to an appraisal of Böhm-Bawerk's scientific work, but contains also a brilliant description and analysis of the great economist's personality with many penetrating observations on what might be called the economics and psychology of economic theorizing. This is probably the most revealing of Schumpeter's biographical essays. It is written with much feeling and shows the close personal and scientific relation with Böhm-Bawerk. In view of that, it seems appropriate in an appraisal of Schumpeter's work to devote some space to a comparison of his system with that of Böhm-Bawerk, especially since in most points here considered, Böhm-Bawerk's views are representative not only of Austrian but of Walrasian and Marshallian economics as well.

[55] Böhm-Bawerk's criticisms and polemics were always polite and urbane in tone as well as truly scientific and constructive in content. He criticized not for criticism's sake but in order to test and defend *The Positive Theory of Capital* against other views. That holds fully also of his Marx critique ("Karl Marx and the Close of His System") which, as Schumpeter said, "will never cease, as far as the theoretical content of the Marxian system goes, to be *the* Marx critique" (*loc. cit.*, p. 474).

[56] Schumpeter, *loc. cit.*, p. 457.

[57] This may sound strange because Böhm-Bawerk stresses the time element so much. But one can deal with the time factor by means of the method of comparative statics. That is what Böhm-Bawerk did.

[58] See also *Business Cycles*, Vol. I, Chapter IV.

[59] From conversation and remarks in classes it appears that he was ready to accept an inventory mechanism *à la* Abramowitz and Metzler as explanation for the short cycle (Kitchin cycle).

on the surface of the sea are incapable of influencing the great rhythm of the tide.

Schumpeter's dynamic mechanism is driven by more powerful forces than the vagaries of the propensity to consume and the acceleration principle. The nature of these forces (technological and organizational innovations, entrepreneurial activity, and the credit mechanism which enables the dynamic innovator to draw productive resources from the static "circular flow" economy) are too well known to make detailed discussion necessary.[60]

In the preface to the Japanese edition of his *Theory of Economic Development* he says: ". . . When in my beginnings I studied the Walrasian conception and the Walrasian technique . . . I discovered not only that it is rigorously static in character . . . but also that it is applicable only to a stationary process. These two things must not be confused. A static theory . . . can be useful in the investigation of any kind of reality, however disequilibrated it may be. A stationary process, however, is a process which *actually* does not change of its own initiative, but merely reproduces constant rates of real income as it flows along in time. If it changes at all, it does so under the influence of events which are external to itself, such as natural catastrophes, wars, and so on. Walras would have admitted this. He would have said (and as a matter of fact, he did say it to me the only time I had the opportunity to converse with him) that . . . economic life is essentially passive and merely adapts itself to the natural and social influences which may be acting on it, so that the theory of a stationary process constitutes really the whole of theoretical economics. . . . I felt very strongly that this was wrong, and that there was a source of energy within the economic system which would of itself disrupt . . . equilibrium. If this is so, then there must be a purely economic theory of economic change which does not merely rely on external factors. . . . It is such a theory that I have tried to build and I believe . . . that it contributes something to the understanding . . . of the

capitalist world and explains a number of phenomena . . . more satisfactorily than . . . either the Walrasian or Marshallian apparatus." [61]

I have strong doubts that the sharp distinction between disequilibrating forces working from within the economic system and those operating on the economic system from the outside contributes anything to the understanding of economic development. But the concrete mechanism of economic change, as described and analyzed by Schumpeter, undoubtedly constitutes a great advance over traditional neoclassical economics.

In these respects he felt himself to be, and actually was, closer to Marx than to Walras, Böhm-Bawerk, and, even more, than to Keynes.[62] Indeed, all his life he was attracted by the grandeur of the Marxian system, although he was by no means an uncritical admirer of Marx and, in recent years, he scornfully disapproved of what he derisively referred to as "the Keynesianization of Marx," that is of the attempts at interpreting Marx in terms of the Keynesian system; this he regarded as a complete emasculation of the Marxian system. There are two other characteristics of Schumpeter's system which seem to put him closer to Marx than to Walras, Böhm-Bawerk, and Marshall. These are, first, the important role assigned to social relationships and to the institutional framework (as against "purely economic" factors) and second, the historical slant and intent of his theory.

These differences between Schumpeter on the one hand and Böhm-Bawerk and other "pure" economists on the other are, however, only a matter of degree. He had no sympathy whatever for the vague, almost metaphysical "collectivism" of which there is so much in Marxist writings. By this I mean "the special and exclusive outlook upon the whole of social life" claimed by the Marxists — an outlook which postulates social forces that operate on

[60] These things have been often discussed. There is now available the excellent and convenient study by R. V. Clemence and Francis S. Doody, *The Schumpeterian System* (Cambridge, Mass., 1950).

[61] Pp. 2 and 3.

[62] In this preface to the Japanese edition of the *Theory of Economic Development*, he mentioned that it was *not* clear to him at the outset "what to the reader will perhaps be obvious at once, namely, that this idea and this aim [to construct a theory of economic development which relies on forces internal to the economic system] are exactly the same that underlie the economic teaching of Marx" (p. 3).

and influence individual behavior and are some-how independent of the totality of individual actions.[63] Schumpeter always adhered to what he called "methodological individualism," [64] i.e., the principle that social phenomena and forces must be defined and interpreted in terms of interrelations and interactions, often of great complexity, between individuals and their sub-jective motivations.

According to Schumpeter, Böhm-Bawerk's theory — and here again Böhm-Bawerk stands for modern theoretical economics — is not "un-social," but the "sociological framework" is only "lightly indicated." [65] It should be ob-served that Böhm-Bawerk sharply distinguishes between the individual household economy (Robinson Crusoe economy), the competitive price economy, and the centrally planned (so-cialist) economy.[66] It is true, however, that Böhm-Bawerk and other marginalists are largely concerned with analyzing economic relationships which hold wherever men apply scarce resources to unlimited wants, irrespective of the particular social organization of society. Schumpeter did not deny that there are such all-embracing regularities, but he was of the opinion that they are of more limited validity than traditional economic theories assume. In that sense his theory is more "social," i.e., it

differentiates more according to the social framework than that of Böhm-Bawerk and other modern theorists.

The difference comes to a head in connection with the problem of interest, capital accumu-lation, and the business cycle. In the *Theory of Economic Development* and in his famous controversy with Böhm-Bawerk on the rate of interest,[67] Schumpeter argued that the rate of interest is institutionally and dynamically de-termined. There would be no interest either in a stationary or semistationary price economy nor in a centrally planned (socialist or single household) economy (whether stationary or progressive), while according to Böhm-Bawerk, the rate of interest is a basic economic cate-gory, independent of the concrete social and institutional arrangements. In this particular respect most economists, including many mod-ern socialists, would side with Böhm-Bawerk, holding that as a calculating or accounting cate-gory (though not as a distributive share) the rate of interest has a place also in the socialist economy.[68]

It should not be overlooked that Schum-peter's contribution to interest theory is not confined to the somewhat questionable proposi-tion that in a stationary state the rate of in-terest would be zero. He might well have ad-mitted that there must be a positive rate of interest in a stationary state, but insisted that the interest rates which we find in practice are raised above the stationary level by the dynamic forces described in his theory.

The controversy concerning the rate of in-terest is, however, only one facet of the whole problem. The differences between Schumpeter's scheme of things and that of Böhm-Bawerk (and Böhm-Bawerk here stands again for a large part of neoclassical economics) goes deeper; it concerns the whole conception of the process of capital accumulation and economic progress. Let me briefly indicate the difference.

---

[63] See, for example, Sweezy's edition of Böhm-Bawerk and Hilferding (*loc. cit.*), especially Sweezy's introduction, pp. xx–xxii, and Hilferding, chap. iii, "The Subjectivist Out-look" (p. 184 ff.) where the "social and unhistorical" stand-point of Marx is contrasted with the "unsocial and unhistori-cal" standpoint of Böhm-Bawerk and of orthodox theory in general. Marxism inherited this social metaphysics from German idealistic philosophy (Hegel), and it shares it with systems like that of Othmar Spann, who derives it from the same source. I know that the Marxists as well as Spann would deny violently and indignantly that their views have anything in common with one another, although they origi-nate from the same source. This illustrates the truth of the observation that there is nowhere so much hatred as be-tween members of the same family.

[64] See the lengthy discussion in *Wesen und Hauptinhalt*, Part I, chap. vi, "Der methodologische Individualismus."

[65] See Schumpeter's biographical essay on Böhm-Bawerk, *loc. cit.*, p. 489. In Marshall's work the social framework is more fully elaborated than in Walras' or in Böhm-Bawerk's writings.

[66] There is a chapter on interest in the socialist economy in his *Positive Theory of Capital*. There is also the im-portant article "Macht oder ökonomisches Gesetz?" (*Zeit-schrift für Voltswirtschaft*, Vol. XXIII, Vienna, 1914, re-printed in *Gesamte Schriften*, Vol. I, ed. F. X. Weiss) which deals with the problem of the extent to which economic laws can be interfered with by government action.

[67] *Zeitschrift für Volkswirtschaft*, Vol. XXII, 1913.

[68] Keynes's interest theory is superficially similar to Schumpeter's inasmuch as he conceives of the rate of in-terest as a purely psycho-monetary phenomenon. But his position on this issue is basically ambiguous and contra-dictory. As is so often the case, one has to distinguish be-tween Keynes's formalized system and a confusing though suggestive welter of surrounding remarks, which contains much that not only goes beyond but also contradicts the liquidity theory of interest of his formalized system.

According to Böhm-Bawerk and most other modern economists (including especially F. H. Knight) [69] the process of capital accumulation is essentially, or at least potentially, smooth and continuous. People save and savings are invested. Thus the capital stock grows and output increases. In addition, the production function changes, new methods and processes are invented all the time, and output increases for that reason too. These writers recognize, of course, that the process of economic development through capital accumulation and advances in technological knowledge is often interrupted. The business cycle and the recurrence of economic depressions are not ignored. But these phenomena are regarded as inessential deviations, due to monetary disturbances and the like — disturbances that could be avoided or at least reduced to insignificant proportions by appropriate policies.

Schumpeter would not deny that some progress can be realized in a smooth and orderly fashion by continuous accumulation of capital and gradual improvement of technology. But he thinks it could not amount to much. The really big changes which shape the course of economic development are not made, cannot be made, gradually and continuously; they must be forced upon the stationary, circular flow economy in intermittent pushes. The business cycle (at least the major cycle), which for many other theorists is the result either of monetary surface phenomena (avoidable aberrations of monetary policy [Mises, Hayek], or of lags and frictions (Hawtrey) or of the vagaries of multiplier and acceleration principle and the like, becomes in Schumpeter's theory an integral part of the process of economic development in the capitalist system. The complicated mechanism which produces this result and its constituent parts, the path-breaking role of the innovator-entrepreneur and of the host of imitators who follow suit, the function of productive credit inflation and forced saving succeeded by autodeflation and all the rest, is well known. Capitalism for Schumpeter becomes, thus, a narrower concept than for Böhm-Ba-werk and most neoclassical economists. It is not synonymous with an individualistic price economy and still less with an economy which uses capital on a large scale; it is a very special type of price economy, namely, that one which is so organized that the indicated rhythmic mechanism can operate. ". . . Capitalism is defined by three features . . . : private ownership of the physical means of production; private profits and private responsibility for losses; and the creation of means of payments — bank notes and deposits — by private banks. The first two features suffice to define private enterprise. But no concept of capitalism can be satisfactory without including the set of typically capitalistic phenomena covered by the third." [70]

The complicated interaction of social and economic forces reappears again, on a higher level, as it were, in the theory of the socio-political disintegration of capitalism as fully elaborated in his *Capitalism, Socialism and Democracy*, although clearly foreshadowed in earlier writings. Schumpeter finds that economically speaking the capitalist system has served the human race very well indeed. It has raised the volume of output and standard of living tremendously. Glaring inequalities of income could easily be removed without serious impairment of the productivity of the economic machine. He saw no economic reason why capitalism should not continue to function with equal success in the future. But, at the same time, he was convinced that capitalism was doomed, because by its very success it is bound to destroy its own supporting and protecting social structures. This piece of social dynamics is not widely accepted, nor does it seem to be a necessary consequence of the rest of Schumpeter's theoretical structure. But it throws into high relief the great complexity and the close interrelations of economic and social forces that are so characteristic of Schumpeter's work.

It was said above that Schumpeter's theory is more historical than that of Böhm-Bawerk and of most other modern economists. Schumpeter was always deeply interested in histori-

---

[69] I hope Professor Knight will not object to being grouped with Böhm-Bawerk. His objections to the concept of a period of production and the like seems to me of minor importance in the present context.

[70] "Capitalism in the Postwar World," in *Postwar Economic Problems*, edited by S. E. Harris (New York, 1943), p. 113.

cal problems and a strong supporter of the historical method of understanding social and economic phenomena. He had historical feeling and perspective, and a tremendous historical knowledge. Many of his writings had a historical slant. His *Wesen und Hauptinhalt* (1908) and *Theory of Economic Development* (1912) are, however, entirely unhistorical, although the theory expounded in the latter book is the basis of later historical interpretations. Schumpeter was, however, not a "historicist" in the sense in which Hegel and Marx [71] were, that is to say, he did not enunciate sweeping historical laws, although he evidently played with the idea of predetermined historical evolution, and was much intrigued by Marx's historical construction. But his devotion to exact methods and rigid scientific discipline did not permit him to go far in the direction of historico-philosophical speculation. He found much truth in the "materialistic interpretation" of history. Economic factors go a long way to explain the course of history,[72] but not all the way: an acceptable "philosophy of history" must "leave adequate room for the quality of leading personnel and in the special case at hand [he was speaking of Bolshevist Russia] for the quality of the leading individual," namely, Stalin.[73]

This is, then, in bare outline Schumpeter's socio-economic world picture, an exceedingly complex structure indeed. The basic ideas were conceived at a very early time, but much of his work throughout his life was spent in elaborating details, making adjustments here and there, and testing his theory against the facts of history; but unlike Böhm-Bawerk he did not defend his theory in extensive polemics.[74] More-

over (again unlike Böhm-Bawerk, whose self-denial and moderation in that respect he had praised so highly), Schumpeter permitted himself the luxury of spending much effort in fields and on subjects that were not at all, or only loosely, connected with his main work. In fact, there is no branch of economics in which he was not deeply interested and well versed, and few to which he has not made important contributions.

Static theory was covered by his first book and by many articles, especially in his earlier period. To the theory of money he made an important contribution in his celebrated paper "Das Sozialprodukt und die Rechenpfennige" (1917) and elsewhere. In its dynamic aspects the theory of money, credit and banking is, of course, an integral part of his theory of economic development and as such found extensive treatment in numerous writings. There are two long chapters on "Money, Credit, and Business Cycles" in the forthcoming *History of Economic Analysis*. There are, furthermore, his sociological studies, mainly in the essays on the theory of social classes (1927) and imperialism (1919) and in his *Capitalism, Socialism and Democracy* (1942), which are, it is true, closely connected with his basic model, but go far beyond it in several directions. And above all, there are his biographical essays and his extensive studies in the history of economic thought culminating in the posthumous *History of Economic Analysis*. Once more, unlike Böhm-Bawerk, he deals not only with those aspects of the work of other economists and of other theoretical systems which have a direct or indirect bearing on his own structure, but tries to understand them, men as well as theories, in their totality.

The wide range and complexity of Schumpeter's scientific work reflects accurately the universality and complexity of his mind. He begins the preface of his first book with the quotation "Alles verstehen, heisst alles ver-

---

[71] For a penetrating analysis and criticism of historicism, see Karl Popper's three highly instructive articles, "The Poverty of Historicism" (*Economica*, 1944–45), and his book, *The Open Society and Its Enemies*, especially Vol. II, *The High Tide of Prophecy: Hegel and Marx* (London, 1945; 2d rev. ed., Princeton, 1950).

[72] Interesting remarks can be found in his essay "Sozialistische Möglichkeiten von heute" (1920), where it is argued that political revolutions always follow after economic revolutions, never precede them — admitting, however, that the Russian case is an exception, a statement that recurs in his *Capitalism, Socialism and Democracy*.

[73] *Capitalism, Socialism and Democracy*, 2d ed., p. 399.

[74] Schumpeter did not believe in the usefulness of polemical discussion. Typical are the following remarks in his article on Sombart ("Sombarts Dritter Band," i.e., third volume of *Der moderne Kapitalismus*, Schmoller's *Jahrbuch*,

Vol. LI, 1927). "The fight about methodology [the *Methodenstreit* initiated between Menger and Schmoller] is obsolete, although there is occasional inclination to fight rearguard actions. . . . Science has got over that, not by fighting out epistemological issues and by subsequent conversion of both sides to a common creed, but in this manner that practical work on concrete problems proceeded in the way indicated by the nature of the task on hand" (p. 350).

zeihen" — "Tout comprendre c'est tout pardonner." This adage is indeed a clue to his mind. He understood every theory, every standpoint, every method, and found in each something true and useful, realizing clearly, at the same time, their defects and limitations. He was extremely open-minded, saw all sides of every question without being eclectic, that is to say, without trying to reconcile the irreconcilable, or merely to assemble unconnected and uncoordinated theorems and facts.

Let me illustrate by a few examples. He was deeply interested in pure static theory and was a real connoisseur of mathematical refinements in that area, a "theoretical *gourmet*" as he himself put it. He was, nevertheless, fully aware of the limitations, or what he thought were the limitations, of static theory and was very critical of what he regarded as uncritical applications, e.g., those typically made of the theory of monopoly and monopolistic competition in the area of welfare economics. He was enraptured by the econometric method, but again became quite impatient with certain econometric analyses of the trade cycle.[75] He had a very high opinion of the productive power of capitalism and an ingrained dislike for socialism. At the same time, he was not blind to what he thought were the cultural drawbacks of capitalism and went out of his way to prove that socialism could work and was compatible with democracy.[76]

The complexity, diversity, and universality of Schumpeter's mind is the key to a proper understanding of the man and his work. It explains a certain lack of systematic arrangement and neatness in his writings which became more pronounced in later years and is especially evident in his book on *Business Cycles*, where he tried to deal with the capitalist process in all its complexity. The great wealth of ideas which constantly streamed through his mind, and his acute awareness of all sides of every question, and of the limitations of each standpoint and method, made it very hard for him to present his views on any subject neatly and systematically. He was not always able fully to integrate his ideas, and he easily gave the impression of being undecided about important issues or even contradictory. He was fully aware of these shortcomings in his presentations and envied those writers who, because they held simpler views, were not troubled by such difficulties.

His somewhat involved literary style, which can be perhaps best described as "baroque," gives adequate expression to the complex structure of his mind. It is characterized by long sentences, numerous qualifying phrases, qualifications of qualifications, casuistic distinctions of meanings. These qualities of his style are especially pronounced, as one would expect, in his German writings, because the German language offers more freedom for complicated constructions.[77]

VII. Why is there no "Schumpeter School"?

I have often asked myself the question and have heard it raised by others, why there are no Schumpeterians in the sense in which there are Keynesians, or even Böhm-Bawerkians and Marshallians, not to mention Marxians. Schumpeter had many ardent admirers and scores of devoted students. Wherever he taught he attracted the cream of the student body, and literally hundreds of economists in all lands have been profoundly influenced by his teaching and writing. But there is no Schumpeter school.

It would be tempting to explain this in terms

---

[75] See his contribution to the National Bureau Conference on Business Cycles, November 1949.

[76] Schumpeter was, however, never a socialist, if by that word we designate those who *advocate* socialism, which is in Schumpeter's own words "an institutional arrangement that vests the management of the productive process with some public authority." ("Capitalism in the Postwar World," *loc. cit.*, p. 113.) It would not be necessary to dwell upon this fact, which should be obvious to any reader of Schumpeter's book on socialism, if it were not also a fact that frequently the opposite assertion is made. For example, the editor of the German translation of *Capitalism, Socialism and Democracy* says in his introduction: "Schumpeter ist Sozialist" and a little later again refers to him as "that socialist"! (Professor Edgar Salin, in "Einleitung" to *Kapitalismus, Sozialismus und Demokratie*, Bern: A. Francke, 1946, p. 8.)

It is true that Schumpeter was pessimistic with respect to capitalism's chances of survival. But he did not say that socialism was inevitable. In the preface to the second edition of his *Capitalism, Socialism and Democracy*, he defends himself against the reproach of "defeatism" (p. 11). To call him a socialist is like calling Cassandra a Greek partisan because she prophesied the fall of Troy!

[77] On the stylistic traditions of the German scientific language see the interesting remarks by H. H. Gerth and C. W. Mills in their preface to the translation of Max Weber's *Essays in Sociology* (New York: Oxford University Press, 1946, pp. 5 and 6).

of external circumstances: Schumpeter was born in a less fortunate part of the world than Keynes, a comparison with whom is especially instructive because he (1883–1946) was Schumpeter's exact contemporary. Schumpeter's real fatherland, the Austro-Hungarian monarchy, disintegrated while he was still in the beginning of his scientific career. The new Austria did not offer him an opportunity for academic success; in Germany he arrived on the eve of a horrible revolution, which did not leave him enough time to take root; and seven or eight of the eighteen years in the quiet haven of Harvard were largely lost, as far as the formation of a school was concerned, through the emotional and intellectual disturbances incident to war and preparations for war. This may sound plausible. But I do not think it is the real explanation. Whatever the influences of the course of his life on his external success as well as on his character and personality — and they must have been considerable — the basic, internal structure of Schumpeter's mind and work offers a better explanation for the fact that he did not found a school.

Schumpeter's universality and open-mindedness and the complexity of his system made the crystallization of a Schumpeter school difficult. *Tout comprendre c'est tout pardonner* is not a powerful rallying cry. What he said of Marshall — that "unlike Mill, he would never have said that some problem or other was settled for all time to come and there was nothing about it that called for further explanation either by himself or another writer" [78] holds fully of Schumpeter himself. "I never wish to say anything definitive; if I have a function it is to open doors not to close them" — he said in the informal farewell address to his students in Bonn.[79] He was, thus, prevented by a self-imposed injunction from constructing a neat simplified version of his theory as Keynes did.[80]

The construction of such a simplified system is evidently necessary for the formation of a compact group of disciples. But above all, unlike Marshall and Keynes, Schumpeter was constitutionally unable "to give his readers exactly what they craved — a message which was both high-minded and comforting — and at the same time to answer to the call of his conscience." [81] He did not and could not, like Marshall, "cheerfully sympathize, from a warm heart, with the ideals of socialism, and patronizingly talk down to socialists from a cool head." [82] With him it was rather the other way round; he disliked intensely the ideals of the socialists but found much truth in their teaching. Again, he was unlike Marshall and Keynes in that it *was* "primarily intellectual curiosity" that "brought [Schumpeter] into the economist's camp. He was [*not*] driven to it from ethical speculations by a generous impulse to help in the great task of alleviating the misery and degradation . . . among the . . . poor." [83]

To summarize: The main reason why no Schumpeter school developed is that Schumpeter was neither a reformer nor an enthusiastic partisan of capitalism, socialism, planning, or any other "ism"; he was a scholar and an intellectual. It is hardly a compliment to economics as a science, but it seems to me to be a fact that nonscientific factors play such an important role in the formation of economic schools. In the purely scientific sphere Schumpeter's open-mindedness and universality, the lack of fighting spirit for any particular approach, the fact that he found something useful and acceptable in almost every theory and method helped to prevent development of a Schumpeter school.[84]

[78] "Alfred Marshall's *Principles*," *American Economic Review*, June 1941, p. 237.

[79] A typescript of that speech is in the possession of Wolfgang Stolper, who kindly showed it to me.

[80] There is good reason to believe that Keynes did this quite consciously, in order to get the immediate action which the situation in his opinion demanded, although he never took the simplified Keynesianism — *vulgär Keynesianism*, to use the technical Marxian phrase (which should not be translated as "vulgar") — quite so seriously and uncritically as do many of his followers.

[81] See Schumpeter, "Alfred Marshall's *Principles*," *loc. cit.*, p. 244.

[82] *Ibid.*

[83] *Ibid.*, p. 239. The quotation, referring in the original to Marshall, has been reversed above, in order to apply to Schumpeter.

[84] It could also be argued that the times were not propitious for a popular success of his theories, because the heyday of capitalism or at least of that phase of capitalism which Schumpeter describes had passed when the *Theory of Economic Development* appeared. This, however, seems to me questionable. During the nineteen-twenties, capitalism was still very much alive almost everywhere — at least *ex visu* of the twenties, if not in the light of what happened later, which nobody foresaw at the time. In the United States capitalism is vigorous even at this time. At

Schumpeter himself was conscious of all this. In his farewell address to his students in Bonn he said: "I have never tried to bring about a Schumpeter school. There is none and it ought not to exist. . . . Economics is not a philosophy but a science. Hence there should be no 'schools' in our field. . . . Many people feel irritated by this attitude. For in Germany alone there are half a dozen economists who regard themselves as heads of such 'schools,' as fighters for absolute light against absolute darkness. But there is no use combating that sort of thing. One should not fight what life is going to eliminate anyway. Unlike politics and business, immediate success should not matter in science. . . . I for my part accept the judgment of future generations."

This was his philosophy in these respects. But he would have been less human than he was, if his feelings had been as austere and re-signed as his philosophy. In fact, he was far from unreceptive to external success and popularity; and, although he rarely showed it, he often suffered from lack of response and appreciation. He was a good laugher and could enjoy exuberantly a stimulating conversation, a good story, a brilliant joke, but he was fundamentally not a happy man. And at the bottom of his unhappiness and resignation was, I believe, the cleavage between his high and austere ideals on the one hand and his human feelings and impulses on the other.[85] Again, he was aware of this, and he envied those who — like the utilitarians and Victorians, like Marshall and Keynes — are not plagued by an unbridgeable gulf between their ideals and their emotions, who manage "at the same time to answer the call of their conscience" and to be "comforting" to themselves and to others.

---

any rate, I prefer the more subjective explanation given in the text.

[85] There were also other, partly external, factors in the situation. On these compare Arthur Smithies' subtle and understanding analysis of Schumpeter's personality in the *American Economic Review* for September 1950 and above, pages 11–23.

SCHUMPETER AS A TEACHER AND ECONOMIC THEORIST

Paul A. Samuelson

THERE were many Schumpeters: the brilliant *enfant terrible* of the Austrian School who before the age of thirty had written two great books; the young Cairo lawyer with a stable of horses; the Austrian Finance-Minister; the social philosopher and prophet of capitalist development; the historian of economic doctrine; the economic theorist espousing use of more exact methods and tools of reasoning; the teacher of economics.

From the long-term viewpoint the first of these roles is the most important. Schumpeter will unquestionably be labeled by future historians of thought as a business-cycle theorist who placed primary stress on the role of the innovator. Of this he was well aware. He always remained faithful to his youthful vision, not only because of its intrinsic merits, but also — I venture to think — because he was too self-conscious an artist to let old age clutter up the aesthetic life line laid down by the genius of youth.

But enough will be written of this long-term contribution of Schumpeter. Here I should like to concentrate on Schumpeter as a teacher, and on Schumpeter as a patron of economic theory. It was in these two capacities that I knew him best. But aside from that, you might say of Schumpeter that, although he had an absolute advantage both as a scholar and a personality, his comparative advantage was if anything almost greater as a personality. His books speak for themselves but only his pupils can recapture the impact of his colorful personality.

II

I saw Schumpeter for the first time at the 1934 Christmas meetings of economists in Chicago when, as an undergraduate, I accidentally walked in on a meeting where he was speaking. I saw him for the last time at the 1949 New York meetings, where in marvelous form he was expounding good sense about the Walrasian theory of money and bringing life back to an audience wilted by two hours of confusing technical discourse. The intervening fifteen years constituted almost half my lifetime — the important years according to Schumpeter's strong view on the biology of scholars. For Schumpeter these same fifteen years constituted less than a quarter of his life-span; and it is remarkable in view of his own theories on the aging of the creative impulse that they did not represent an anticlimax to his career.

This was the period of his two-volume *Business Cycles*, of his *Capitalism, Socialism and Democracy*, and of his yet-to-be-published *History of Economic Analysis*. A grand work on economic theory was part of his plan: a work on Money, and a separate volume on Banking; a book on mathematical logic for his old age, his seventies. And as relaxation for really old age, he spoke of writing a sociological novel in his eighties. He even once did field work on the latter: after a long and rather tiring walk, Mrs. Schumpeter with some difficulty persuaded him to ride on the subway back to Harvard Square. This, he reported, had been a very interesting experience; and what was more, when he came to write his sociological novel, he was going to do it again.

Professor Smithies, who knew him much more intimately than I ever did, has indicated in his obituary essay the importance in Schumpeter's life of having been born in the closing era of the Austro-Hungarian empire. With the disappearance of that world, he became completely qualified to play the important sociological role of the alienated stranger. The America of Mickey Rooney and coca-cola he knew almost nothing about; in 1913, while at Columbia, he first saw a football game, and that was enough to last him the rest of his life; if anything, he went out of his way to exaggerate his naïveté with respect to all such matters.

As a judge of short-term events, this could not help but prove a serious handicap; in compensation, his long-term view may have gained.

On the psychological side, Schumpeter's was a temperament not uncommon among gifted minds, and perhaps peculiarly characteristic of those who have been precocious in their youth. Obviously, he was ambitious to make his mark and it was no accident that the figure of the innovator should have intrinsically appealed to him. There was in him a consciousnes of great powers, and this served as an irritant urging him toward creative activity. Moreover, this was not an irritant that ceased to operate on weekends and holidays; I don't suppose that he ever crossed the Atlantic without spoiling the trip by taking along a book on tensor calculus or partial differential equations, which inevitably he succeeded neither in reading nor ignoring.

This feeling of great personal powers was of course of tremendous importance in connection with his professional work. It also showed itself in every aspect of his life: he was quite prepared to talk expertly on anything from Etruscan Art to medieval law; to read, or feel that he could read, Italian, Dutch, and Scandinavian; to outline a theory of metaphysics. This lack of inhibition was extremely important in giving him the freedom to make daring and interesting sociological hypotheses concerning phenomena on the fringes of politics and economics.

The one field in which he did show real humility was in connection with mathematics — a statement that may seem surprising to some. It is true that he never tired of pointing out to the non-mathematical the virtues for economics of mathematics. It is also true that he would often refer with a wave of his hand to quite difficult problems as if they were elementary and easy. But nonetheless he was quite aware of his own lack of facility with mathematics and cheerfully admitted the difficulties he had in mastering and retaining mathematical techniques.

I think to the end he regarded it as a slightly mystical fact that a mixed-difference-differential equation of the Frisch-Tinbergen type involves complex exponentials which in a miraculous manner give rise to sinusoidal periodicities. He waited eagerly (the uncharitable might almost say credulously) for some new mathematical method to turn up that would solve the mysteries of the ages: the tensor calculus, linear operators, symbolic logic, etc.

Moreover, it was his conviction that mathematics itself had grown up as a servant of physics and was not adapted to economics; so that real progress in economic theory would require new methods tailor-made to economics. In this expectation he foreshadowed in a sense what actually came to pass in the von Neumann-Morgenstern *Theory of Games*, which dispenses completely with the tools of modern mathematical physics and falls back upon the more fundamental notions of point-set theory and topology. Schumpeter held this expectation all the more confidently because of his conviction that the processes of logical thought had themselves been biologically developed in the human species as the result of a Darwinian process in which man had to learn to solve successfully the *economic* problems of living: Schumpeter expected therefore that logic and economics would turn out to be closely interrelated. Such an inference may have a slightly far-fetched flavor but it illustrates the character of his speculations. It is not unrelated to Schumpeter's views concerning the naturalness of econometrics: in an early issue of *Econometrica*, he argued that the economic marketplace is by its nature concerned with monetary magnitudes of a measurable sort so that while other disciplines may gradually feel their way toward exact quantitative analysis, economics has this problem thrust upon it from the very beginning.

Call this faith of Schumpeter's naïve if you will. Still it was a beautiful thing to see. And it kept him young. Every scholar, as he grows in years, experience, and judiciousness, faces two insidious enemies which in the end usually take over: disillusioned skepticism and loss of enthusiasm. Schumpeter held these at bay. Only in the last year of his life did Schumpeter express before the National Bureau of Economic Research Conference on Business Cycles the view that mathematical models in business-cycle research had been relatively sterile: that as between the alternative methods of cycle research, (1) theoretical, (2) statistical, and (3) historical, the last was by far the most important. It is not necessary here to ask whether there is any antithesis between these alternative methods, whether there is not one single problem of empirical induction which is necessarily to be attacked by means of hypothesis formation and abstraction so that (2) and (3) are methodologically indistinguishable in principle and both inseparably intertwined with (1), with the only real issue being the pragmatic one of degree. The only point of the incident is that it represents one of those rare occasions when Schumpeter gave what was from his viewpoint "comfort to the enemy." For the real enemy to him was first and foremost those who opposed — and I now employ the words uttered a thousand times by him in the classroom — "the use of exact methods in economic analysis." [1]

Patron of mathematical economists is perhaps the best way of describing his rôle. He was quite the opposite of those celebrated scholars who rarely make an error and who instill in their best students an inferiority complex. Schumpeter's very imperfections gave hope and drive to his students.

Conscious of his scholarly achievements outside of mathematical economics, he very wisely refused to make small contributions to this field. Subconsciously he may have realized that the last part of the 19th century was a bad time for a theorist to be born. It was either too late or too soon — too late to lead the pack in the 1870 "revolution," and too soon to participate fully in the post-1925 era. In Austria, England, and America the first quarter of the 20th century proved fairly arid for economic theory.

However, if a bad time for theory, the first years of this century were tremendously fertile for trade-cycle analysis, culminating around the beginning of World War I in a series of brilliant studies by Spiethoff, Schumpeter, Aftalion, Mitchell, Hawtrey, and Robertson. Primarily as a pioneer in this development will Schumpeter be remembered.

[1] Aside from the merits of Schumpeter's view, I do not think we have to invoke old age as an explanation for this uncharacteristic performance. He loved to oppose the popular side; and in the Cowles Commission, I respectfully suggest, he met a faith not less fervent than his own, thereby reversing completely his usual motivation.

III

Let me turn to Schumpeter as a teacher. Schumpeter was a great showman. In all probability he spoke before more economists the world over than any other scholar in history, so I do not have to try to describe his manner. But good as was his average performance, he was really at his best in his own classroom. I don't suppose that ever in his life he *read* a paper in the literal sense. He spoke from notes only very rarely. On really serious occasions, such as his Presidential Address at the 1948 Meetings, he was in a sense caught between stools and his best spontaneous speaking was inhibited.

What his German speech was like I cannot judge. His English was, of course, easy, grammatical, and flowery; but with an accent that was *sui generis*. On that occasion at the 1934 meetings referred to above, he was quite incomprehensible to one who had never been out of the Middle West. On every subsequent occasion my ear seemed to have acquired the proper key so that I never again had the slightest difficulty. This experience, however, seems to have been quite typical.

Schumpeter liked to talk too well to be at his best in leading a small seminar. He loved to lecture! And to large audiences. If left to himself, he would probably have swallowed up imperialistically all fields of economics and lectured on all subjects. At Harvard, I dare to think, he was not left to himself in this respect; but, nonetheless, for the semester after his death he had been scheduled to give a course on Economic Theory, one on History of Economic Thought, and one on Socialism — and all this when he was past the age of retirement!

In 1935 when he first took over Taussig's famous Ec-11, the basic Harvard graduate course in economic theory, the class met at 2 o'clock in Emerson Hall. After, and not before, the students had assembled for the class hour, in would walk Schumpeter, remove hat, gloves, and topcoat with sweeping gestures, and begin the day's business. Clothes were important to him: he wore a variety of well-tailored tweeds with carefully matched shirt, tie, hose, and handkerchief. My wife used to keep track in that period of the cyclic reappearance of the seemingly infinite number of combinations in his wardrobe: the cycle was not simple and it was far from random.

The hour after lunch is the most dangerous of all to the lecturer, but no one ever felt tempted to enjoy a siesta in his class. Humor always eludes description and defies analysis. In Schumpeter's case it is clear that he never told jokes and had no prepared-in-advance booby traps; he was never dead-pan and ingenuous, but somehow made the class itself seem witty, so that even earnest Radcliffe students felt themselves to be engaging in brilliant sortie and repartée. He was free of the congenital vice of the veteran college professor: he never repeated his stories, as I know from careful count kept over a span of years. Only after some years of teaching have I learned to appreciate the real significance of this.

I do not know what the effect has been of the postwar flood of graduate students, but back in the 1930's his typical class was about 50 in number. He did not lecture in the strict European sense of a unilateral monologue. He called on people in the class, and he was constantly interrupted by his audience. If anything, he tolerated too many interruptions from grade-chasers, fools, and exhibitionists. In the beginning years when he was carrying on Taussig's famous course, he aimed particularly at carrying on the Socratic method of Taussig.

This requires some explanation, which I offer with some diffidence since I was the very first of the post-Taussig generation. The year 1935–36, my first at Harvard, was also the first year of the age of Schumpeter: Taussig had given one half of Ec-11 the previous year; Bullock too had just finished his last course; Gay had still one more year to go; and Carver was long-since emeritus. The Socratic method of teaching, which Taussig had perfected to its highest art, had tremendous prestige and was universally imitated — even down to the rawest instructor in elementary economics.

What did it consist of? For one thing, the teacher never presented the answers to questions to the student. The student was supposed to work out all answers by himself, but he was never to be told whether he had or had not arrived at the correct answer. Furthermore, different members of the class were called upon to discuss the question at issue, and it was part

of Taussig's greatness that he would plan out his campaign in advance, knowing exactly who could be counted on to give the appropriate stupid reply and who must be avoided lest he give the show away. Taussig, himself, was a rather austere gentleman of the old school so that most of the class sat in fear and trembling until he had announced his immediate victim, whereupon all the rest relaxed to enjoy the fun.

All this is of course grossly over-simplified and not a balanced view of the method, but it will suffice for the present purpose. What shall we conclude about the Socratic method? That it represented a performance of consummate skill and artistry on the part of Taussig, none can deny; and, apparently, those who went through it had an unforgettable experience. It is equally clear that in the hands of most teachers — and not just beginners — it was a disastrous method: disastrous both to students and teacher. Moreover, even at its best it was not — and here I am expressing my own opinion — a very good method for teaching graduate economic theory of the modern type. If you believed as Taussig did that economics consisted of a few great thorny problems — such as "the" index-number problem, "the" problem of value, etc. — that no one had ever solved and that no one ever would solve, but concerning which there were a number of aspects to be explored along the lines laid out by Ricardo and others — then it was a good method. You never got anywhere very fast, but since there was nowhere to get to anyway it didn't really matter very much, just so long as you had a good ride through the traditional back-country.

All this that I am saying is, I realize, heresy. I have never said it before, but I have thought it; and so too did many of the people of my generation, who had constantly thrown at them the almost-mystic accounts of the Taussigian method, which none could describe but to the excellence of which all testified.[2]

---

[2] I am the more emboldened to say it because once when Taussig was a dinner guest at the Society of Fellows, a year or two before his death, he told me that in his own opinion his economic theory course had not, since the time of the First World War, been very good. Caught up in war-time duties, he felt himself getting out of touch with developments in economic theory; and being about 60 years old at the war's end, he preferred to throw himself into International Trade rather than pick up the modern theoretical developments.

Schumpeter was perhaps not at his best in conducting a first course in graduate economic theory, and after two or three years he confined himself to more advanced courses. For one thing, he was considered too difficult for an important fraction of the class, many of whom had scarcely heard of Marshall and J. B. Clark before coming to Harvard, to say nothing of Pigou or Frisch. Aside from the intrinsic difficulties of economic theory, there was the added fact that Schumpeter darted about, "opening doors" on new theories and topics. Furthermore, he was addicted to the cardinal vice of introducing mathematical symbols into the economic classroom; and it must be confessed that his blackboard equations were not a model of neatness. Sometimes we spent half an hour looking for a lost Walrasian equation or getting rid of a redundant one.

I have said that he was consistently amusing and in a way that counted against him. Whereas he never gave a lecture that a one-day visitor would have found dull, the regular class attendant became a little numbed and jaded and began to wish for a little more systematic instruction. At the time I was a fairly conscientious note taker, but I find not infrequently in my class notes the following type of entry for a full hour's lecture:

A. Particular Expenses curve: Array (cumulative) of average cost curves of different firms. It is not a supply curve.

And that is all.

But now that I have stated the case against him, let me restore the balance. His 1935 theory course more nearly resembled the courses now being given in every graduate school than did any course then being given in America, excellent as were many of the contemporaneous courses. He took you out of the flat dull textbook world and into the three dimensional world of living economics and economists; his enthusiasm over the latest article to appear in the *Review of Economic Studies* on the elasticity of substitution was real and catching. In the last analysis, the poor students were the ones who were critical. The good ones — and in the long perspective isn't it they who primarily matter? — found his course the most valuable of all. I believe it was David McCord Wright who once summed up the general re-

action: a year or two after taking Schumpeter's course, you began to appreciate what you had got.

The subject matter of his 1935–36 Ec-11 course was excellent. It involved readings in Marshall, Wicksell, Pigou, Böhm-Bawerk, Knight, and Wicksteed. In addition, much was made of Chamberlin, Robinson, and current journal articles by Hicks, Harrod, Sraffa, and others. Such advanced authors as Cournot, Edgeworth, and Hotelling were at least sampled. The "Cost Controversy" was, understandably for the time, given great weight — probably too much weight we would now say. Monopolistic competition received a great deal of attention, as one could expect from the time. The order of topics followed was: Individual Firm, Industry, Monopolistic Competition, General Equilibrium, Marginal Productivity (including capital theory), Welfare Economics (which he never got to by the year's end). In awarding final grades, he completely depreciated the currency by his liberality, as has become legendary.

Curiously enough, he rarely mentioned his own theories. The nature of entrepreneurship and profits was discussed; but only once did I hear him discuss the reasons why the interest rate would be zero in a stationary state, and then only in an advanced seminar and under heavy pressure from Paul Sweezy and others.

Although he departed from the practice of his teacher Böhm-Bawerk, in that he rarely bothered to answer criticisms alleging the impossibility of a zero rate of interest, he never abandoned his early views.[3] On the occasion of his sixtieth *Festschrift*, I had occasion to review the various logical contradictions allegedly involved in his notion of a zero rate of interest. None of the following stood up under careful logical analysis: (1) the bizarre notion that a zero interest rate has the logical implication that all goods must be free; (2) the incorrect belief that at a zero rate of interest capital will necessarily not be maintained or replaced; (3) the quaint belief that someone who has *no* intention of ever repaying his debts will at a zero rate of interest borrow an infinite amount and squander it on riotous living, but will at a positive rate of interest borrow none

[3] See Professor Haberler's essay below. — Ed.

or only a finite amount; (4) the terror that an asset, such as land, which over perpetual time will yield a perpetual yield, should, in the absence of a discount factor, fail to have a finite value in relation to current flows — as if this were something horrendous or absurd, and as if this same mathematical infinity were necessarily avoided by the usual assumption of an ever falling rate of interest; [4] (5) the dogmatic extrapolation of the laws of technology and of tastes so that the question (of non-vanishing net productivity) is begged by revealed hypothesis. One may consider attainment of a zero rate unlikely or even (under likely empirical assumptions) impossible, but this is no warrant for the still-frequently-met indictment of deductive error and logical contradiction.

In his general views on economic theory, he seemed surprisingly un-Austrian. On the whole, he was much more Walrasian. He always referred to Léon Walras as by far the greatest economist of all time.[5] He usually spoke of Marshall as "Papa Marshall," and although he was always respectful toward Marshall's worth, he obviously regarded him as overrated. Edgeworth he thought underrated, partly because he had written articles rather than books.[6] As a man, he found Irving Fisher a little comical; as a scientist, he revered his achievement. This was typical of Schumpeter: although himself a genius, he paid exuberant tribute to talent and promise; rather fastidious in his personal likes and dislikes, he never let these stand in the way of giving real encouragement to able economists, whatever the color of their haberdashery.

Though Schumpeter left behind him no band of zealots bent on differentiating his views from those of traditional economic theory, he did leave behind him the only kind of school appropriate to a scientific discipline — a generation of economic theorists who caught fire from his teachings.

---

[4] A concrete case will illustrate the point. Suppose total labor and land are fixed and inventions cease so that the interest rate is determined by the "net productivity of capital" as given by the marginal-productivity partial derivative of a Cobb-Douglas production function with exponents .75 for labor, .13 for land, and .12 for capital. If such a society always accumulates 15 per cent of its income, the interest rate will fall toward zero but never reach it. Nonetheless, if we evaluate the requisite integrals, we find that under conditions of certainty any dollar of perpetual income (such as a consol or land) will in this case have *infinite* present discounted value. Shall we hurriedly shoot the mathematician lest the world come to an end? Or infer that the rate of possible accumulation must be limited relative to technology so as to avoid the infinity?

[5] By virtue of Walras' vision of general equilibrium. In the next rank, Schumpeter placed Smith, Cournot, and (strangely) Quesnay. As a scholarly personality, Kurt Wicksell was his ideal.

[6] He used to tell of visiting Edgeworth in the *ante bellum* Edwardian days and having rock pheasant and champagne at breakfast in All Souls, which was adequate recompense for the dullness of Edgeworth's lectures. At about the same time, Schumpeter, in the full flower of his brilliant youth, visited Marshall, only to be advised not to continue work in economic theory! On another pilgrimage, he asked Mrs. Foxwell whether her "father" was at home. Later when he asked to see the famous library, Foxwell, grieving over his recent necessitous sale of it, merely pointed sadly to his two young children and the shoes on their feet.

SCHUMPETER'S EARLY GERMAN WORK, 1906–1917 [1]

Erich Schneider

IT is significant that Joseph Schumpeter entered our field in the year 1906 with a study on mathematical methods in theoretical economics.[2] This, his very first work, contains the points from which his own original research took its departure. Reading it today, one gains not only an impression of its author's comprehensive familiarity with the literature on mathematical economics that had by then been published, but of the influence which the study of these works exerted on young Schumpeter. Reared in the atmosphere of the Vienna School, he was attracted far more by the views of such as Cournot, Jevons, Edgeworth, Marshall, and above all Léon Walras. What Walras meant to him is seen plainly from the obituary for the founder of the Lausanne School which he published four years later in the same journal. "When we look back today on the life of this scholar," he wrote, "we are struck by the simple grandeur that lies in uncompromising devotion to a single task. The impression is as of a natural phenomenon, powerful, self-evident, of foreordained necessity. The study of problems in pure economics — such was the content of that career, to the exclusion of all else." Schumpeter was really describing his own scientific ideal, one to which he clung to the end of his life. Walras was his great model, the man whom he held in higher esteem than any other. He once told me that whoever failed to study and understand Walras was unlikely ever to become a good economist. And, indeed, his first great work, which attracted world-wide attention to him at the age of only twenty-five, came into being against a background of Walrasian thinking. His *Das Wesen und Hauptinhalt der theoretischen Nationalökonomie* (Nature and Main Content of Theoretical Economics, Leipzig, 1908) breathes the spirit of Lausanne rather than Vienna. The book, written in the brilliant style peculiar to Schumpeter, is at once a program and a profession of faith. "I hold aloof from practical politics and recognize no purpose other than knowledge. . . . We seek to understand rather than to engage in polemics, to learn rather than to criticize, to work out the elements of truth in every theorem rather than simply to accept or reject" (Preface, pp. vi, vii). The work is essentially a study in methodology and epistemology. One looks to it in vain for a systematic presentation of theory. It seeks, rather, to set forth the principles that should, in the author's view, govern the pursuit of theoretical economics as such. Solutions of concrete problems are presented only by way of example and in illustration of his methodological reasoning. The book, nevertheless, touches on all the central problems of theory, and foreshadows the approaches toward their solution which Schumpeter elaborated in his later works. Even this first outline contains nearly all the thoughts that only later came to full maturity. The concepts of statics and dynamics, the imputation problem, questions of price theory, the distribution theory, the principles of the theory of money, the method of variations, interest as a phenomenon in economic development — all these are found in this work. To be sure, much of what Schumpeter then had to say on these questions — e.g., the definition of static and dynamic economies — appears in a different light today and was viewed differently even by him later on. He still held at the time that the phenomenon of economic development was not susceptible to the same kind of exact treatment as the problem of static equilibrium, and in this respect the latest elaboration of dynamic theory has not upheld him. Nor has his thesis of the nonexistence of interest in a stationary economy proved tenable. But that is not what matters. The value of the book must be judged by the message it brought to its contemporaries at the time it was published. In a period that paid little heed to exact theory,

[1] The editor is indebted to Heinz Norden for translating this essay from the German.
[2] *Zeitschrift für Volkswirtschaft, Sozialpolitik und Verwaltung*, Volume 15 (1906), pp. 30–49.

Irving Fisher
and Joseph Schumpeter
1934

Gottfried Haberler
and Joseph Schumpeter
1948

Joseph Schumpeter
1947

it shone as a beacon, lighting the way for many — indeed, revealing to many the advantages of that way. Schumpeter himself was full of firm faith in the triumphant advance of exact theory: "I am as far removed from uncritical acceptance of authority, from adherence to ancient dogma, as from any ruthless mania for destruction, from melancholic or complacent skepticism, as well as exaggerated optimism. I look with confidence to the new day in science that, if I am not greatly mistaken, is beginning to dawn" (Preface, p. xxii). Time has justified his faith. It was with the greatest satisfaction that he took part in the founding of the Econometric Society, whose program reflected the very ideals he had championed. The aspirations of a scattered handful had become a world-wide movement. I shall never forget how his eyes lighted up when he told me about the founding of this society in 1930.

II

There is a second great intellectual trend that is reflected in Schumpeter's early work — a trend that deeply impressed him and lent decisive impulse to his own research: This is the theoretical work done since the late eighties in the United States, chiefly under the influence and leadership of J. B. Clark and Irving Fisher. His study, "Die neuere Wirtschaftstheorie in den Vereinigten Staaten" (Recent Economic Theory in the United States), published in *Schmollers Jahrbuch* for 1910, reveals how intensely its author was even then following everything that was published in America in the field of economics. He assigned a leading place to the work of Irving Fisher. Schumpeter felt that Fisher's notion of combining economic theory with accounting and actuarial science was particularly happy: "Accounting is, after all, the result of long practical experience, properly justifying the expectation that its practices accurately reflect, so to speak, one aspect of economic life; while the formulas of actuarial science are in part no more than the crystallization of certain lines of economic reasoning, and in other part useful supplements to that reasoning. All this is reason enough why we should study this field, stemming directly from practical life. To have done this thor-

oughly for the first time is to Fisher's very high credit. It was an endeavor that bore instant fruit" (pp. 939–40). Schumpeter always evinced a lively interest in theoretical constructions that grow from a precise knowledge of cost accounting, that shape their concepts by those of actual practice. He sensed that this was one of the essential points of departure in the creation of any realistic theory.[3] For that very reason he rejected Irving Fisher's concept of capital: "Fisher's concept of capital is not the concept of business life, for the businessman's capital is and remains solely a sum of money" (p. 940). And in his *Theorie der wirtschaftlichen Entwicklung* (Theory of Economic Development, Leipzig, 1912), he has this to say on his own concept of capital: "Our concept is that of business practice, carried to a logical conclusion and purged of contradictions" (second edition, p. 185).

To an even greater degree than Fisher, however, the figure of J. B. Clark plays a role of central importance in the thinking of the youthful Schumpeter. He was particularly fascinated by Clark's theory of distribution and his theory of economic development. It was in the theory of distribution that he saw Clark's main achievement. "It has set its stamp on the present phase of distribution theory in America. Clark's unifying influence makes it possible to formulate in general terms at least one basic principle that may be described as dominant in American distribution theory. It will be seen, at the same time, that modern theory in every country, at least ultimately, proceeds from the same premises" (p. 941). As early as 1906, in his second published work, "Professor Clarks Verteilungstheorie" [4] (Professor Clark's Theory of Distribution), he subjected to searching scrutiny Clark's views laid down in the latter's *The Distribution of Wealth*. A year later, in a comprehensive study entitled "Das Rentenprinzip in der Verteilungslehre" (The Rent Principle in Distribution Theory) in *Schmollers Jahrbuch*, Volume 31, 1907, he again came to grips with the problem of distribution. Even later he reverted repeatedly to

[3] Cf. his article, "The Common Sense of Econometrics," *Econometrica*, Volume 1 (1933).

[4] *Zeitschrift für Volkswirtschaft, Sozialpolitik und Verwaltung*, Volume 15 (1906), pp. 325 ff.

this subject: in 1909, in a study entitled "Bemerkungen über das Zurechnungsproblem" (Notes on the Problem of Imputation) in *Zeitschrift für Volkswirtschaft, Sozialpolitik und Verwaltung*, Volume 15, 1909; and in 1917, in a memoir entitled "Das Grundprinzip der Verteilungstheorie" (The Basic Principle of the Theory of Distribution) in *Archiv für Sozialwissenschaft und Sozialpolitik*, Volume 42. "The principle of Clark's distribution theory is that of marginal productivity. It might be best described in general terms as 'the theory of marginal productivity.' This principle may be formulated approximately as follows: Under free competition and in a static state of the economy, the share of each production factor in the value of the total product is determined by its marginal yield" ("Die neuere Wirtschaftstheorie in den Vereinigten Staaten," p. 29). In a note Schumpeter remarks that Wicksteed, in 1894, gave an important mathematical formulation of this theorem that has attracted far too little notice. "Wicksteed's Theorem," as we call it today, engaged his lively interest down to the thirties. Time and again he read with deep interest the Walrasian version of the theory of marginal productivity, in the *36ᵉ Leçon* of the *Éléments* — an interest that was reawakened by Henry Schultz's well-known article, "Marginal Productivity and the General Pricing Process" (*Journal of Political Economy*, Volume 37, 1929). In his early work he was interested chiefly in the interrelationships between the American and the Austrian concept: "When one applies the necessary corrections to Professor Clark's law, one inevitably reaches the law of marginal utility, *sans phrase*, and the imputation theory of von Wieser, and one realizes the full extent to which the latter renders the rent principle superfluous" ("Das Rentenprinzip in der Verteilungslehre," p. 633). Later on, his interest in the Walras-Pareto-Barone version of the theory of marginal productivity came to the fore. Space does not permit a more detailed discussion of these developing trends in the lifework of our author.

III

We must hasten to deal with the second great problem complex inherent to Clark's theories that was to mean so much in Schumpeter's own work: Clark's theory of economic development. "It is Clark alone who has undertaken to offer a rigorous theory of economic development, thus extending the field of theory all the way to the limits of economic life" ("Die neuere Wirtschaftstheorie in den Vereinigten Staaten," p. 961). "The distinction between statics and dynamics is essential to his theory.[5] In a static state [better: "stationary"] all economic activity is identical [repeats itself continuously] in character. In a dynamic state, however, a new function is added — the function of making decisions that modify the prior course of the economy, that concern new production methods, organizational forms, commercial combinations. A static economy pursues its wonted way as though automatically. In a dynamic economy alone is there room for individuals who display leadership. Call this function 'labor,' if you will — it remains a new kind of labor. Call its yield 'wages,' if you will — that does not change the fact that it is a reward for work that is *sui generis*, that it follows laws distinct from the wages of static labor. True, Professor Clark did not elaborate his notion in detail. He offered only a few brief outlines, and his formulation may not be above criticism. Entrepreneurial profit cannot be simply characterized as remuneration for improvements in the productive process which sooner or later benefit everyone and precisely thereby cease yielding profit to the entrepreneur. Yet at bottom the notion is probably correct and contains the basic explanation, κατ'ἐξοχὴν, of entrepreneurial profit. If this be so, it obviously offers additional proof of the fruitfulness of the distinction between static and dynamic economies. For only in the light of this distinction does the core of this thought stand out sharply against its background" (pp. 957–58). The background against which Schumpeter projected his own theory of development becomes entirely plain here. Unquestionably he was also stimulated by W. G. Lanworth Taylor's *The Cinetic Theory of Economic Crises*: "He [Taylor] emphatically refuses to search for the causes of crisis in the elements of a static system. Instead, he views

---

[5] We would be more likely today to distinguish between a stationary and an evolutionary economy. — E.S.

crises purely as a reaction to the upsets in the static equilibrium of an economy caused by economic development. He describes the elements of the material and psychological environment, defines development as changes in that environment resulting from inventions, etc., and explains crisis as a process by which a new state of equilibrium is restored. If this interpretation is correct — and it is not easy to see clearly, because of the brief and sketchy character of the study, and because it is presented in a rather less than lucid manner; and if I am not misled by certain prejudices that may be traceable to my own work; then Taylor comes closer to a true understanding of the phenomenon of crisis than any other author I know" (pp. 960–61).

I have quoted these sections at length to point up the close kinship between Schumpeter's conception and that of contemporary American theory at that time. Schumpeter's original thinking in this field must have begun about 1908 or 1909. The first outline of his basic ideas is found in an essay entitled "Über das Wesen der Wirtschaftskrisen" (The Nature of Economic Crises) published in 1910 in the *Zeitschrift für Volkswirtschaft, Sozialpolitik und Verwaltung*, and forming, in his own words, "part of a larger work, as yet unpublished, on the subject of economic development" (p. 271). We must, he wrote, "proceed from a static state of the economy, if the processes of development are to be made sharply distinct from the static elements, if there is to be no obscurity arising from the chance that the factors which are to serve as the points of departure for the whole investigation may already contain elements of the phenomenon to be explained" (p. 277). "The essential character of economic development lies in the fact that means of production which heretofore served certain static uses are diverted from this course and placed in the service of new purposes. We describe this process as the effectuation of new combinations. And these new combinations do not prevail of themselves, as it were, as do the wonted combinations in a static economy. They require a degree of intelligence and energy that characterizes only a minority of the economic subjects. It is in the effectuation of these new combinations that the true function of the entre-

preneur lies" (p. 284). Schumpeter then poses and answers this question: "Why does economic development proceed jerkily rather than smoothly, upward movement being followed by downward movement, the latter alone opening the way to further prosperity?" (p. 295). Even these few quotations show that the main pillars of his *Theorie der wirtschaftlichen Entwicklung* (Theory of Economic Development), published in book form in 1912, were already contained in this article, clearly formulated and reduced to their essential outlines. What came later was no more than an elaboration of these basic ideas. The essay entitled "Die Wellenbewegung des Wirtschaftslebens" (The Wavelike Movement of Economic Life), published in 1915 in Volume 39 of the *Archiv für Sozialwissenschaft und Sozialpolitik*, represents another repetition of these basic ideas "in different and simpler form, as I presented them early this year in a lecture at Harvard University, stripped of technical detail, as a mere interpretation of some great and well-known facts."

IV

Only brief reference will be made to Schumpeter's early interest in questions of monopoly, duopoly, and bilateral monopoly. They are touched on in refreshingly original fashion as early as *Das Wesen und Hauptinhalt der theoretischen Nationalökonomie* (pp. 263–72). In this field, Cournot and Edgeworth exerted the greatest influence on him. Later on, he reverted time and again to this complex of problems, though only in 1928, in his well-known article, "The Instability of Capitalism," which appeared in the *Economic Journal*, did he deal with it at greater length.

V

We must yet discuss the last two great achievements of Schumpeter's early period: His *Epochen der Dogmen- und Methodengeschichte* [6] (Epochs in the History of Doctrines and Methods [of Economics]), published in 1914; and his great article, "Das Sozialprodukt und die Rechenpfennige. Glossen und

[6] *Grundriss der Sozialökonomik* (Outline of Social Economics), First Edition, Section 1 (Tübingen, 1914).

Beiträge zur Geldtheorie von heute" (Social Product and the Unit of Account. Notes and Contributions to Present-Day Monetary Theory) in *Archiv für Sozialwissenschaft und Sozialpolitik*, Volume 44, 1917. Whoever reads the utterly unique *Epochen der Dogmen- und Methodengeschichte* inevitably asks himself how it was possible for a young man of thirty-one to write such a history of ideas on our discipline, based on the most intimate knowledge of a vast mass of sources and an altogether uncommon maturity of judgment. To this day our science knows no other achievement to match it. Bear in mind that the three fundamental works, *Das Wesen und Hauptinhalt der theoretischen Nationalökonomie*, *Theorie der wirtschaftlichen Entwicklung*, and *Epochen der Dogmen- und Methodengeschichte*, appeared in the brief span of six years! What immense intellectual vigor was at work here! Spiethoff was right when he wrote in his obituary in *Kyklos* (Volume III, 1949): "One scarcely knows which is the more amazing, that a man of twenty-five and twenty-seven should shake the very foundations of his chosen science, or that a man of thirty should write the history of that discipline!"

VI

With his treatise, "Das Sozialprodukt und die Rechenpfennige," our author for the first time embarked on the field of monetary theory in the narrower sense, a field he cultivated later on with particular interest. It is true that certain elements were already foreshadowed in *Das Wesen und Hauptinhalt der theoretischen Nationalökonomie* (pp. 276–98); but only the great study dating from 1917 offers a comprehensive presentation of Schumpeter's thoughts. It grew from the conviction "that it is meaningless, precisely in the field of monetary policy (*Währungspolitik*), to tackle practical problems until clarity on the basic problems of money has been attained and the paralyzing influence of discrepancies in basic approach has been eliminated. More than in any other field, practice can here rest on theoretical insight" (p. 628). And this theoretical insight Schum-

peter gained by tackling the basic problems from an analysis of the circular flow. He thereby opened up an approach to research in monetary theory that has proved particularly fruitful. It is true that today we see many things in a different light from what Schumpeter then saw; but this pioneer study will always retain its importance as a milestone on the road toward true knowledge.

VII

This concludes our survey of Schumpeter's early German works. They are works that are inspired by an unremitting quest for truth. Schumpeter sought to convince by the power and logic of his argument, and nothing else. He was concerned with the facts, never with personalities. Nor was he a zealot, stubbornly clinging to certain one-sided approaches. True, his heart belonged to the quantitative aspects of economics and thus to the mathematical approach; yet he was very well aware that there were other aspects to the phenomena of economics, aspects that must be mastered by other methods. His greatest loathing was reserved for methodological controversy, which he regarded not only as sterile, but as a direct obstacle to the progress of our discipline. One of his articles, "Die 'positive' Methode in der Nationalökonomie" (The 'Positive' Method in Economics) in *Deutsche Literaturzeitung*, 1914, in which he subjected to criticism F. Simiand's work, *La méthode positive en science économique* (Paris, 1912), concludes with the following words: "When at long last will the day come that will bring home the realization to all of us that weapons to cope with the vast mass of facts must first be forged, each by itself? — that this vast mass possesses countless different aspects, demanding countless different approaches? When at long last shall we have learned our scientific craft to the point where we can grasp what our neighbor is doing and calmly till our own field rather than attack him?" This "methodological tolerance" runs straight through the lifework of this genius, serving as a shining example to all who work in the perfection of our discipline.

SCHUMPETER AND QUANTITATIVE RESEARCH IN ECONOMICS

J. Tinbergen

THE difficulty of giving a correct appraisal of so many-sided a talent as Schumpeter was is evident. The following impressions relate to only one aspect of the writings of this complicated and almost mysterious mind; they try to find out what his attitude was toward the type of economist we may call "model builders" in the econometric sense.

Schumpeter was among the enthusiastic founders of the Econometric Society. In fact, the very first contribution to *Econometrica* — apart from the "Editorial" — was his "The Common Sense of Econometrics,"[1] one of the masterpieces of vision, eloquence, and harmony, characteristic of his work. In the paper he expresses a warm sympathy for, and a strong belief in, econometric research. It is striking, therefore, that upon a careful study of his own largest publication since then — *Business Cycles*[2] — one finds a mental attitude vis-à-vis econometric work which is not only rather critical, but to some extent alien to it. A critical attitude can never be a reason for concern: keen analysts will always have to make critical comments of anything that others have wrought, and only at the benefit of further progress. What strikes one to some extent is, however, that the mental approach to the problems which seems to be behind many parts of *Business Cycles* looks so different from the approach common to most econometricians. If this approach is correct, it seems to me to be worth while to consider it further, since it might contribute to the mutual understanding of econometricians (as I see them) and others, Schumpeter in his broad approach perhaps representing both.

The space devoted to typical econometric research in this one-thousand-page book is relatively small. The place given to the description of facts, to a somewhat primitive chart-reading, and to institutional consideration is very much larger. The treatment, even of theoretical points, is quite different from the econometric habit of a rigorous subdivision according to the relations discussed — e.g., a sharp distinction between the demand and the supply side, to quote the simplest case.[3]

But it is not only the outer form of his treatment which strikes the econometrist as non-econometric. The difference goes much deeper; it is, in fact, the impression of his whole attitude vis-à-vis the setting of the problems and their solution. I shall try to make my position clear from a number of cases in point.

First, as to the setting of the problem "how to explain the business cycle phenomenon?" I think the general econometric view now is to state that the phenomenon of the rather irregular movements we are accustomed to call business cycles must be understood as the coöperation of essentially two elements, both relevant to the explanation, viz., a mechanism capable of performing characteristic cyclical movements ("Eigenschwingungen" as the German physicists call them) and exogenous "shocks" as initial movers. Schumpeter shows a scarcely-hidden preference for the shocks to be the "true" "causes" and tends to belittle the importance of the mechanism. Discussing the hog cycle, he concludes:[4] "What we behold when looking at those hog graphs that are so remarkably regular is *nothing but* [my italics] the — wavelike, to be sure — working of a particular apparatus of response."

Similarly, about the coffee market he says:[5] "*Only* [my italics] the form of these fluctuations is shaped by the structural properties of the coffee resonator. . . ."

[1] *Econometrica*, I (1933), p. 5.
[2] Joseph A. Schumpeter, *Business Cycles: A Theoretical, Historical and Statistical Analysis of the Capitalist Process* (New York and London, 1939, 2 vols.).
[3] Cf., in particular, his treatment of separate markets in Chapter x, for which subject this technique would seem the ideal one.
[4] *Business Cycles*, II, p. 533.
[5] *Ibid.*, p. 530.

When discussing his own theory, that of the innovations, the emphasis is also more on these "shocks" than on the mechanism.

The point is more important than a mere difference of emphasis would be. In the mind of the econometrists, the mechanism deserves the main attention especially, because what we can influence is much more the structure of the mechanism than the occurrence of the shocks. Business-cycle policy, in whatever form, always comes down to changing the structure of the "response mechanism" or the "resonator" — the word is very well chosen by Schumpeter — so as to increase its damping degree and hence to "nip in the bud" the cumulative processes provoked by the shocks.

By the way, it may be questioned whether the shocks of innovations are so much the leading ones. His monolithic theory is remarkable enough for one like Schumpeter, with his sense of the complexity of things. Are not agricultural shocks also very important and could they not even explain especially the Kitchin? [6] It is, in this respect, interesting to quote from *Business Cycles* that, among prices, food and textile prices (and those of textile machinery) show the Kitchin more markedly than metal prices. The same is true for the demand for shipping (where grain transports play an important rôle) as distinguished from the cost of shipping (where coal prices are predominant).

Also his opinion on the nature the mechanisms under discussion shows remarkable deviation from the usual econometric approach. Discussing the possibility, put forward by the "self-generating theories," that the causation of prosperity lies (to some extent at least) in the conditions prevailing in depression, he adds: [7] "This line of reasoning may perhaps serve . . . in order to account for revival *up to normal* [my italics], *but obviously cannot serve beyond that*."

Anybody who is familiar with the theory of econometric models, to which the italicized passages do not apply, wonders what exactly Schumpeter may have had in mind here.

Throughout his treatment of the business-cycle mechanism, he is very much in favor of a-cyclic, or at least heavily damped, mechanisms. This may, from a realistic point of view, be very wise. From a purely theoretical point of view it would not seem justified, however. His assertions that undamped mechanisms are like a *perpetuum mobile*, or his comment on Kalecki's model that the starting impulse might have been some trouble in the apple-growing industry at the time Adam and Eve dwelt in Paradise — however refreshing this latter idea be — seem to indicate such an unjustified theoretical belief against periodic endogenous movements.

Another passage in his discussion of econometric models, when dealing with reinvestment cycles, also strangely collides with econometric results. He seems to think that an explanation of the cycle based on the "echo principle" has as a necessary condition that the lifetime of all machines be the same. [8] He seems to be unaware of the fact that the very relation he emphasizes, viz., that between reinvestment and the general economic situation, is sufficient to explain even undamped reinvestment cycles with distributed lifetimes.

Throughout he considerably, in my opinion, understates the degree of generality of the validity of the theorems on cycles put forward by econometrists. When discussing — may I add, generously—the shipbuilding model I once put forward, he states, among other things: [9] "Freight rates are not an invariant function of tonnage alone and, as soon as this is recognised, there is an end of this particular cycle."

If the function varies, or if other variables come in, there need not at all be "an end" to this cycle. If one of these other variables be the price of new ships — another objection made — the same answer applies, in particular when this variable, according to Schumpeter's graph XXII (p. 535), appears to be, with great approximation, a function of freight rates. Neither does the theory of the shipbuilding cycle rest on the necessary assumption that the reaction of carriers "to freight rates be mechanical." [10]

A question perhaps more of terminology would seem the statement that the cycle just

[6] Cf. J. Tinbergen and J. J. Polak, *The Dynamics of Business Cycles* (Chicago, 1949), p. 214.

[7] *Business Cycles*, I, p. 139, note.

[8] *Ibid.*, p. 190.

[9] *Business Cycles*, II, p. 534.

[10] *Ibid.*

discussed is not an endogenous one, because it depends on some disturbance "that starts them." [11]

The didactic value seen by a number of "model builders" in the clear distinction between the explanation of (i) the period, (ii) the shape, and (iii) the amplitude of some of the simple cycles, each of them having separate determinants, does not seem to have impressed Schumpeter either, when he concludes about the coffee cycle that "the form of these fluctuations is shaped by the structural properties of the coffee resonator, of which the *lag* is one." The lag is typically responsible for the period, but not for the form; the disturbing shocks are determinants to the form.

Finally, a difference of opinion on the economic contents of one particular relation in a certain model may be quoted. In that model it was assumed that the volume of production is — apart from a lag resulting from the production period — determined by the *rate of increase* of profits and the *rate of increase* of other incomes (as far as not saved) as the only determinants. The present author is of the opinion that this assumption is rather strange; in fact, in no other model so far presented has it ever been adhered to. Schumpeter, according to an anticritical note,[12] evidently considered it rather reasonable.

Are these few remarks an expression of some "dépit" that Schumpeter was rather critical, in 1939, vis-à-vis some of the econometric models of cycles that had been put forward since his warm recommendation of the econometric method in 1933? If so, the only reaction of the reader should be: Evidently many model builders have to learn something from Schumpeter's universal knowledge and insight, the more so since one cannot expect him to have been biased against their work! At any rate, this is an important conclusion that the present writer wants to draw. But there is another, a somewhat puzzling one: Evidently Schumpeter "lived another life" than most econometrists. What exactly did econometrics mean to him? Did he feel at home with it, or did he not? What is the sense of the divergencies just stated? In the opinion of the writer it cannot be explained only by the grief Schumpeter expresses [13] concerning "the difficulties which exact methods of analysis are sure to meet."

As I have said, these remarks may be of some slight use in clearing a few misunderstandings about econometric models. It is only too bad that Schumpeter himself cannot answer them. They by no means do justice to the book on which they bear, and they are not meant to do so. In fact, even the chapters to which they refer are so crowded with important remarks on the theory of cycles as well as on actual economic life that, taken as a whole, they can only confirm the impression of Schumpeter's thorough knowledge and experience.

[11] *Business Cycles*, II, p. 534.
[12] *Business Cycles*, I, p. 185, note 1.

[13] *Business Cycles*, II, p. 530. Cf. also Professor Samuelson's and Professor Smithies' essays in this volume. — Ed.

THE MONETARY ASPECTS OF THE
SCHUMPETERIAN SYSTEM

Arthur W. Marget

THE editors of this book suggested, as a title for this paper, "Schumpeter's Contributions to the Theory of Money." I have entitled it, instead, "The Monetary Aspects of the Schumpeterian System." The choice is deliberate. It is based on the proposition that one of the most remarkable features of the towering intellectual structure which Schumpeter envisioned, and did so much to realize, was its really extraordinary architectonic unity. It follows that it is impossible to evaluate, or even understand, the nature of Schumpeter's contributions in the monetary field in isolation from the other parts of his magnificent over-all vision.[1]

The Grand Design

The ground-plan of Schumpeter's structure, in its monetary aspects as well as in its "real" aspects, is the Quesnay-Walras concept of a "circular flow" of economic life, conceived of as a system of *flows of monetary expenditure directed toward objects sold against such expenditure*. The words I have italicized represent an example of that aspect of Schumpeter's genius which might be characterized as an almost unparalleled capacity for genuinely creative interpretation of his predecessors.[2] They go a very long way toward explaining at once why Schumpeter reverenced Walras so profoundly and why an inheritance which remained an archetype of sterility as long as it was viewed through distorting lenses of Paretian manufacture became, at the hands of Schumpeter, a living matrix for fresh creation.

This is best seen if we concentrate our attention on the *grand design* of the structure which was to be erected on this Walrasian ground-plan, rather than on its details. That Schumpeter was himself a builder of parts of the structure, as well as the architect of the whole, is beyond question. Specification of these parts would therefore be indicated as a matter of simple justice, even if it were not particularly indicated by that combination of modesty with respect to his own achievements and generous recognition of the achievements of others which would make it so easy to fail to notice his own achievements as a builder of specific analytical instruments in the field of money.[3]

But it is the majestic *sweep* of his concep-

[1] The monolithic quality of Schumpeter's achievement will be emphasized, rather than obscured, by the mass of detail and the staggering range characterizing his monumental *History of Economic Analysis*, which Mrs. Schumpeter has been kind enough to allow me to read in manuscript. I regret all the more, therefore, that I have been able to make only the most cursory inspection of the manuscript of the monograph on *Money* (in German, almost all of it untyped) on which Schumpeter worked until 1934 or 1935. The latter monograph is being prepared for publication in both German and English.

[2] In the present instance, the extent to which such an interpretation in itself represented a constructive achievement, by opening the way to an adequate appreciation of the leads for further construction implicit in the *details* of the Walrasian system of monetary analysis, may best be judged by comparing the results summarized in this paper with those results which followed from the clear *mis*interpretation of Walras' teaching which has been almost the general rule, even in our own day. In this connection, see my *Theory of Prices* (hereafter referred to as *TP*), II, 70–72, III, n. 50, 168, n. 51, 328, n. 27, 358–63, 417, n. 23, 459, n. 127, 622–23, and the references there given.

[3] For those to whom such specification may be welcome, it should be sufficient here to call attention to such items as (1) Schumpeter's role in the history of the "income approach" generally (*TP*, I, 338, 343, 350, II, 114–16); (2) his presentation of the first algebraically formulated "income equation" of the general Fisherine form (*TP*, I, 339, n. 111, 409, 511, II, 104, 115, 117, n. 65, 735, 753, n. 57); (3) his priority, among contemporary economists, in the formulation of the concept of "income velocity" (*TP*, I, 338, 359–60, 365, n. 51, 379, 511, II, 114, n. 59); (4) his establishment of the relation between his "income equation" and the concept of a "consumers' goods price-level," *in conjunction with* the explicit specification of an equation for the prices of producers' goods (*TP*, I, 486, 497–99, 512, n. 75, II, 118, n. 67, 330, n. 33), and the relation of both to the problem of differential price-change and the associated changes in the structure of incomes and output — including the phenomenon of "forced saving" (*TP*, I, 497–98, II, 118–19, 315, n. 200); (5) his establishment of the relation of the concept of "aggregate demand" (*Gesamtnachfrage*) to "stream" equations of the general Fisherine form (*TP*, II, 117, 121, n. 75, 686, n. 13); (6) his provision of an explicit "sequence" model tracing the successive impact of money-flows, and his relating thereof to devices of "general" value theory such as production functions and particular demand schedules, as well as to the theory of output as a whole (*TP*, II, 316, n. 205, 431–34, 600, n. 103); and (7) his "monetary theory of interest" (*TP*, II, 63, n. 26, 119, n. 70).

tion of the problem, rather than his creation of specific analytical weapons, which makes him almost unique among monetary theorists: indeed, his only peer in this respect was Léon Walras, whom he acknowledged as his master in the field of monetary theory as in the field of economic theory generally. It is therefore the lines of Schumpeter's grand architectural design for monetary analysis (a term which he himself defined as "*a theory of the economic process in terms of expenditure flows*") that will be stressed in what follows, leaving for reference to other sources an indication of the principal points at which he was able, with his own hands, to bring the actual work of building closer to completion; the points at which he indicated the way in which further construction was to proceed, and thus (in the phrase that keeps recurring in his evaluation of the work of his own predecessors) "pointed beyond himself"; the principal points at which one would have to write simply "work under construction"; and the points with respect to which, as far as his own work is concerned, one has the same feeling that one has in scrutinizing some of the baffling scrawls — chiefly in a personal variant of "Gabelsberger" (an Austrian type of shorthand) — which he was in the habit of dashing off as ideas came to him: points on which, that is to say, one simply cannot be sure how far he himself had gone, or what new turn his thought was taking.[4]

The following, then, is an outline of the grand design for the structure of monetary analysis which was to be erected on the Walrasian ground-plan:

1. Viewed as a system of flows of money expenditure and of objects sold against such expenditure, the Walrasian system is to be thought of as a system of inter-dependent *markets*. It is, moreover, the flow of *money* which establishes the inter-dependence between the markets. It is *money* which entrepreneurs disburse to create income to the factors of production; it is therefore *money* which the factors of production, in their turn, disburse out of income in purchase of the products of industry.[5] Money, in short, is the means whereby a link is established in *time* between the successive discretely realized events of the economic process.[6]

2. Money, however, has no organs of locomotion in itself. It flows (or ceases to flow) in response to *decisions* made by *economic units*: the economic unit being, by definition, the decision-making agency, whether it is a consumer, a business firm, a financial institution, or a government. It is these decisions which determine (a) whether money received (currently or in past periods) is to be spent currently, or to be kept unspent; (b) whether, if it is to be spent currently, it is to be spent on one type of commodity or service (or financial instrument) or another; and (c) (in the case of financial institutions and governments) whether there shall be additions to, or subtractions from, the total stock of money-spending power, and what particular elements in the community shall receive or be deprived of money-spending power as a result of these decisions. It is the task of economic analysis, monetary and "non-monetary," to explain why these decisions are

---

[4] On these points, the "references to other sources," as the reader will discover, are chiefly *via* references to my own *Theory of Prices*. To the reader who may be offended (or amused) at what may seem to be a particularly naive example of the completely *un*-Schumpeterian practice of citing one's own previous writings, I offer a two-fold excuse (in addition to the obvious one of saving space as a result of the fact that single references to *TP* will provide a much larger number of detailed page-references to Schumpeter's writings directly). First, since one of the purposes of *TP*, incidental to its main constructive purpose, was to provide "a documented illustration" of the *processes by which the received body of monetary analysis came to be what it is*, references to Schumpeter via *TP* will, I hope, answer an objection that readers of this paper might otherwise have raised: namely, that I have here attributed a degree of uniqueness to Schumpeter's contribution which does injustice to other great figures in the history of monetary analysis. Secondly, I am, indeed, not prepared to confess to the sin (if it is a sin) of *consciously* attributing to Schumpeter, either in this paper or *TP*, more of positive construction than can actually be found, in various states of articulation, in his own writings; but I am aware of the possibility that my unbounded admiration for his work may

have led me *unconsciously* to father upon him developments of his basic ideas which he himself might not have acknowledged as his own offspring. The specific references to *TP* may at least serve "to indicate where his [Schumpeter's] personal responsibility begins, and where it ends" (*TP*, II, 110, n. 47).

[5] See *TP*, II, 351–63 (the passage in Schumpeter's *Business Cycles* cited on p. 362, n. 31, is a particularly clear example of Schumpeter's use of the Walrasian concept of the establishment of "mutual interdependence" in time by the inter-market flow of realized money expenditure), and 416–21.

[6] See *TP*, II, 347–52.

what they are, and to indicate the consequences of the decisions, once taken, for the further functioning of the economic process.[7]

3. The inevitable inclusion of *consumers* in the list of groups of decision-making economic units makes equally inevitable the segregation, for analytical purposes, of the flow of consumers' money income and consumers' money expenditure, and the flow of objects sold against such money expenditure by consumers. But it would be completely wrong in principle to suppose that economic analysis, monetary or non-monetary, can confine itself to an apparatus in which these are the only magnitudes to be studied. The direct contrary is indicated with particular force by the arguments for believing that it is precisely in the area of *entrepreneurial* decisions with respect to the level and direction of money spending that the main-spring of economic *change* is to be found.[8]

4. Walras himself was not primarily concerned with the use of his system of flows of money-expenditure and of objects sold against such expenditure for the description and explanation of the processes of economic *change*. But it is characteristic of Walras' genius, and adequate justification for an estimation of him as having in fact "created the modern theory of money," that the groundwork which he established lends itself perfectly to the further developments which are required in order to be able to analyze the causes and consequences of economic change.[9] Thus, the fact that the process to which Walras devoted his major attention was a *"stationary"* process does not alter the fact that it was, after all, a *process*, unfolding in time, with a definite time sequence of money receipts and of money expenditures out of those receipts.[10] Thus, also, the fact that, for Walras' own major purpose, the level and direction of the flows of money and of objects sold against money were pictured as unchanging, does not alter the fact that Walras' own analytical apparatus provided elements which can be used to explain *changes* in the level and direction of these flows.[11] The development of these elements in the Walrasian system, and their supplementation whenever such supplementation is indicated, is precisely the task to which our own generation should devote itself.

5. The fact that the Walrasian system is, from first to last, a system of *money* flows means that there is no important aspect of economic life without a monetary aspect.[12] Thus,

---

[7] Schumpeter accepted these propositions so completely in his own work that he found it necessary to stress them explicitly only after the Keynesian "revolution" had revived ancient controversies which then came to be discussed under the heading of the new *terms*, "microeconomic *versus* macroeconomic" analysis (cf. *TP*, II, 498–504). Schumpeter's statements with respect to the methodological principles involved are therefore to be found chiefly in the course of his attacks on certain aspects of the Keynesian system: specifically, (1) on the limitations of *unsupplemented* "aggregative" analysis of the Keynesian type; (2) on what he regarded as the Keynesian misapplication, to social aggregates, of concepts, such as demand and supply schedules, which had had a quite different role and meaning in earlier analysis; and (3) on the Keynesian failure to relate changes in the supply of *money* adequately to the acts of *volition* involved. See, e.g., the references given in *TP*, II, 117, n. 66, 110, n. 48, 163, n. 41, 204, n. 131, 437, n. 67, 542, n. 44; also Schumpeter's later paper, "The Decade of the Twenties," *American Economic Review, Proceedings*, XXXVI (1946), 3, on "the proposition that analysis of the economic phenomena of any given period must proceed from the economic facts that produce them and not from the monetary aggregates that result from them." Yet it is worth recording that a premonitory instinct had led Schumpeter to issue a warning even in his pre-Keynesian writings against a type of error in analytical procedure which was to become dominant after the publication of the *General Theory*. See, e.g., *TP*, II, 204, n. 131; and contrast the emphasis, in Schumpeter's pre-Keynesian paper on "The Analysis of Economic Change," this REVIEW, XVII (1935), 9, on the need for studying "the process of investment and the corresponding process of *credit contraction*" in relation to "the actual behavior of borrowers and lenders," with the *General Theory*'s treatment of the "elasticity of supply of money" (cf. *TP*, II, 642–44).

[8] Study of the passages referred to under (4) in note 3, above, should demonstrate the *balanced* nature of Schumpeter's emphasis on *both* the proposition contained in the first sentence of the paragraph and the propositions implied by the last two sentences. Any other interpretation of his analytical system could be justified only by wrenching his utterances out of their proper context. When, for example, Schumpeter insisted ("The Analysis of Economic Change," *loc. cit.*, 9) that "the stream of expenditure by householders on consumers' goods is *one of* [italics inserted] the most indispensable elements in the analysis of the business cycle," he did so on the assumption that readers would not ignore the ensuing paragraphs on the necessity for studying variations in the amount and direction of *entrepreneurial* spending. On the relation of the "mutually interdependent" flows of "consumer expenditure" and "producers' expenditure," respectively, to the processes of economic *change*, cf. Schumpeter's *Business Cycles*, 549 f.

[9] Cf. *TP*, I, 406, n. 46, 505, n. 47; II, 71, n. 48, 112–13, 361, n. 30, 364–66, 421, n. 31, 427–36.

[10] Cf. *TP*, II, 352, 357–63, 417–20, 622–24.

[11] Cf. *TP*, II, 71, n. 46, 284, n. 132, 315, 328, 331, n. 35, 361, n. 30.

[12] The specific references which follow should be sufficient to establish the role of Schumpeter in the history of the

the conclusion that any adequate theory of the determination of the *rate of interest* must, in an important sense, be a *"monetary* theory of interest" is a conclusion which is forced upon anyone who will face a fact which Walras himself emphasized: namely, that the market on which rates of interest, properly so called, are determined is the market on which *"le capital"* is *lent* in the form of money (*capital-monnaie*) and not the market on which *capital goods* (Walras' *les capitaux*) are sold.[13] By the same token, however, the fact that "real" means of production *are* sold against money, and that the purchasers of these means of production expect to sell for money the output obtained therefrom, must mean that any adequate theory of output must deal with the effects of monetary expansion and contraction on the level and structure of output.[14] Similarly, any adequate theory of the determination of *prices* must be able to account for those changes in the *level and structure of money prices* which result from changes in the level and direction of the flow of money-expenditure in relation to the flow of objects sold against such expenditure.[15]

6. It is in the very nature of analysis in terms of an interdependent system of money-flows that the separate money-payments which represent purchases and payments in individual transactions must, at some stage in the analysis, be *summed*, in such wise as to yield a series of "aggregative" concepts.[16] This is inherent, for example, in the concept of "consumer expenditure," even if we are concerned only with the expenditure of a single consumer: it is, indeed, the fact that an individual's monetary expenditure is distributed over uses which are either competitive or complementary that makes the concept of economic interdependence inevitable even within this single analytical sector.[17] But the case for the creation of significant "aggregative concepts" becomes much more evident when we pass from the total money expenditure of an individual consumer to the expenditure of all consumers (or of all consumers of a given economic class), or from the expenditure of one business firm to the expenditures of all business firms (or of all business firms in a particular industry). In this sense, indeed, the case for the use, at some stage of the analysis, of "aggregative" concepts is simply that, without such concepts, it is impossible to realize that picture of a system of interdependent markets, in terms of a system of flows of money expenditure and of objects sold against such expenditure, which, as indicated under (1) above, is so essential a feature of the Walrasian ground-plan.[18]

7. It is a fair corollary from the principle of general economic interdependence that our picture of flows of money expenditure and of objects sold against such expenditure cannot, with analytical safety, leave out any important area of flows of money expenditure. In this sense, our "aggregation" of separate flows of money expenditure (or of sectors of such expenditure) either must be *complete* or must be accompanied by a special argument to show why, for the purpose of a particular argument under discussion, it is safe to work with an aggregation of money flows that is less than complete.[19] An illustration of the point is provided

---

development of an adequate recognition, in our own day, of the importance of the role played by money in the economic process, as against the position that money is merely the "veil" to be torn aside for purposes of serious analysis (cf. *TP*, II, 111, n. 51): one has, indeed, only to recall that Schumpeter's insistence on the importance of money in economic analysis earned for him the charge, by Böhm-Bawerk, of having delivered himself to "mercantilist" heresy (cf. *TP*, II, 63, n. 26). But it is equally important to record the fact that no one protested more vigorously than did Schumpeter against an over-emphasis on monetary factors whenever such a protest was called for. See, e.g., the comments in his paper, "Mitchell's Business Cycles," *Quarterly Journal of Economics*, XLV (1930), on the "provable error" implied in the "view that economic life is changed to its very core by the intervening of money."

[13] On Walras, in addition to the references given in *TP*, II, 71, n. 47, see the references given in my "The Monetary Aspects of the Walrasian System," *Journal of Political Economy*, XLIII (1935), 184, notes 79 and 80. On Schumpeter's "monetary theory of interest," see the references given under (7) in note 3, above.

[14] See the references given under (4) and (6) in note 3, above.

[15] In addition to the references given under (4) and (6) in note 3, above, see *TP*, II, 331, n. 35, 335, n. 47.

[16] In addition to the references to Schumpeter's use of the concept of "aggregate demand" given under (4) in note 3, above, see *TP*, II, 285–96, on "aggregate money demand" as "the sum of realized money demands." On the implications of other "aggregative" concepts which appear in Schumpeter's analytical system, such as "the sum of prices" and "the sum of products," see *TP*, II, 118, n. 67, 295, n. 159, 341–45.

[17] Cf. *TP*, II, 296, n. 161, 320, n. 3.

[18] Cf. *TP*, II, 323–29.

[19] Cf. *TP*, II, 326, n. 23.

in the last two sentences of paragraph (3) above. But this point, important as it is, does not cancel the point made in the first sentence of that paragraph, in support of the *segregation* of certain types of expenditures. On the contrary: our analytical system must be flexible enough to *aggregate* money-flows, whenever such aggregation is both safe and useful analytically, without losing, in the process of aggregation, the heuristic value of a significant *segregation* of specific types of money-flows.[20] In the simplest possible terms: the proposition that x is equal to $a+b+c+d$ does mean that we cannot, without separate proof, reason as if variations in x could be fully accounted for by variations in a and b alone; but it does *not* mean that, since x is equal to $a+b+c+d$, it is x which we should use as our analytical weapon, and not $a+b+c+d$.

8. The prices of commodities and services which are realized in the world about us are *money* prices; and the realization of these prices is in all significant cases effected by money payments which are the components of the money flows whose magnitude and direction it is the task of economic analysis to explain.[21] At the same time, by far the largest part of the received corpus of "general" price theory is concerned precisely with the "explanation" of *prices* in terms of decisions by "economic units" (see par. 2, above) such as the consumer and the business firm.[22] If this corpus of "general" price theory is to have any claim to explain the prices actually realized in the market, it must be brought unequivocally in relation to the conception of the realization of prices as effected by flows of monetary expenditure for objects sold against such expenditure.[23] Here, obviously, is a crucial point at which monetary theory and "general" economic theory must be brought together.[24]

9. All representations of the "circular flow of economic life" have rested upon specific assumptions as to the nature of the *institutional arrangements* which condition the functioning of the economic process.[25] No "theory" of that process, therefore, can be regarded as adequate if it presses its claim to "generality" to the point of abstracting from the influence exerted by institutions on the functioning of the process, and of failing to provide an analytical framework capable of dealing with these institutional effects in all necessary detail.[26] It is the responsibility of *monetary* analysis in particular to see to it that the nature and functioning of *monetary* institutions (especially banking institutions) be studied from the standpoint of their effect upon the magnitude and direction of money flows.[27]

---

articulation and resolution of the formal issues involved, (1) to avoid errors of a type which have served to cloud the very meaning of the relevant analytical devices, and (2) to proceed to a direct incorporation of the weapons of "general" value theory into an explanation of the economic process in terms of money flows. For examples of (1), see *TP*, II, 197, n. 116, 198, n. 121, 229, n. 19, 324, 454, n. 115, 533, n. 28, and the references given in note 7, above, to this part of Schumpeter's critique of Keynes' *General Theory*. For examples of (2), see the references given under (6) in note 3, above.

[25] On the antiquity of discussions of the relation of *institutions* to "the economic processes that, controlled and controlling, take place within them," see Schumpeter's "Wesley Clair Mitchell (1874–1948)," *Quarterly Journal of Economics*, LXIV (1950), 144, n. 6.

[26] Cf. *TP*, II, 432, n. 51, 442, n. 85, 462–71, 717, n. 102, 771.

[27] The central role played in Schumpeter's analysis by commercial ("credit-creating") banks in establishing the "monetary complement of innovation" *via* their effect upon the dimensions and directions of money flows is too well-known to require emphasis here. (Cf. *TP*, II, 434; and see also Schumpeter's essay on "Capitalism in the Postwar World," in *Postwar Economic Problems*, ed. S. E. Harris (1943), 113, where the "creation of means of payments — banknotes or deposits — by private banks" is put on a par with "private ownership of the physical means of production" and "private profits and private responsibility for losses" as a feature without which "no concept of capitalism can be satisfactory.") What is worth emphasizing, however, is that Schumpeter was not content with the mere reiteration of a generalization with respect to the role of banking institutions in affecting the dimensions and directions of money flows. For him, the generalization meant specifically that, in any analysis of the actual economic process, we must be concerned directly with the detailed consequences of such specific institutional facts as a "structural change in banks' assets," the degree of dependence of large-scale business upon bank borrowing, the effects of the "institutional set-up" of the banking structure upon the intensification of business down-turn, and the existing "mortgage situation, both urban and rural" ("The Decade

---

[20] Cf. *TP*, II, 320–29.

[21] Cf. *TP*, II, 240, 274, 550.

[22] Cf. *TP*, II, 240–63, 550–51.

[23] Cf. *TP*, II, 29, n. 76, 130, n. 93, 221–404, 549–624.

[24] The *elements* required for a formal solution of the problem here indicated have behind them, as usual, a distinguished lineage, which includes names as notable as those of Auspitz and Lieben, Cairnes, Newcomb, Cournot, Walras, Marshall, and Fisher (*TP*, II, 263–74). The significance of Schumpeter's performance in this connection lies, not in an articulation of the analytical issues and their explicit resolution, but in the way he was able, even without such an

10. The very conception of the circular flow as a *process* unfolding in time, and the necessity for building, on the foundation of the concept of a stationary "circular flow," an analytical super-structure which will deal adequately with the processes of *change* (par. 4, above), means that we cannot be content with a type of analysis which consists entirely of the representation of successive positions of equilibrium ("comparative statics," in one of the senses of that term).[28] On the contrary, we must start from the proposition that what happens in so-called "transitional" processes may very profoundly alter the actual course of subsequent events. We therefore require an analytical apparatus that will do full justice to the mechanics of *change*, in the sense of providing a description of every step in the processes of change at which decisions are taken that could change the level or direction of those flows of money and of objects sold for money which, in an economy such as ours, are the realized events of economic life that economic analysis must be able to explain.[29]

11. Before we can say that we have "explained" the processes of economic life, we must have an adequate *record* of the processes which we claim to have explained. It is only from such a record, moreover, that we can learn

which of the factors that analysis ("theory") tells us *could* operate in the real world to produce a given result have in fact operated to produce such a result in particular historical situations, and with what degree of relative force they have operated in each situation.[30] This means that there is no escaping the necessity for constructing an "econometric" (in the sense of "numerical" — or statistical — rather than "mathematical") complement to purely theoretical analysis. This inescapable requirement presents at once a challenge and a hope. It presents a challenge to economic analysis to frame its concepts in such a way that these concepts will be "operational" with respect to the "econometric" part of our task.[31] It presents a hope that, given an unambiguous statement of both the analytical and the statistical requirements for the adequate description and explanation of those flows of money expenditure and of the objects sold against such expenditure which are at once the vehicle and the embodiment of the functioning of the economic process, we shall some day realize the dream of both the early econometricians (beginning with the sponsors of "Political Arithmetick," such as Petty) and the constructors of analytical "tableaux economiques" (from Quesnay on)

---

of the Twenties," *loc. cit.*, 6, 9). It is, indeed, worth contrasting Schumpeter's insistence that "the explanatory value for the crisis of this element [the mortgage situation] is ten times as great as that of the most elegant difference equation" with Keynes' deliberate abstraction in his *General Theory*, from the influence of "institutions," in general, and of what he called "technical monetary detail," in particular (cf. *TP*, II, 462, n. 1, and 464, n. 4).

[28] As in the case of the relations between "microeconomic" and "macroeconomic" analysis, we are dealing here with propositions which Schumpeter accepted for himself so completely in his own work that he felt it necessary to stress them explicitly only after Keynes' *General Theory* had popularized precisely the type of analysis here characterized as inadequate. See, e.g., Schumpeter's criticism of the *General Theory's* avoidance of "all complications that arise in process analysis," and, in particular, Keynes' "aversion to *periods*," in "John Maynard Keynes, 1883–1946," *American Economic Review*, XXXVI (1946), 511; and cf. *TP*, II, 452, 454.

[29] Cf. *TP*, II, 473–77. In addition to the references there given, cf. W. W. Leontief, *The Structure of American Economy, 1919–1929*, p. 20, on the implications of "the suppression from our record of all those statistical data which describe the mechanism of interindustrial relations," in the face of the fact that "it is exactly this mechanism which determines the size of the net income flow and its variations."

[30] On "theory" as "not an unscientific or provisional substitute for facts, but an instrument — spectacles, so to speak — needed in order to discern the facts" — i.e., on theory "not as hypothesis, but as a tool," see "Mitchell's Business Cycles," *loc. cit.*, 155, 169, and "Wesley Clair Mitchell," *loc. cit.*, 143–44. Cf. *TP*, II, 504–12.

[31] It is of considerable importance to note that Schumpeter regarded this challenge as valid not only with respect to the type of economic theory usually called "*business cycle* theory" (cf. "A Theorist's Comment on the Current Business Cycle," *Journal of the American Statistical Association*, XXX [1935], 167), but also with respect to the concepts of "general" economic theory. Indeed, he made a special point of grading the performance of economic theorists according to the pains they had taken to make their concepts "statistically operative": i.e., such that they could yield "not merely quantitative, but also numerical results." See, e.g., his comments on Fisher ("Irving Fisher's Econometrics," *Econometrica*, XVI [1948], 220, 228), and on Cournot and Marshall ("The Common Sense of Econometrics," *Econometrica*, I [1933], 8–9; "Mitchell's Business Cycles," *loc. cit.*, 156–57; "Alfred Marshall's Principles: A Semi-Centennial Appraisal," *American Economic Review*, XXXI [1941], 247–48). Relevant also, in this connection, is Schumpeter's repeated insistence on the necessity for establishing a mutually fructifying relation between economic theory and the records and practice of business *accounting*. See, e.g., "Irving Fisher's Econometrics," *loc. cit.*, 224; and cf. *TP*, II, 511.

who have undertaken to provide a description and explanation of economic events in the world we know.[32]

The Econometric Implementation

Schumpeter, who made it a point of pride as well as of honor to trace the ancestry of the fundamental ideas underlying his "analytical engine" to some of the greatest names in the history of economics, would have been shocked if anyone had suggested (in the recurrent fashion of which the most recent example was given us in the later 1930's) that what he was offering, in his "monetary analysis," was a "New Economics" that was to undo the work of all his predecessors. He would have been no less shocked if anyone had suggested that what made a "New Economics" of his grand design for monetary analysis was its specific association with an insistence that it must be given an econometric implementation in the form of a statistical *tableau economique:* a result that would provide numerical information, for the purpose of diagnosis of the economic process, "analogous to the information a doctor assembles in the course of his investigation when we go to him for a check-up." [33] And even if he could have been brought to condone a characterization of his insistence on the necessity for an econometric implementation of his grand analytical design as amounting to the formulation of a "program" for a "New Economics" in the more modest sense of an "economics of the future" which would grow organically out of, and embody the best in, the "economics of the past," he was not a man to set up a tub-thumping campaign to further such a "program." "Any 'New Economics,' " he insisted, "can come about not by program, but only by achievement." [34]

Nothing is more characteristic of the man than that he never seems to have entertained the slightest expectation that this achievement might be accomplished by a determined sect of fanatical disciples, self-styled "Schumpeterians," who would succeed in constructing a "numerical" implementation of the "theory of the economic process in terms of expenditure flows" that would thenceforward be labeled "Schumpeterian." It is certain, moreover, that, if such a sect had emerged, he would have discouraged it from describing its work as the implementation of *his* analytical system.

He would have done so not merely out of modesty, a sense of history, and respect for the proprieties. He would have done so primarily because he was too well versed in the history of his subject to have missed one of its chief lessons: namely, that what has divided economists in the past has, as often as not, been nothing more than differences in emphasis; that a degree of tolerance toward alternative approaches far greater than that which in fact prevailed would have given us progress far more rapid than that which in fact was made; and that a variety of methods of posing and resolving varied problems is likely, in the long run, to provide a far more inclusive and effective organon for the solution of problems recognized as *common* problems than would insistence on a single method of posing and resolving problems characterized by their sponsors as the only problems worth the economist's attention.[35]

For the furtherance of the econometric implementation of the grand analytical design, therefore, one should look for a framework of econometric research which would provide the *largest area of initial agreement as to what it is important to measure, and to measure currently;* one would then hope that the elabora-

---

[32] On Petty and other writers of the seventeenth century as "econometricians" who made "a conscious attempt to weld into one indivisible argument theorems and statistical facts," see Schumpeter's "The Common Sense of Econometrics," *loc. cit.*, 6–7.

[33] Cf. "The Decade of the Twenties," *loc. cit.*, 1.

[34] "Mitchell's Business Cycles," *loc. cit.*, 152; cf. also "The Common Sense of Econometrics," *loc. cit.*, 12. In the light of what is said below concerning Schumpeter's appreciation of the work of Wesley Mitchell, it is worth noting that he presented the proposition quoted in the text as a summing up of Mitchell's own teaching, having called attention to the fact that "by starting in his first chapter with a survey of the work done since the discovery of the problem

as well as of the solutions now current, he [Mitchell] testifies to his belief in the continuity of science, thereby condemning implicitly any program of 'starting anew.'" The date, it may be observed, was 1930 — six years before the *annus mirabilis* which established a different fashion of viewing such matters.

[35] Cf. "Wesley Clair Mitchell," *loc. cit.*, 145: "The simple fact is that it takes many types of mind to build a science; that these types hardly ever understand one another; and that preference for the work one is made for easily shades off into derogatory judgment about other work which is then hardly ever looked at seriously."

tion and the filling in of this framework, by many hands with varied scientific interests, would in the end not only give us the numerical measures suggested by the particular analytical set-up with which he started, but would also suggest, as we proceed, the "need to add to our analytic engine the new parts which it requires." [36] Where shall one look for the common starting point?

Joseph Schumpeter died at his desk, as it were, pen in hand; and no one can be quite sure what he would have written as his final legacy had he known that he was to go so suddenly. But there is a page, among the last that he wrote for his posthumous *History of Economic Analysis*, which some of us, at least, will choose to regard as that part of his legacy which provides an answer to the question I have just raised. He was discussing the state of economic analysis under totalitarian regimes, and was asking whether, despite the intellectual terror which is inseparable from such regimes, there is not some framework which could provide a common operational framework for economic analysts of intellectual integrity, whatever limitations, external or internal, may be imposed upon them otherwise. *And he found that common framework in "The National Income Accounts."*

The suggestion that Schumpeter would have found the "common starting point" for the construction of an econometric *tableau économique* for our times in the *National Income Accounts* will come as a surprise only to those whose understanding of the history and present substance of technical economics would run somewhat as follows: (1) the "national income accounts" are to be explained by something called "income analysis"; (2) by "income analysis" is meant, and should be meant, exclusively the analytical system first presented in Keynes' *General Theory* and developed by Keynes' disciples; (3) hence, the "national income accounts" are in a peculiar sense associated with the Keynesian analytical system (Schumpeter's general evaluation of which is too well-known to require re-statement here).

But of course this syllogism is completely invalidated, on the analytical side, by its absurd minor premise. And, on the historical side, one can hardly be accused of failing to do justice to such contributions to National Income Accounting as have been made in recent years by individuals who happen to have been Keynesians, if one insists, in the interest of simple justice, that something more than a faulty syllogism of this kind is required in order to determine to whom credit is due for the inspiration that led to the empirical achievements which are here under discussion.

Schumpeter would, most emphatically, not have claimed the credit for himself.[37] So far as figures of the American scene are concerned, he would, I think, have assigned the chief credit without hesitation to the great contemporary whom, in his own words, he so greatly "loved and admired" — Wesley Mitchell.[38] Surely it is to Mitchell, and to the inspiration which

[36] See Schumpeter's "English Economists and the State-Managed Economy," *Journal of Political Economy*, LVII (1949), 382. Note should be taken of Schumpeter's reference to the work of Leontief in this connection.

[37] I am speaking here specifically of credit for having provided the direct impetus to the empirical work involved. If the principal element of novelty in the recent work on the National Income Accounts ("Social Accounts," in the phrase adopted from Hicks' *The Social Framework* [1942]) is held to be its emphasis on the *"structure of the constituent transactions"* which make up the "broad totals" previously emphasized in empirical work on the National Income (cf. *Measurement of National Income and the Construction of Social Accounts*, United Nations, 1947, pp. 7, 23, 26), there is of course an obvious conceptual relation to Schumpeter's insistence, throughout the Keynesian controversy, on the importance of breaking down the broad aggregates with which the *General Theory* proposed to operate into subgroups which would enable us to locate the points at which *change* is inaugurated, and to trace the steps in the process resulting from this change (see the references given in note 7, above). But a "conceptual relation" is quite different from direct stimulus to a specific type of empirical work.

[38] It will be noted that I am speaking here of "the American scene." Schumpeter did not hesitate to say that "a great part — perhaps the chief part — of the contributions that *English* economists have made to economic analysis during the last few years consists in researches of the type that is best exemplified by national income accounting" ("English Economists and the State-Managed Economy," *loc. cit.*, 371). I am not familiar enough with the British scene to be able to trace any personal filiation between the recent British work on National Income Accounting and the earlier work on the National Income by such a figure as A. L. Bowley. In any event, Schumpeter must have been pleased by the spirit which led Richard Stone to remark that "from an historical point of view, it is interesting to note that modern investigations in this field [of "The Social Accounts"] come close both in form and purpose to the political arithmeticians of the seventeenth century with whom such studies originated" (*Measurement of National Income and the Construction of Social Accounts*, 26).

Mitchell passed on to his co-workers at the National Bureau of Economic Research (whose first publication was precisely on the National Income) that we must look for the source from which American work on the measurement of "National Income and the related accounts" received its great impetus in our generation.[39]

It is, indeed, precisely at this point that one finds a striking example of the convergence of results of the work of "many hands with varied scientific interests," indicated above, when the "hands" and the "interests" involved are guided by a spirit of scientific and personally disinterested scholarship. For Mitchell is to be mentioned here not only as the true fountain-head of the American work on the National Income Accounts; he is to be mentioned here also (as Schumpeter himself mentioned him) as one who, in his discussion of "The Monetary Mechanism" and *The Flow of Money Payments*," indicated the outlines of a *"theory of money flows* which . . . anticipates much of what is best in modern income accounting and aggregative analysis."[40] To complain, with respect to some of the details of this aspect of Mitchell's performance, that Mitchell himself did not provide the kind of "effective conceptualization" of his "theory" that might have been provided by a "professional theorist" would be to ask of individual achievement the humanly impossible. One might just as well complain that Schumpeter, who *did* provide a considerable part of the "effective conceptualization" required, of a kind and quality one would expect from a "professional theorist," did *not* provide the mass of material for that "numerical" implementation of the common grand design for which Mitchell must be given undying credit. What is remarkable about Mitchell's

"theory of money flows" is that, for all his primary concern with the actual "numerical" implementation of his conception of the economic process, he was able to present a working drawing for the *"theorist"* — and precisely the "theorist" concerned with *"The Flow of Money Payments"* — of a degree of suggestiveness and insight that entirely warrants Schumpeter's characterization of it as a "great performance."[41]

It is therefore not a criticism of the architects and the builders of modern National Income Accounting, but a recognition of the protean flexibility of the instrument itself, to suggest that one of the things most needed now is precisely (1) its econometric articulation as a system of *money* flows and (2) the more precise elaboration of its relations to the functioning of *"the monetary mechanism."* No one who understands the implications of the first point will fail to understand the importance which some of us attach to the empirical work on Money Flows of which Professor Morris Copeland has been the chief instigator.[42] And no one who understands the implications of the second point will fail to see the necessity for sharpening methods for the inclusion of data, such as those of the Federal Reserve System, on the break-down of *cash balances classified by economic type of holder* ("Ownership of Demand Deposits"), with all that this should mean for the ultimate securing of data with respect to *the rate of payments out of these cash balances,* and thereby the location of the precise points at which one of the most important type of "hitch-up" in money-flows may occur,

[39] Since any historical account of progress toward an econometric implementation of the grand design, precisely in relation to what came to be called later "National Income Accounting," would have to accord a place of honor to Leontief's pioneer monograph on *The Structure of American Economy* (1941), it should be recorded that Leontief concluded the preliminary research for his project in 1931 while he was "holding the position of Research Associate in the National Bureau of Economic Research" (*op. cit.,* Preface). A further apposite touch is Leontief's description of his work as an "attempt to construct, on the basis of available statistical materials, a *Tableau Economique* of the United States," with its specific reference to Quesnay (p. 9).

[40] "Wesley Clair Mitchell," *loc. cit.,* 150–51.

[41] "Wesley Clair Mitchell," *loc. cit.,* 151.

[42] See M. A. Copeland, "Tracing Money Flows through the United States Economy," *American Economic Review, Proceedings,* XXXVII (1947). The fact that Professor Copeland's work was inaugurated under the auspices of the National Bureau of Economic Research would itself establish a line of descent from Mitchell's influence. In this particular case, however, the line is more direct; for, as Professor Kuznets has suggested ("National Income: A New Version," this REVIEW, XXX [1948], 154), there is a connection between the project inaugurated by Professor Copeland and the rough estimates presented by Mitchell in 1947 in connection with the latter's proposition that "for the smooth working of the business economy it is as necessary that the immensely larger flow of payments among business enterprises shall be maintained as it is necessary that the smaller flow of payments from consumers to retail merchants shall be continued" (*Business Cycles: The Problem and Its Setting,* 151).

and the establishment of the reasons and the consequences of such "hitch-ups."[43]

One could provide further illustrations of empirical material (such as that provided by the Federal Reserve System's continuing study of Consumer Finances) that must be integrated into our ultimate econometric implementation of that grand design for a system of monetary analysis conceived as a "theory of the economic process in terms of expenditure flows" which represents Schumpeter's central contribution in the monetary field. But it would be a denial of the spirit of that contribution to suggest that, through a collection of rigid specifications in advance, we could say just how the final accomplishment will be achieved and just when.[44] Schumpeter's own tracing of the origins of his grand design to names such as that of Quesnay, and the vision of its econometric implementation to names such as that of Petty, is an indication of his own recognition of the slowness with which definitive achievement can be expected to accrete in a subject such as ours.

As far as contemporary contributions are concerned, I have already cited his tribute to Mitchell as an indication of his recognition of the necessity for contributions by "many hands with varied scientific interests" to the common goal. I need not attempt here a list of others, among his contemporaries, whom he would have regarded as having contributed most to both the analytical substance and the econometric implementation of the grand design; but I cannot pass the point without expressing the firm conviction that high on the list would be the name of Irving Fisher, whom Schumpeter regarded not only as the "greatest scientific economist" that America had produced, but also as "the most important of the pioneers of econometrics since William Petty."[45]

It would be difficult to find, in any discipline, three masters as different as Mitchell, Fisher, and Schumpeter in temperament, outlook, and the specific content of their respective achievements. But the three men had at least two qualities in common. None of them established a "sect": we do not speak of Mitchellians, Fisherians, or Schumpeterians, as we speak of Marxians and Keynesians.[46] And of each of them, and of their work, one can say what Schumpeter himself said of Mitchell and his work:

Work of this kind has no natural end and of necessity always points further into an indefinite future. . . . Here was a man who had the courage to say, unlike the rest of us, that he had not all the answers; who went about his work without either haste or rest; who did not care to march along with flags and brass bands; . . . who taught us, by example, and not by phrase, what a scholar should be.[47]

[43] On the role played in monetary analysis by the analytical break-down of cash-balances by economic type of holder, and its integration into a generalized system of money-flows, see *TP*, I, 404–409, II, 509, and the references given in n. 116, thereto. The fact that Walras himself introduced the concept of a break-down of cash-balances by economic type of holder into his own "ground-plan" is a further illustration of his instinct for analytical construction of a kind capable of really significant development. Cf. *TP*, I, 406, n. 46. On the empirical side, F. A. Lutz's *Corporate Cash Balances, 1914–43* (1945), takes on particular significance when regarded as a pilot study in the use of the accounting records of business firms to provide the desired empirical complement to those "contemporary theories of the value of money and of the role of money in business fluctuations" in which "the behavior of cash balances of consumers and business enterprises plays a central part" (see Ralph A. Young's preface to the Lutz study, p. vii).

[44] Cf. the modest comment by Professor Copeland on his own work on Money Flows as representing merely the results of "an early stage in a maiden effort" ("Tracing Money Flows through the United States Economy," *loc. cit.*, 49). See also the comment of Richard Stone in *The Measurement of National Income and the Construction of Social Accounts*, p. 27, third complete paragraph.

[45] "Irving Fisher's Econometrics," *loc. cit.*, 219, 220. Fisher's merits, precisely in connection with the construction of elements both of the "grand design" and of its econometric implementation, were not lessened in Schumpeter's eyes merely because of Fisher's own failure to present "as a tectonic unit" the "imposing structure" of which they can be made an integral part. It is true, Schumpeter remarked, that these elements "are the pillars and arches of a temple that was never built. . . . But those pillars and arches will stand by themselves. They will be visible long after the sands will have smothered much that commands the scene of today" (p. 231).

[46] Cf. Schumpeter himself on the fact that "there are no Fisherians" in the sense indicated ("Irving Fisher's Econometrics," *loc. cit.*, 231).

[47] "Wesley Clair Mitchell," *loc. cit.*, 155.

SCHUMPETER'S THEORY OF INTEREST

Gottfried Haberler

SCHUMPETER'S theory of interest, which was fully expounded in the first edition of his *Theory of Economic Development* (1912) but had been clearly foreshadowed in his first book, *Das Wesen und Hauptinhalt der theoretischen Nationalökonomie* (1908), is fairly well known, although it has not been widely discussed in English. Nor has it been widely accepted, but most critics recognize, explicitly or implicitly, that the extreme version of the theory of interest is not an essential part of Schumpeter's dynamic system.[1]

A thorough understanding of Schumpeter's views on the problem of the interest rate requires, I believe, that we distinguish between an extreme and a less extreme version of his theory.

The extreme version culminates in the proposition that in a stationary or quasi-stationary economy, in the *Kreislaufwirtschaft*, the rate of interest would be zero, and that the positive rate which we observe in reality is entirely the result of the well-known dynamic mechanism that Schumpeter has described and analyzed so brilliantly.

The less extreme version admits that there would exist a positive rate of interest in the stationary economy, but insists that dynamic forces not only are likely to raise the interest rate above its stationary level but add, qualitatively, entirely new features to the static picture.[2]

The extreme version of his theory is hardly acceptable. Although Schumpeter spent much time and effort in defending it (e.g., in his famous controversy with Böhm-Bawerk),[3] he frequently made remarks which indicate clearly that he was aware of the fact that this version was by no means essential for his dynamic mechanism.

On the other hand, adherents of what might be called the ruling theory of interest — Böhm-Bawerkians, Fisherians, Knightians, etc. (the differences between them are minor, at any rate much less important than the fierce controversies in which they were or still are embroiled would suggest) — might well admit that there are few branches of static, equilibrium theory that require such drastic alterations, in order to preserve a semblance to reality under realistic dynamic conditions, as does the static, equilibrium theory of interest. Schumpeter was always keenly conscious of, and felt most uncomfortable with, the unreality of many assumptions underlying most static theorizing on the interest rate: existence of a uniform rate, absence of uncertainty, free capital market in the sense that everybody can borrow as much as he wants to at the ruling rate. These are, indeed, most unrealistic assumptions which have far-reaching implications.

II

The discussion of Schumpeter's theory has been concerned almost exclusively with the crit-

[1] L. Robbins' criticism in his article "On a Certain Ambiguity in the Conception of Stationary Equilibrium" (*Economic Journal*, June 1930) is typical. A more sympathetic treatment is to be found in Samuelson's paper, "Dynamics, Statics and the Stationary State" (this REVIEW, 1943). There is a considerable literature in German, which is, however, largely concerned with methodological questions and has not contributed much to the basic issues. Those German theorists who belong to the neo-classical school — Marshallian, Austrian, or Walrasian — and have concerned themselves with the theory of capital and interest, like Eucken, Schneider, and Stachelberg, have not accepted Schumpeter's theory.

[2] It is more correct in the present context to speak of a stationary rather than static economy. In his later writings, Schumpeter sharply distinguished between the two. In the introduction to the Japanese translation of *The Theory of Economic Development* (1934), he says that he "discovered

not only that [the Walrasian System] is rigorously static in character (this is self-evident and has been again and again stressed by Walras himself), but also that it is applicable only to a stationary process. The two things must not be confused. A static theory . . . can be useful in the investigation of any kind of reality, however disequilibrated it may be. A stationary process, however, is a process which *actually* does not change of its own initiative. . . . If it changes at all, it does so under the influence of events which are external to itself, such as national catastrophes, wars and so on." (p. 2)

[3] *Zeitschrift für Volkswirtschaft*, Vol. 22 (1913).

In addition, we ought to say "*quasi*-stationary," because changes due to such catastrophes as well as to minor accidents to population growth and even to improvement of the production process are not excluded from the stationary state.

icism of the extreme version. That is unfortunate, because in this way attention has been diverted from more fruitful problems connected with the less extreme version.

The extreme version follows from two assumptions which can be formulated as follows: (a) There is no systematic time preference. (b) In the absence of the dynamical mechanism which Schumpeter describes (i.e., the innovator-entrepreneur financed by inflationary bank credit), the marginal productivity of capital is zero, or, in Böhm-Bawerkian language which Schumpeter used, there is no room for more productive roundabout ways of production; it is impossible, in other words, to produce more than a dollar's worth of future income for each dollar's worth of present income that is saved and suitably invested.[4]

Both propositions are highly complex statements about facts which are easily misunderstood but not readily verified or refuted. But whether true or not, it is not difficult to derive their implications. If the two conditions obtain, the consequence is, indeed, a zero rate of interest. That is perhaps most easily seen, if we think in terms of the diagrams introduced by I. Fisher,[5] where present (real) income is measured on the vertical axis and future (real) income on the horizontal axis. Time preference is then defined in terms of the indifference map drawn in that diagram: If the slope of the indifference curves along a straight line from the origin bisecting the income plane is 45° to both axes (perpendicular to the bisecting line), if in other words the marginal rate of substitution of present for future income is unity *in case present and future income are equal*, we say that there is no time preference. If the indifference curves at the bisecting line are flatter, i.e., if the rate of substitution of future for present income is greater than unity, there is positive time preference. If the indifference curves are steeper, time preference is negative (the opposite of what is usually assumed).

If there is no time preference, the system cannot be in a stationary equilibrium (i.e., cannot come to rest on the bisecting line) except at a zero rate of interest. The equilibrium will, however, be a stationary one (i.e., the equilibrium point will be located on the bisecting line in our diagrams) only if the marginal productivity of capital is zero. The latter magnitude is represented in our diagram by a transformation curve which shows what combinations of present and future income can be produced. Let us assume that this curve has the usual shape, namely, that it is concave toward the origin ("decreasing returns of future income in terms of present income and vice versa"). The slope of this curve at any point is the marginal rate of transformation of present income into future income. If the slope is 45°, the marginal productivity of capital is zero: By giving up one unit of present income, only one unit can be obtained in the future. If the slope of the transformation curve at the point where it crosses the bisecting line is less than 45° (with respect to the horizontal axis), in other words, if the marginal productivity of capital is positive, the equilibrium point, that is the point where the transformation line touches an indifference curve, will be to the right of the bisecting line, i.e., future income will be greater than present income; in other words, the system is not a stationary one but is an investing and expanding one and the rate of interest (which in equilibrium is equal to the time preference and the marginal rate of transformation) is positive.

Schumpeter did not express his theory in those terms, but from conversations with him I got the impression that he was not unwilling

---

[4] In Knight's formulation: It is not possible to exchange, by production, a finite segment of present income for an infinite stream of future income. Since Knight has admitted the possibility of physical disinvestment not only for an individual but for the economy as a whole, i.e., the possibility (within limits) of converting an infinite stream of future income into a finite segment of current income, there is only a verbal difference between his formulation and the formulation of those who, following Böhm-Bawerk (although not necessarily accepting the concept of an average period of production for the individual process or for the economy as a whole), speak of an exchange of a finite sum of present for a finite sum of future income or goods.

[5] See his *Theory of Interest, passim*. Professor Fellner reminds me that a word should perhaps be said about the income concept. As is well known, Fisher defines income as consumption, not as consumption plus investment. In the present context, what is given up is, indeed, present consumption, not income. What is substituted is future consumption *or* income (since future income may again be invested). If we keep that in mind, we need not worry about the precise definition of income in the present connection.

to accept this transcription of his theory into the Fisherian model.[6]

How about the realism of the two basic assumptions? I shall say only a few words on the much discussed question as to whether there is a widespread typically positive time preference or, what is much the same thing, the motives of saving; how many people would save at a zero rate of interest, etc? I should like first to draw attention once more to the fact that I define time preference by the slope of the indifference curves along the bisecting line, that is to say, under the assumption that present and (expected) future income are about equal. Time preference is said to be absent, if the slope of the indifference curves *there* is 45°. There can be no question that, even without time preference in the defined sense, somewhere to the right of the bisecting line (not necessarily in the immediate neighborhood) the rate of substitution of future for present income becomes greater than unity, implying that it would require a positive rate of interest to induce an individual to make a further shift toward the future (i.e., to save).[7]

But I personally do not doubt that the majority of people do have a positive time preference in the proper sense, at least for more distant periods.

The reason why this is so often denied is, I believe, that the implications of the assumption that there is absolutely no time preference, not even with respect to the remote future, are seldom fully realized. Let me briefly indicate what I mean: It has often been pointed out that a zero rate of interest would imply an infinite value of permanent or nearly indestructible instruments, such as land, railway tunnels, dams, and the like. Let us assume the value of land is not literally infinite, but very high. Would it then not be tempting to sell a little land and use the proceeds for having a good time? Essentially the same argument was used by L. Robbins (*op. cit.*) for other types of capital goods. Some people would consume some of their capital, and that would recreate a positive rate of interest. No good, replies the remorseless logician — the argument is circular, it implies time preference! Whoever has no time preference ought to forego present pleasures even if the reckoning comes only in infinite time! The logician is, of course, right; he has won a point, but has he not lost the argument? Does not the reasoning show that there is, in fact, always time preference?[8]

---

[6] In spite of his love for pure theory, he was always reluctant to encase his theories of economic development — and his interest theory he regarded as an integral part of it — in an abstract, mathematical model. For example, he was never quite happy with Professor Frisch's mechanical model of his theory. (See R. Frisch, "Propagation Problems and Impulse Problems in Dynamic Economics," in *Economic Essays in Honour of Gustav Cassel*, London, 1933, pp. 203–4). At least as far as his dynamic theory was concerned, he agreed with Keynes that "in ordinary discourse . . . we can keep 'at the back of our heads' the necessary reserves and qualifications and the adjustments which we shall have to make later on, in a way in which we cannot keep complicated partial differentials 'at the back' of several pages of algebra . . .'" (Keynes, *General Theory*, p. 297). He often was torn by conflicting emotions: On the one hand, there was his love for precision and his enthusiasm and admiration for mathematical ingenuity; on the other hand, his impatience with the lack of judgment, ignorance about the complexity of the real world and with the irresponsibility which econometricians often display by the rash and premature application of their models to practical problems. He felt like Keynes that "too large a proportion of recent 'mathematical' economics are mere concoctions, as imprecise as the initial assumptions they rest on, which allow the author to lose sight of the complexities and interdependencies of the real world in a maze of pretentious and unhelpful symbols" (*General Theory*, p. 298). It was largely post-Keynesian writings which aroused such resentment in him. However, Keynes himself may well have shared in these feelings.

[7] Absence of time preference cannot be defined as a rate of substitution of unity between present and future income irrespective of the time shape of the income stream, that is,

as an indifference map consisting of straight lines at 45° angle. If it were so defined, we would have to say that time preference (positive or negative) always exists. See the excellent discussion in Hayek, *The Pure Theory of Capital*, Chapters 17 and 18.

Lack of precision in the definition of time preference has caused endless confusions in interest theories. Böhm-Bawerk's extensive controversies with L. v. Bortkiewicz and I. Fisher on the question whether his "third ground" (productivity of capital) by itself could explain a positive interest rate without the aid of the first two grounds (time preference), and also Wicksell's intervention into that dispute ("Zur Zinstheorie, Böhm-Bawerk's Dritter Grund" in *Die Wirtschaftstheorie der Gegenwart*, Vol. 3, pp. 199–210, Vienna, 1928, which was Wicksell's last work) suffered seriously from ambiguities in that matter, and Schumpeter's discussion of the problems is by no means impeccable in this respect.

[8] In the above mentioned controversy between Böhm-Bawerk and Bortkiewicz and I. Fisher, the last two were right: They could demonstrate that Böhm-Bawerk, when he claimed independence for his third ground, tacitly introduced time preference by assuming that the planning period or time horizon is always limited, in other words that people do not plan for infinite periods. Böhm-Bawerk explained laboriously and inelegantly but conclusively in an appendix of almost a hundred pages to the third edition of his

Turning now to the marginal productivity of capital, two questions must be distinguished: We have *first* the problem which has in recent years been much debated by Knight and the Keynesians as to whether investment opportunities would not quickly be exhausted, if technological knowledge ceased to advance, if no territorial discoveries were made and the population did not increase. The *second* question is whether in an individualistic economy investment can be achieved on the whole or in large part only by means of the Schumpeterian dynamic mechanism, the innovator-entrepreneur supported by inflationary bank credit. In other words, does every major investment scheme, every important lengthening of the period of production or new roundabout way of production require an entrepreneurial feat, or is there at any time or most of the time a large, if not inexhaustible, reservoir of "routine investments" available which are within the grasp of Schumpeter's "static production managers"?

On the first question, we have a group of optimists and of pessimists opposed to one another. The optimists are the Böhm-Bawerkians and Knightians who believe that there is always a practically inexhaustible stock of investment opportunities available even without new discoveries and inventions. The pessimists are, of course, those Keynesians who believe that investment opportunities would be quickly exhausted, if they were not constantly replenished by discoveries and inventions. Schumpeter took a middle position.[9] It seems to the present writer, however, that (for reasons which will presently become obvious) it would have been more consistent for Schumpeter to side definitely with the Keynesians on this issue. I personally am inclined to agree with the

optimists, at least to the exent that at any time in modern history there were (and still are) plenty, though perhaps not a literally inexhaustible stock, of investment opportunities available, even without new inventions. Let us, furthermore, not forget that, as Schumpeter points out, many inventions are in the long run capital saving. If the automobile had not been invented, who can tell whether investments in railroads and canals would not have absorbed more capital than was actually invested in automobiles, roads, garages, and so on? [10] It would be my guess that, if technological progress came to a halt today, there would be productive investment opportunities for many, many years to come.[11]

On the other question mentioned above, Schumpeter's opinion was that in an individualistic economy [12] large new investments are al-

[10] It is another question, as Schumpeter also pointed out (cf. *Business Cycles*), whether at present many investment opportunities are not of such a nature that, given the existing political climate and current economic policies and regulations, they are effectively closed to *private* enterprise and fall into the domain of *public* investment.

[11] Needless to say, Schumpeter had no sympathy whatsoever for the secular stagnation thesis. But the reason was not so much the belief that at any given moment there are inexhaustible investment opportunities in existence, but the confidence that in a free enterprise economy entrepreneurs would always find and create new investment outlets, and especially his conviction that by and large people save in order to invest and that, therefore, if investment opportunities should give out, saving would also vanish (see below).

He probably agreed with Knight ("Diminishing Returns from Investment," *Journal of Political Economy*, Vol. 52, March 1944, *passim*) that investment and advance of knowledge cannot be entirely separated, because investment, even along previously known lines, always teaches new lessons.

[12] It would be somewhat question begging to say in a "capitalistic economy" because his definition of capitalism includes this particular feature. "Capitalism will be defined by three features of industrial society: private ownership of physical means of production; private profits and private responsibility for losses; and the creation of means of payments — bank notes or deposits — by private banks. The first two features suffice to define private enterprise. But no concept of capitalism can be satisfactory without including the set of typically capitalistic phenomena covered by the third." ("Capitalism in the Postwar World" in *Postwar Economic Problems*, ed. S. E. Harris, New York, 1943, p. 113.) As it stands the statement is, however, not tautological. For Schumpeter gives reasons why he thinks that an individualistic private enterprise economy would decay and "capitalist society cannot exist" (*Business Cycles*, p. 1033), if there were not a constant stream of innovations and the credit mechanism of introducing them were destroyed. This theory may be wrong or exaggerated, but it is not question begging.

Positive Theory (*Exkurs*, XII, pp. 338–434), which hardly anybody ever read, that he assumed the finiteness of the time horizon as an indisputable fact and reserved the expression "time preference" for the subtle psychological myopia with respect to the future.

[9] See, especially, Chapter XV, Section G, *Business Cycles*, Vol. II, pp. 1032 *et seq.* On Schumpeter's position on this issue, see D. McCord Wright's illuminating remarks in "Schumpeter and Keynes" (*Weltwirtschaftliches Archiv*, Vol. 65, 1950, pp. 188–90). Cf. also Wright's stimulating discussion of the problem in "The Prospects of Capitalism" (*A Survey of Contemporary Economics*, 1948) and "Professor Knight on Limits to the Use of Capital" (*The Quarterly Journal of Economics*, Vol. 58, 1944, pp. 331 *et seq*).

ways made and can be made only by means of his dynamic mechanism. This theory seems to me difficult to uphold in an uncompromising form. But it is a type of proposition which can be partially true. If the optimistic view with respect to the availability of investment opportunities in the absence of technological progress is correct, if there are all the time (or most of the time and for a long time to come) investment opportunities available from past innovations, then it is difficult to accept that large new investments require again and again truly entrepreneurial acts in Schumpeter's sense. Once railroads have been built and electrified and tunnels and roads constructed by entrepreneurial geniuses, the static production managers can continue to copy these things for an indefinite period.[13]

Schumpeter was, however, not entirely uncompromising on this issue. (He never was in such matters; that was precluded by his empirico-positivist *epistemology*.) He envisaged the possibility that progress may be progressively "mechanized" (see *Business Cycles*, p. 1034 and Chapter III, and *Capitalism, Socialism and Democracy*), which would diminish the importance of the entrepreneurial role.

In my opinion, he could have made even greater concessions without damage to his main argument. He could have admitted that there are always practically unlimited investment opportunities of a routine character available which are well within the grasp of the static producer. He might have even conceded that occasionally, as a matter of exception, genuine innovations are introduced by others than by his dynamic entrepreneurs and may be "financed from the depreciation accounts" of old enterprises rather than by inflationary bank credit.

It is true the extreme version of his interest theory would be rendered untenable by these concessions. If they are made, the elimination of Schumpeter's dynamic mechanism would not result in the emergence of a stationary state with a zero rate of interest. The interest rate would not disappear but possibly, though not necessarily (see below), it would fall to a lower level and progress would be slowed down greatly but would not cease altogether. However, his theory that capitalist society as we know it could not long survive such a change (or would be drastically transformed) stands on its own feet and is not affected by the concessions mentioned above. The same is true of the less extreme version of his interest theory, to an examination of which I now turn.

III

The milder version of Schumpeter's interest theory can be set out most easily by stating briefly the "traditional" equilibrium theory and showing where Schumpeter's views deviate and what his theory adds to the classical picture.

By the classical or traditional theory, I mean the "pure," static, equilibrium theory of interest as developed by Böhm-Bawerk, Fisher, Wicksell, Knight, to mention only a few prominent writers on the subject,[14] as distinguished from monetary aberration and disturbances, Wicksell's discrepancies between natural or equilibrium rate, on the one hand, and money or market rate, on the other, and related complications.

According to the traditional theory, there are always investment opportunities available. There always exists the possibility of producing more by longer roundabout ways, in other words, to obtain a larger future income for a given amount of present consumption or, in Knight's formulation, to exchange a segment of

[13] This issue was debated by Taussig and Böhm-Bawerk. Taussig argued that the introduction of any "longer round-about-method of production" is a dynamical change which requires a change in technological knowledge and an entrepreneurial act ("Capital, Interest and Diminishing Returns," *Quarterly Journal of Economics*, May 1908), to which Böhm-Bawerk replied that there are always longer round-about ways known which could be undertaken, if only the capital were available (*Positive Theorie des Kapitals*, 3rd ed., Innsbruck, 1912, *Exkurs*, I, p. 17 *et seq.*).

[14] As stated earlier, the difference between those authors seems to me not very great. There is at any rate a common core of propositions on which they all could agree.

It is interesting to observe that Walras' theory of interest has certain similarities with that of Schumpeter. He too regards interest as originating in a progressive economy only. Wicksell criticized him on this point (*Wert, Kapital und Rente*, Jena, 1893, p. 142), while Hicks treats it, perhaps too generously, as a mere slip ("Léon Walras," *Econometrica*, Vol. 2, 1934, p. 346) which could be easily corrected by dropping the assumption made by Walras that "the reinvestment is technically given" and assuming instead that depreciation allowances are reinvested, or rather invested, according to the same principles as new savings.

current consumption against a narrower infinite stream of income in perpetuity. These opportunities are successively utilized as savings become available. If new inventions and discoveries are made, the new investment opportunities either swell the stock of as yet unutilized outlets for saving, provided their expected rate of return is less than the current interest rate; or if this expected yield is greater than the going interest rate, they are utilized, the interest rate is pushed up, and some hitherto utilized methods become extramarginal. If new methods of production are discovered which require less capital than the old methods in use — "capital saving inventions" — they will replace the old methods, probably gradually as the existing equipment wears out, capital is set free, the rate of interest falls, and the margin of investment is pushed out.

In its less extreme interpretation, Schumpeter's theory would accept this picture in principle. It would admit that even in the absence of his dynamic mechanism some investments would be made and intramarginal improvements effected. It would concede that there would be a positive, though probably comparatively low, interest rate. But it would insist that in our world actually not much is being achieved in this smooth and orderly fashion. And it would emphatically deny that economic progress since the industrial revolution can be explained in this way. Not only did things not happen this way — few economists would deny that — but the economic and technological revolution of the 19th and 20th centuries could never have been accomplished, if investment funds had been limited to voluntary savings and depreciation allowances, and if it had not been possible for "outsiders," for an ever-changing group of entrepreneur-innovators, to force themselves and their projects into the circular or quasi-circular flow by means of inflationary bank credit created *ad hoc*.

New ventures are always risky. There is, therefore, no guarantee — in fact there is no likelihood — that established producers or firms in possession of sufficient funds from depreciation quotas or from income will be willing, to any great extent, to finance such new ventures.

Even capital-saving inventions which enable the production of existing well-known products with the use of less capital are not sure of being introduced by those producers who are already in the field although, ideally, they could be introduced smoothly, without any sacrifice in the form of postponement of consumption being required, by redirecting depreciation quotas.

These "frictions" will necessarily be greater in the case of all those innovations, probably the great majority, that do require new saving and especially of those which involve the introduction of new products, consumers' goods as well as capital goods that do not fit into the existing industrial pattern but require the creation of new industries.

Schumpeter's theory is in this respect in sharp contrast to the theories of Mises and Hayek, which also grew up on the basis of the Böhm-Bawerkian capital theory. While they are of the opinion that the capital stock of an economy could never be permanently enriched by inflationary credit and forced saving, because what is constructed during the upswing of the cycle will necessarily be lost in the following depression, Schumpeter's theory emphatically asserts that such a permanent enrichment is not only possible but always occurs in prosperity periods. His theory was much more akin to that of, say, Spiethoff or Robertson than to those of his fellow Austrians.

There can be hardly a doubt that there is much truth in his theory and that his dynamic, "disequilibrium" approach to the problem of development and of the business cycle is much more realistic and fruitful than the excessively static "equilibrium theory" of Mises and Hayek. But surely a model like Schumpeter's has to be taken *cum grano salis;* it can be more or less true in the sense that it need not fit every period or every single cycle within a certain period. His mechanism can be disturbed or cease to function, and other forces can produce cyclical fluctuations of the same general nature. Schumpeter was not unaware of all that, although he often was emphatic in his claim of having fully and definitively explained economic fluctuations of different amplitude and length as well as long-run trend since the industrial revolution until our times. He was, however, fully conscious of his obligation as a scholar to substantiate and verify his theory by historical and statistical research, something one cannot say of all business-cycle theorists. Since everybody knows it, we need not dwell upon the fact that his effort in this direction is of truly imposing magnitude and scope and has not been surpassed by any other writer who had to work single-handed in that field.

IV

Our discussion has strayed away from the subject of this paper, the rate of interest. This is, however, quite natural and proper because the rate of interest becomes a comparatively unimportant detail in the dynamic picture. But although it is a detail within a detail, a word might be said on whether it is generally true, arguing on the basis of the less extreme version of Schumpeter's theory, that in the dynamic economy — dynamic in the sense that the Schumpeter mechanism is at work — the rate of interest is always higher than in the stationary or quasi-stationary state.

If, as a consequence of Schumpeter's dynamic mechanism, many investment projects are undertaken which otherwise would remain unused, the interest rate will be driven above its stationary level. Increased uncertainty and rising prices will work in the same direction, at least as far as the money rate (as distinct from the "pure" or "equilibrium" rate) is concerned.

But there are countervailing forces at work. Inflationary bank credit supplements the supply of investible funds from voluntary saving and this, one should expect, will depress the interest rate. Moreover, the dynamic process creates large incomes which become the most important source of voluntary saving.

Schumpeter's theory of saving is the complete antithesis of the current Keynesian view. He denied that saving is a function of income. In his first book in 1908, long before the appearance of the *General Theory*, he discussed the hypothesis that saving is an increasing function of income and came to the conclusion that "saving is undoubtedly no such [i.e., no 'simple'] function of income." [15] From this argument it appears that by "simple" he meant not an increasing function of income. He argued that consumption habits change with rising income in such a way that people in higher income brackets often save less percentagewise or even in absolute terms than those in lower income levels.

In *Capitalism, Socialism and Democracy*, he argued that normally people save in order to invest. "It is not only that the bulk of individual savings — and, of course, practically all business savings which, in turn, constitute the greater part of total saving — is done with a specific investment purpose in view. The decision to invest precedes as a rule, and the act of investing precedes very often, the decision to save." [16]

In view of these conflicting tendencies, it is hardly possible to make a general statement with any confidence either that in a dynamic economy the rate of interest will be higher or lower than in a stationary or quasi-stationary state (both terms in Schumpeter's sense). Fortunately, however, this is an unimportant, indeed an idle, question. If it is true that during the capitalist epoch of the last two centuries not only the economies but the whole social structure of the Western World were continuously transformed and revolutionized in the manner which Schumpeter describes — and there can be hardly a doubt that this is true to a large extent — it does not matter whether the rate of interest was a few per cent higher or lower than it would have been if that dynamic mechanism had not existed.

[15] *Wesen und Hauptinhalt*, p. 308.
[16] P. 395. That seemed to him the basic argument against the secular stagnation thesis: If investment opportunities give out, saving too will vanish. He was careful, however, to stress that temporary hitches in the flow of saving into investment often occur in depression periods and that government deficit financing is the proper remedy for such conditions.

SCHUMPETER'S CONTRIBUTION TO BUSINESS CYCLE THEORY

Alvin H. Hansen

MACRO-ECONOMICS began with monetary and business-cycle theory. Schumpeter was one of five Continental economists whose work on business cycles laid the foundation for modern macro-economics, and it is worth while to emphasize the fact that this important foundational work in the currently most popular branch of economics was done around the first decade of this century, to be specific in the years 1898 to 1912.

Macro-economics — the branch of economic analysis which deals with the general level of output and income in the economic system as a whole — is often associated nowadays with Keynesian economics. It is true that the *General Theory* contributed to, and opened up new areas for investigation and research in, macro-economic analysis. But there is even now in Anglo-American circles a widespread underestimation of the Continental contribution to macro-economics.

English speaking economists were, until relatively recently, generally unaware or blind to this significant development in economic thinking. The first English translation of Cassel's *Theory of Social Economy* in 1924 began to break the ice; and Keynes' *Treatise on Money* (1930) may be regarded as a belated, and, in a measure, confused, effort to catch up on Continental thinking. These publications and the increasing emphasis on the investment approach aroused an interest in the basic literature and led to the English translation of Schumpeter's *The Theory of Economic Development* in 1934, and Wicksell's *Interest and Prices* and *Lectures on Political Economy* (Vol. II, *Money*) in 1935 and 1936. Most of the rest of the important Continental literature still remains untranslated into English.

Schumpeter was one of the most brilliant and original of the five Continental writers who originated nearly all of the really basic ideas in modern business-cycle theory (the most significant omission being the multiplier and the consumption function). To be more specific, these basic ideas were first clearly pointed up in the following publications: Wicksell's *Geldzins und Güterpreise* (1898), Tugan-Baranowsky's *Studien für Geschichte der Handelskrisen in England* (1901), Spiethoff's "Vorbemerkungen zu einer Theorie der Überproduction," *Jahrbuch für Gesetzgebung, Verwaltung und Volkswirtschaft* (1902), Aftalion's "Essai d'une Theorie des crises générales et périodiques," *Revue d'economie politique* (1909), and Schumpeter's "Über das Wesen der Wirtschaftskrisen," *Zeitschrift für Volkswirtschaft* (1910) and *Theorie der wirtschaftlichen Entwicklung* (1912).[1]

The leading basic conceptions which were developed in this literature were: (1) the essential characteristic of the cycle movement is a fluctuation in the rate of output of fixed capital (Tugan-Baranowsky); (2) investment outruns saving in the boom phase of the cycle (the difference being financed by tapping idle balances and creating new bank credit), and in the depression phase saving outruns investment (Tugan-Baranowsky, Wicksell); (3) investment opportunities rise when the rate of return on real capital exceeds the money rate of interest (Wicksell); (4) favorable investment opportunities are created in a dynamic society experiencing rapid technical progress, rapid growth in terms of resources and population, and rapid expansion into new territories (Spiethoff); (5) a society using large quantities of fixed capital experiences a marked lag between the decision to expand output and the realization of the desired end (Aftalion); (6) a society using a large amount of durable capital goods will discover that mild oscillations in final demand cause large fluctuations in the

---

[1] I cite here only the significant publications on the subject. In each case, those here cited were followed by other, often more expanded, publications.

derived demand for fixed capital (Aftalion);
(7) the economic system is like a rocking
horse, capable of performing cyclical adjustment movements in response to external shocks
(Wicksell); (8) a dynamic society is constantly being drawn away from neighborhoods
of equilibrium by reason of the pioneering activities of daring innovators whose lightning
successes entice a swarm of imitators into a
wild outpouring of new investment activity
(Schumpeter).

Here are all the elements (the multiplier
alone is missing) of a modern cycle theory including the materials for the construction of
econometric models, such as the cob-web theorem and the quarter-cycle accelerator-induced
lag.

Here are rich materials for the business-
cycle theory mill: external shocks and internal
relationships between the variables that constitute the structure of the economy. Within
this framework, it is innovational activity
(Schumpeter) which accounts for the "wave
movement" in economic life.

Schumpeter's theory of innovation would
have no meaning apart from the "fixed-capital
investment framework" created by the Continental business-cycle school. Schumpeter's
"new production function," the child of innovation, would have no meaning in the *Kapital-
lose Wirtschaftstheorie* — the "economic theory
of *a*capitalistic production" — particularly the
theory of English economics "of the fifty years
after 1870." [2] But it was a vital part of the
dynamic theory which was evolving on the
Continent in the first decade of this century.

Schumpeter's innovations supply, indeed, the
heart-throb that pumps intermittent flows of
investment into the economic system, a system
with a structure of internal relationships between economic variables (time lags or time
rates of change) capable of responding in a
cyclical manner to such intermittent disturbances.

With respect to Schumpeter's cycle theory
I shall direct attention to four matters, all of
interest and some not altogether free from obscurity; and in my brief discussion I shall not
pretend to reach definitive conclusions. They

are: (1) Should his theory be classified as exogenous or endogenous? (2) Schumpeter's explanation of the upper turning point; (3) the
three-cycle schema; and (4) the relation of his
two-volume *Business Cycles* of 1938 to his
Theory of Economic Development of 1912.

A perennial and inexhaustible subject for
discussion (which Schumpeter himself did not
clearly resolve in his vast two-volume work on
business cycles) is the question whether Schumpeter's cycle theory is an exogenous or an endogenous one. It is exogenous in the respect
that it places primary emphasis upon changes
in the data. Yet it is also an endogenous theory
in the respect that it runs in terms of an internal, self-perpetuating process — a process inherent in the inner nature of a dynamic economy whose impelling force — innovation —
cycle after cycle renews the wave-like movement. The business cycle is regarded as the
ebb and flow of innovation, together with the
repercussions flowing therefrom. It is an endogenous process determined by the inner nature of a dynamic economy; but it is exogenous
in the sense that innovation *is* a change in the
basic data.[3]

Exogenous theories place primary emphasis
upon changes in the data; endogenous theories,
upon the lagged reactions of the economic
structure (with a system of internal relationships) to changes in the data. It is sometimes
said that there is a tendency in business-cycle
literature in general to stress the role of exogenous factors (changes in the data) as the cause
or causes of expansion; and to stress the role
of endogenous factors (lagged response spring-
ing from a system of constant relationships) at
the upper turning point. This statement seems
to fit Schumpeter's analysis reasonably well.

Expansion is brought about, in Schumpeter's
view, by innovational activity. An innovation
is defined, broadly speaking, as a fundamental
change in the data. Innovation is an historic
and irreversible change in the way of doing
things. It is not a matter of varying the *quantities* of the factors; it is a change in the production function. "We will simply define innovation as the setting up of a new production
function." [4] This means not only new tech-

---

[2] See Lionel Robbins' Introduction to Wicksell's *Lectures*,
p. xiv.

[3] Cf. Tinbergen, above. — Ed.
[4] *Business Cycles*, pp. 87–88.

niques, but also new products, new forms of organization, new markets. It involves not only new ways of doing things but is generally associated with new firms and new men. All this points up the exogenous elements in Schumpeter's theory.

Innovation wells up in a great tidal wave, and then recedes. The business cycle, as Schumpeter saw it, is nothing more or less than the ebb and flow of innovation, together with the repercussions flowing therefrom. An economy which experiences innovations necessarily displays wave-like movements. Innovation involves capital investment which "appears *en masse* at intervals." Innovational activity tends to come in "clusters," in "bunches," because of the herd-like action of followers in the wake of successful innovation. Whenever a few successful innovators appear, a host of others follow. The appearance of a few innovating entrepreneurs facilitates the appearance of others, and these, the appearance of more in ever-increasing numbers. This is the basis of the "wave-like movement" of economic life. The expansion proceeds by "rushes" because of the herd-like sweep into new openings. Innovation is thus discontinuous, like the throw of dice. The new contribution appears "discontinuously in groups or swarms." The central drawing force, the primary cause of cyclical movements, is the appearance of an innovation which sets going the herd-like movement of entrepreneurs.

But there is also the endogenous process of adaptation to this driving force. Under the impulse of innovational activity, the economic system draws away from the neighborhood of equilibrium. But the farther it moves away from equilibrium the stronger is the fall back to equilibrium. In the downward readjustment the economy is likely to "overshoot." Again the economy is pulled back toward equilibrium. After this process of adaptation and adjustment, this recovered neighborhood of equilibrium offers a favorable climate for a renewed surge of innovation. Thus in a very fundamental sense, Schumpeter's theory runs in terms of an endogenous, self-perpetuating process — a process inherent in the inner nature of a dynamic economy. Frisch, by combining Schumpeter's and Aftalion's systems, has given us an interesting example of a self-perpetuating endogenous cycle movement.[5]

With respect to the termination of the boom, Schumpeter did not accept the view of Spiethoff (also that of Robertson and others) that it is a question of investment saturation. Rather he followed Juglar's lead — the "only cause of the depression is prosperity." This statement he interpreted to mean that depression is nothing more than the economic system's reaction to the distortions of the boom; it is the "adaptation to the situation into which the boom brings the system." Innovations inject disturbances into the system. These disturbances cannot be currently and smoothly absorbed. They are "big" and they disrupt the existing system and enforce a distinct and often painful process of adaptation. The boom development is "lopsided, discontinuous, disharmonious." The depression is a process of adaptation to the changed conditions ushered in by the boom. The economic nature of the depression lies in the diffusion of the achievements of the boom over the whole economic system through the process of the struggle for equilibrium.[6]

He liked Fisher's concept, "rate of return over cost,"[7] and in his biographical article on Fisher[8] specially refers to Keynes' acceptance of Fisher's formulation. But he did not build his own theory, of either the expansion or the upper turning point, on the investment demand function as formulated by Wicksell and later by Fisher. Moreover, he paid scant attention to the acceleration principle. Thus, while his explanation of the upper turning point could in a sense be regarded as an endogenous theory, it did not rest on any of the econometric models derived from Aftalion's acceleration principle. In his classes, however, he often commented on Samuelson's article on the interaction of the multiplier and the accelerator, and he also took cognizance of Metzler's econometric inventory models. But just how he would have incorporated these, if at all,

[5] *Economic Essays in Honour of Gustav Cassel*, pp. 171–207.

[6] *Theory of Economic Development*, p. 251.

[7] *Business Cycles*, Vol. 1, p. 129.

[8] *Econometrica*, July 1948, p. 226.

into his system, had he revised his *Business Cycles*, is not altogether clear.

Schumpeter's three-cycle schema has been and remains a matter of controversy. That we have had long-run, secular movements of prices no one doubts, but it is not quite clear how these are to be interpreted in relation to the "Juglar" or major cycles. Schumpeter regards these long periods of buoyancy and relative stagnation as part of a genuine wave-like movement, with the ground-swell of far-reaching innovations at work in the "upswing," and equally far-reaching readjustments being made in the long downswing periods. Whether these secular movements are really long-cycles, whose phases stand in an integral relation to each other, is at least debatable and the weight of competent opinion appears to be against Schumpeter. That the long periods of buoyancy, with rising secular price trends, are periods of fundamental innovations — the railroad age, the automotive and electrical age — seems to me highly persuasive. There is a discontinuity in fundamental innovational activity — a movement into quite new frontiers of technology, the achievement of a fundamentally higher plateau of production methods, a new level of technique, as for example the railroad. The emphasis placed by Schumpeter upon the rate of revolutionary changes in technology is of great importance to an understanding of the modern economic process. It has been stressed by others, including Wicksell and Spiethoff; but Schumpeter, more than the others, has developed this concept into an organic system of analysis, perhaps too rigid a mold, but nonetheless highly illuminating and helpful in the difficult task of understanding the dynamic processes of the modern economy.

Finally, a brief word about the relation of Schumpeter's two leading books on business cycles — *Theorie der wirtschaftlichen Entwicklung* (1912) and *Business Cycles* (1939). The first book, comparatively small, presents a central idea in a bold, imaginative, dashing, colorful, and eloquent style; the second, a massive two-volume work, rich in historical learning, takes cognizance of a vast analytical literature but only as a side issue in the process of unfolding the author's own argument. There is in a way a parallel in the case of Malthus. The *Essay on Population*, a brief but brilliant work, was followed some years later by a two-volume work full of vast accumulations of empirical research. But it was the sweeping hypothesis painted with bold strokes in rich colors which carried the day. The subsequent writing was more painstaking and in a way more thorough, but the literary quality and power of the *Essay* remained unsurpassed. Much the same could be said in high praise of Schumpeter's early work — *The Theory of Economic Development*.

THE IMPACT OF RECENT MONOPOLY THEORY
ON THE SCHUMPETERIAN SYSTEM

Edward H. Chamberlin

THE chapter on "Recent Developments" in Schumpeter's forthcoming *History of Economic Analysis* remained unwritten at the time of his death. It appears that he had, quite naturally in view of its content, left it for the end; and so we are deprived of the systematic evaluation of recent and prevailing trends which he was about to write. Yet he had, of course, already put into print many of his views, and I propose in this short paper to indicate and to comment upon his expressed evaluation of one "recent development" — that of monopolistic and imperfect competition theories — as found in his two major works of 1939 and 1942. I shall maintain that, in spite of a definite hostility to what he saw as its impact on his own system, his later views on monopoly serve well to illustrate the fundamental compatibility between the two.

It is necessary first to look at the *Theory of Economic Development*, where the underlying structure of his system of thought is to be found. There will, I think, be general agreement (including my own) with the statement by R. V. Clemence and F. S. Doody in their recent book, *The Schumpeterian System*, that "the circular flow is a model of a purely competitive system. . . . Despite all the theoretical contributions (in connection with monopolistic and imperfect competition) . . . the Schumpeterian circular flow in its most recent formulation remains essentially what it was in 1911." [1]

There is only a minor qualification, but it is interesting to look at it. There is in fact surprisingly little insistence in the *Theory of Economic Development* on the competitive nature of the circular flow, and no statement that I can find that it is *necessarily* character-

ized by "perfect competition" (the word "pure" had not yet appeared). The primary concern is with an uninterrupted flow which steadily repeats itself in the absence of entrepreneurial innovation. It seems evident that such a flow *could* embrace monopoly of all kinds and degrees without in the least interfering with its static quality. On page 152 the possibility is explicitly envisaged of "a permanent monopoly" (clearly, however, identified with the old *industry* concept) from henceforth embodied in the circular flow.

On the other hand, there can be no doubt that the analysis of the circular flow does commonly proceed by "abstracting from monopoly" (p. 129), so that monopoly revenue becomes a phenomenon only of the innovations which for short periods bring about departures from it. "Since the entrepreneur has no competitors when the new products first appear, the determination of their price proceeds wholly, or within certain limits, according to the principles of monopoly price. Thus there is a monopoly element in profit in a capitalist economy." (p. 152) Such a "surplus" in the form of a monopoly profit is only temporary, however, for if it exists, "a tendency to reorganization in the industry will set in, which will finally restore the rule of the law of cost." (p. 135) Indeed, one of the chief features of the circular flow seems to be the overwhelming tyranny of the "law of cost" which forbids any surpluses. On page 31 it is proved, apparently with complete rigor by the logic of imputation, that in the circular flow "net profit cannot exist, because the value and price of the original productive services will always absorb the value and price of the product." Yet the possibility of ubiquitous surpluses appears at once if only monopoly elements are admitted into the picture; and proof is unwittingly supplied for us by a later demonstration based equally upon imputation theory. On page 143 it is

[1] P.21. For those unfamiliar with the concept of a "circular flow" it may be explained that the phrase is used by Schumpeter to characterize the functioning of a static economy in the absence of "development"; it may be taken as synonymous with a static state.

[83]

shown that the innovating entrepreneur may be constituted a third original productive factor, and that this factor may have imputed to it as a surplus "the value of the new products minus the value which could be realized without it." If we now recognize that the "new" products, and in fact, *any* products in the system, are typically subjected to a competition of substitutes which varies in its effectiveness and may easily be insufficient to eliminate the monopoly profits, the possibility of such "surpluses" very generally in the circular flow is established. And of course it is a familiar part of monopolistic competition theory that monopoly often exists without monopoly profits (under conditions of "tangency"). In summary, imputation theory and the "law of costs" dispose neither of "net profits" nor of monopoly elements.

I believe it is fair to say that the chief concern of Schumpeter about the impact of monopolistic competition theory on the circular flow was the question of determinateness. This is foreshadowed in a footnote inserted in 1934 in the *Theory of Economic Development* (the English translation) on page 40: "This [that an individual acts in one and only one particular way in adapting himself to given conditions] is universally recognized, indeed, only for the cases of free competition and unilateral monopoly in the technical sense of both words. Yet it is sufficient for our purposes. And it has been shown of late that Cournot was not wrong, after all, in holding that there are important cases of determinateness even in the field of 'monopolistic competition.'" The question of *determinateness* becomes the focal point of his whole discussion of "Imperfect Competition" in *Business Cycles*, to which we now turn.

The possibility of "monopoly gains" in the circular flow receives brief explicit mention on page 40; and it is soon stated (p. 41) that "The first and foremost task of economic analysis is to explore the properties of that system." "What we want to learn before anything else" is whether it is determinate, and the proof that it is, is described as the "magna charta of economic theory." The "special case" of perfect competition is first discussed, and it is concluded (p. 56) "that — subject, it is true, to serious qualifications and reservations —

there is a real tendency toward equilibrium states in a perfectly competitive world." In then taking up "imperfect competition" it is significant that he aims merely to reassure those who question such a tendency "when we leave the precincts of the perfectly competitive case," and comments that his "sketch of an answer . . . may be omitted by those who feel convinced already." The ensuing discussion turns mainly on whether and in what degree the various sub-cases under "imperfect competition" give "difficulties" on the score of determinateness.

Now it is easy to understand (though not to accept) this emphasis on determinateness if one is seeking to establish a theoretical norm characterized by "equilibrium" as a point of departure for a theory of business cycles. But I must enter a vigorous protest on two grounds: (1) Even supposing that a case can be made for a generally determinate system which is sufficient "for our purpose," or "for most practical purposes," it remains true in Schumpeter's own words that *"the first and foremost task of economic analysis is to explore the properties of that system."* It is held that a system of "Universal Monopoly" may be determinate (p. 57), and it may be added that a variety of "models" characterized by various types and degrees of monopoly elements and influences will also be determinate. But the *determinateness* of a set of equations, important as it is, is only a small part of what we want to know about them; we also want to know what they are if possible, or at least as much as we can about their form and properties. And it would seem that the properties of the economic system, in terms of monopoly and of competition as well as in other terms, would be of prime importance not merely in general, but with specific reference to the kind of "evolution" it generates, including the cyclical process. (2) Supposing the system not to be determinate in certain aspects or in certain areas, it appears to me to be the job of the economist, as a scientist, to say so — in fact to insist upon giving full importance to the indeterminate properties as well as to the determinate ones. I am myself convinced that oligopolistic elements are very general, and that one of the prime subjects of economic study must be their influence upon prices and upon other economic categories. It appears likely that many situations are indeterminate when account is taken only of the *economic* variables involved, and that they are rendered determinate only by the influence of what would ordinarily be regarded as non-economic factors. There is nothing surprising about this when we consider that "economics" deals with only one aspect of a much wider set of social relationships. The revelation that certain "economic" problems, considered in their own narrow isolation, are "indeterminate" may be a necessary preliminary to putting them into the wider context which will explain why in the real world they do in fact settle down into some form of stable relationship. To this extent economics simply is not an "autonomous science" (p. 41) and will only lose in the end by pretending to be. It must seek out the indeterminate as well as the determinate, and carefully avoid the tempting expedient, currently so popular with the mathematicians, of adjusting the formulation of its problems with the *objective* of assuring a determinate answer.

Returning to the main argument, let us pass over the discussion of bilateral monopoly and oligopoly-without-product-differentiation, and examine the conclusions with respect to product differentiation. In view of a generally adverse judgment, it should not be overlooked that the possible seriousness of the impact of this factor upon economic analysis is envisaged with rare intuition, and that a number of the routes whereby it is often diminished or dismissed are carefully avoided. Thus, although there is some tendency to speak of the "creation" of special markets by sellers as a mere strategic or "short-run" device, there is also the statement that "Differences in location and other factors which will induce customers to prefer, rationally or a-rationally, one firm to another, are of course unavoidable, irrespective of any intention to create them. And there is simply no such thing as a homogeneous commodity motor car or liver pill." (p. 63) A footnote at this point presents criticisms of prevailing treatments of "irrational behavior of consumers" and of product differentiation as necessarily wasteful, either from the standpoint of buyers or of society, with which I heartily concur,

and which I have myself criticized elsewhere [2] as features of the Robinsonian theory, not my own. Furthermore, in spite of a general disposition to pass off the phenomena of monopolistic competition as frictional, in the sense of disappearing in the long run, the statement is made that "it is not denied that, where circumstances are favorable . . . the consequences predicated . . . may even in the long run prevail" (p. 66); and further that "we do not think, as Mr. Hicks seems to do, that we can now contentedly return to the Marshallian apparatus." [3] (p. 66 n.)

However, the general conclusion is that, although "one corner of business reality is adequately taken care of by this theory," "In general . . . that is not so." (p. 64) The corner that is taken care of appears to be that segment of business reality where there is no "oligopolistic difficulty," and where we therefore have "acceptable approximations to straight monopoly." (p. 64) The *general* case, *not* adequately taken care of by the theory, appears to be that of product differentiation combined with oligopoly, described in terms of the sales of one firm being "a function of the behavior both of the firm itself . . . and of all the other firms in the field." (p. 64) I should like first to concur in the judgment as to the quantitative importance of this last case: the evidence seems overwhelming that it constitutes a major sector of the economy.

Yet the arguments by which it is disposed of simply do not dispose of it at all. The main one is that "the demand curves for the products of individual firms will, in general and in the long run, display a high elasticity" which "will enforce approximate realization of the results of perfect competition . . ." (p. 65), followed however by the comment (which must

[2] "Product Heterogeneity and Public Policy," *American Economic Review, Papers and Proceedings*, Vol. XL, No. 2 (May 1950), p. 85.

[3] The reference to Mr. Hicks is to his article, "Annual Survey of Economic Theory: The Theory of Monopoly," *Econometrica*, 3:1 (1935). But the fundamental reason for Mr. Hicks' position is found in *Value and Capital*, where he observes that "a general abandonment of the assumption of perfect competition . . . must have very destructive consequences for economic theory," and after contemplating the "threatened wreckage" with a visible shudder, concludes, "Let us return, then, to the case of perfect competition." (pp. 83–85)

be obvious) that "Strictly, this applies only to cases which differ from perfect competition in nothing else but product differentiation." Thus are we brought back to the "corner" already "taken care of" because of the absence of the "oligopolistic difficulty" — the case is simply that of monopoly with the location of each seller's demand curve independent of his movements along it. An "exception" is then made for what had *appeared* to be the case under discussion, viz., product differentiation plus oligopoly, with the conclusion that, although it may be important in particular industries, "it is hardly ever important enough to interfere substantially with the working of the system as a whole" (p. 65), from which it would appear not to be the general case at all! The only addition made at this point to the general discussion of oligopoly elsewhere is that a demand curve thus conditioned (by oligopolistic interdependence) — "as brittle as that — had better be discarded altogether." It is in fact "discarded" in my own discussion of this case (*Monopolistic Competition*, pp. 100ff.) in that it becomes only a landmark indicating the lower limit of the range of oligopolistic solutions; and in some types of solutions it is completely irrelevant. Wherever oligopoly is a factor, with or without product differentiation, the demand curve of an individual seller is not in the nature of the case a datum, unless it has been made so by an appropriate sub-assumption as to the behavior of the oligopolists. Schumpeter, having taken the position that the demand curve should be discarded in this case of product differentiation plus oligopoly, certainly gives no indication of how the case is to be analyzed and fitted into the whole picture — except perhaps in the end to say, as was indicated above, that it is not very important anyway.

Let us now comment briefly on the proposition that the demand curves are highly elastic. (Let us assume that Marshallian curves are meant; my own — but never Mrs. Robinson's — are frequently of this type.) Clearly, the general theory of monopolistic competition, including as it does *all* sellers except those in purely competitive markets, embraces elasticities ranging from infinity to the lowest value to be found. And since there are all degrees of sub-stitutes, both actual and potential, with conditions varying widely in different areas of the economy, it is quite impossible to make sweeping generalizations as to elasticities. This will appear at once when we bear in mind that monopolistic competition (but not Mrs. Robinson's imperfect competition) explicitly embraces *all* monopoly (my pp. 68, 74; Mrs. Robinson's position is discussed, pp. 208–12), and is not to be associated merely with those situations where "close" substitutes are a possibility. But even if we restrict our attention to cases where demands are highly elastic, there are still two more observations to be made: (1) the results will be quite different from those of pure competition, if for no other reason because of the presence of two new and disturbing variables — the product itself and selling costs; and (2) even without these, although *price* may not be greatly divergent from what it would be with a perfectly elastic demand curve, outputs, profits, and other features of the system may be strikingly different.

Several other points are added, of which only one can be discussed: that problems of short-time strategy appear under monopolistic competition which would be absent under perfect competition, and which in particular constitute the correct explanation of excess capacity, "rather than . . . any particular properties of normal equilibrium in monopolistic competition." The emphasis on short-time strategy is important, especially when it is realized that what happens in the short run affects the long-run equilibrium itself; but what appears to be the conclusion, that on the whole the phenomena of monopolistic competition are *merely* short-run (pp. 67 and 64 n.), cannot be accepted. The particular matter discussed at this point is "excess capacity," which at once introduces major problems of definition. But what is at issue is not at all the phenomena discussed in *Monopolistic Competition* (pp. 100–109), but merely that of equilibrium under conditions of diminishing average unit cost for the firm. I believe it is not too much to say that the key to an understanding of most of Schumpeter's reluctance to accept the schema and conclusions of monopolistic competition lies in his *much earlier* rejection of descending long-period cost curves (cf.

Business Cycles, p. 91 and note). Such curves he attributes again and again merely to lumpiness of factors, and argues (p. 90) that "disregarding the effects of lumpiness or smoothing them out by drawing a monotonic curve through the alternating stretches of rising and falling average costs, we should, strictly speaking, get a curve which would for a small individual firm, be parallel to the quantity axis, *i.e.*, constant unit costs." In accord with this view he also held that utilization of a *plant* at outputs less than that corresponding to the minimum point on its cost curve is not consistent with long-run equilibrium; and it is largely for this reason that he concludes that what "is more than anything else responsible for our impression of a prevalence of decreasing cost . . . is innovation, the intrusion into the system of new production functions which incessantly shift existing cost curves." (p. 91)

Now there is no intention to deny this latter force; but it should not be given an artificially high value for what is certainly a false reason. What is at issue is the correct explanation of the descending phase of the long-run average unit cost curve of the firm. In a footnote on page 64, the distinction is made between a U-shaped long-run average cost curve and an envelope curve which I am unable to follow because to me they are the same thing, since the envelope curve merely involves the variability of all factors in the long run. My own views on these matters are developed at length elsewhere [4] and cannot be elaborated here. Whatever lumpiness exists in fact must be a part of the analysis of these curves, but it is easy to show that the long-run average cost curve has a descending phase even under the assumption of perfect divisibility (barring the usual tautological definition of divisibility which simply removes the problem without answering it). The minimum points of the plant curves *cannot* lie on it except at its own minimum point. This is the old envelope curve controversy, and perhaps the less said about it the better. One final comment: U-shaped cost curves are *incidental* to the theory of monopolistic competition in the same way that the shapes of cost curves generally are incidental to a theory of pure competition; they naturally affect the result when they are introduced, but the fundamental idea of blending monopoly and competition does not involve them.

Only brief space remains for a discussion of *Capitalism, Socialism and Democracy*. For the most part the arguments appearing are the same as or similar to those already discussed, and attention will be directed only to a few points of difference. There are in the first place statements which contrast strongly with the basic defense in *Business Cycles* of "perfect competition" as the theoretical norm. To quote: "If we look more closely at the conditions . . . that must be fulfilled in order to produce perfect competition, we realize immediately that outside of agricultural mass production there cannot be many instances of it . . . [examples] . . . Thus we get a completely different pattern which there seems to be no reason to expect to yield the results of perfect competition and which fits much better into the monopolistic schema. In these cases we speak of Monopolistic Competition. . . . As soon as the prevalence of monopolistic competition or of oligopoly or of combinations of the two is recognized, many of the propositions which the Marshall-Wicksell generation of economists used to teach with the utmost confidence become either inapplicable or much more difficult to prove."

However, in spite of this and similar statements, most of the lines of argument by which the *un*importance of monopolistic competition in the "circular flow" was argued earlier again put in their appearance somewhere or other. What seems to have happened is a shift of emphasis away from statics to dynamics, ". . . the problem that is usually being visualized is how capitalism administers existing structures, whereas the relevant problem is how it creates and destroys them." (p. 84) It had been foreshadowed in *Business Cycles* that the area in which monopolistic competition theory really came into its own was that of "new firms producing new commodities or old commodities by new methods" (p. 67), and it is this problem which now moves into the center of the stage. It is at once linked with the two new

[4] "Proportionality, Divisibility and Economies of Scale," *Quarterly Journal of Economics*, Vol. 62 (1948), p. 229 (see also discussion, *ibid.*, Vol. 63, p. 128), reproduced in *Monopolistic Competition*, 6th ed., as a new Appendix B.

variables introduced by monopolistic competition, the product itself and selling costs: "Economists are at long last emerging from the stage in which price competition was all they saw. As soon as quality competition and sales effort are admited into the sacred precincts of theory, the price variable is ousted from its dominant position," and we have "the kind of competition which counts," . . . viz., that "from the new commodity, the new technology, the new source of supply, the new type of organization." The new products enjoy a monopoly position — the familiar analysis going back to the *Theory of Economic Development* — and monopoly comes in for a substantial defense as the engine of economic progress. Into this thesis we cannot go in detail, and especially into the extent to which monopoly profits may be defended as an *incentive* to change and innovation.[5] However, the general theoretical conclusion that "the bulk of what we call economic progress is incompatible with [perfect competition]" (p. 105) would seem to be incontrovertible. And it follows that "In this respect, perfect competition is . . . inferior (to the ' "monopoloid" species of capitalism'), and has no title to being set up as a model of ideal efficiency." (p. 106) The consequences for both economic dynamics and welfare theory are evident.

To many, certain features of the theory of monopolistic competition would indicate that it is *necessarily* a theory of change, to be asso-

ciated with dynamics rather than with "circular flows." Among these features are the constant change in the product which is implied by its recognition as a variable in the problem, the incessant shifting about of demand curves with the recognition of selling costs as an essential element in the structure of theory, and the fact that each change in the number of producers involves a corresponding change in the number of products in the system (by contrast with either pure or imperfect competition, where the number of products in the system is a datum). Nevertheless, it is clearly possible, and it is also essential, to define the *static* "theoretical norm" to include monopoly as well as competition, since it seems true beyond question that if the economic system were actually to "settle down," there would be nothing in the process to diminish the importance therein of either product heterogeneity or oligopoly.

In summary, while criticizing most of the grounds on which Schumpeter sought to diminish the importance of monopoly elements and to preserve "perfect competition" as the static norm, I have also sought to indicate his perception of their overwhelming importance in a theory of change. In spite of many — and important — differences between his system and my own, the two systems have always seemed to me essentially harmonious in the sense that their differences could easily be resolved, and that a marriage between them would be most fruitful, at least in congenial day-to-day living, and possibly even in the production of economically handsome offspring.

[5] Cf. Professor Mason's essay in this volume. — Ed.

SCHUMPETER ON MONOPOLY AND THE LARGE FIRM

Edward S. Mason

. . . the problem that is usually . . . visualized is how capitalism administers existing structures, whereas the relevant problem is how it creates and destroys them.[1]

ALTHOUGH Schumpeter's views on U. S. anti-trust policy represent a fairly familiar European reaction, in his case these views were heightened by an annoyance with professional colleagues who attempt to apply an economic analysis based on simple "models" to the complicated world of reality; by the possession of a well-developed ideology concerning the evolution and functioning of capitalism that clashes rather violently with typical anti-trust ideology; by adherence to a distinctly aristocratic view of the distribution of talent in the economy and in society; and, finally, by a rather low opinion of the likelihood of developing, in a democracy, a public policy toward the large firm and monopoly that will be anything more than an amalgam of the special interests of particular groups and the rancor of disgruntled intellectuals. These elements combined to make a rather explosive mixture as can be seen by reading Chapters VII and VIII of *Capitalism, Socialism, and Democracy*, which contain Schumpeter's parting shot at anti-trust policy along with certain other distinguishing features of the current scene.

These chapters, which bring together and sharpen earlier views on the role of the large firm in the competitive process, represent one of the most effective as well as most drastic critiques extant concerning traditional patterns of anti-trust thought. The critique is drastic and effective because it plausibly undermines the two main pillars of the traditional ideology: first, that market power is the proper object of attack since power means the ability to exploit; and, second, that the preservation of competition, meaning the exclusion of posi-

tions of market power, will assure the efficient use of resources. The essence of Schumpeter's position is that market power is necessary to innovation and that innovation is the core of effective competition.

The competition that counts is "the competition from the new commodity, the new technology, the new source of supply, the new type of organization (the largest-scale unit of control for instance) — competition which commands a decisive cost or quality advantage and which strikes not at the margins of the profits and their outputs of the existing firms but at their foundations and their very lives. This kind of competition is as much more effective than the other as a bombardment is in comparison with forcing a door, and so much more important that it becomes a matter of comparative indifference whether competition in the ordinary sense functions more or less promptly; the powerful lever that in the long run expands output and brings down prices is in any case made of other stuff."[2]

Schumpeter maintains that his argument is not a case against all anti-monopoly policy but only a particular variety of policy. There may be "cases of restrictive or regulating strategy" that have "that injurious effect on the long-run development of output which is uncritically attributed to all of them."[3] He does not, however, give us much help in determining what business practices or strategies might be expected to produce expansive rather than restrictive results. What he has to say in criticism of existing policy constitutes a challenge that every serious student of the "monopoly problem" must take to heart. But whether his view of competition as the process of "creative destruction" could be made to yield principles applicable by government agencies and the courts in pursuit of a "rational" as opposed to a "vindictive" anti-monopoly policy is a different matter.

II

American anti-trust policy, as distinguished from the anti-monopoly policy of most other

[1] Joseph A. Schumpeter, *Capitalism, Socialism and Democracy*, p. 83.

[2] *Ibid.*, pp. 84, 85.
[3] *Ibid.*, p. 91.

countries, purports to be — and to some extent is — an attack upon positions of market power. Whereas legislation and administrative practice elsewhere has emphasized *abuse of power*, including the charging of unreasonable prices, as the proper object of attack, and has recognized the possibility of "good" monopolies, American practice, within certain areas at least, has attacked market power as such. "The reasonable prices fixed today — may become the unreasonable prices of tomorrow" runs the language of a famous anti-trust decision.[4] And with respect to certain kinds of agreements in restraint of trade, i.e., certain attempts to secure a position of market power, the judicial position has been that they are unreasonable and illegal *per se*.

Needless to say, however, U. S. anti-trust policy has not been entirely consistent. Large firms enjoying a position of market power have remained immune, while associations with much less power have been broken up. Nevertheless, this inconsistency has been recognized, and within recent years the courts have proceeded some way toward its remedy. There is, moreover, a strong current of opinion both within and outside government that would go much further and faster than the Anti-Trust Division or Federal Trade Commission have been willing or able to go. Schumpeter was frequently inclined to confuse this current of opinion as to what anti-trust policy *should* be, with the reality. Nevertheless, insofar as market power is really the subject of attack, Schumpeter's strictures apply to anti-trust policy as enforced as well as to what may be called the core of anti-trust ideology.

Market power, that is to say, some protection from a competitive forcing of prices toward short-run marginal costs, was, in his opinion, essential to successful innovation. This is recognized in the case of patent protection, but patents form only one example of a much larger class of restrictive devices without which the introduction of new processes, new products, or new forms of organization would frequently become impracticable. Innovation, by definition, is the introduction of new, that is to say, untried processes or prod-

ucts. What the new will involve in the way of costs or revenues is uncertain. If through business strategies, e.g., tacit agreement among leading firms not to enter each other's fields of specialization, or even by overt agreement to limit competition in certain areas, the risk attendant on large investment to introduce new products or processes is lessened, innovation *may* be encouraged.

That there is *some* truth in this contention can hardly be denied. A history of the growth of most large firms that have been important innovators in their field would probably reveal, in addition to the patent protection they may have enjoyed, the use of various strategies and practices that in any proper anti-trust interpretation would be called restrictive.[5] But how important these strategies and practices were to these firms as innovators, and whether on balance growth was encouraged or checked in the relevant industries and in the economy as a whole, would be difficult for even the most painstaking research to establish with assurance. The history of the firms and industries which Schumpeter cites in support of his thesis — the old Standard Oil Company, the Aluminum Company, rayon and motor cars — is capable of yielding a rather different story.

Schumpeter is on surer — and also more important — ground in his evaluation of the results of innovation, that is to say, the relation of innovation to effective competition. Here he denies completely the significance for public policy purposes of any standard of evaluation derived from pure competition, marginal cost-price relationships, or other formulations of static economic analysis. His general position is best stated in a proposition quoted with approval by Pigou.

A system — any system, economic or other — that at every point of time fully utilizes its possibilities to the best advantage may yet in the long run be inferior to a system that does so at *no* given point of time, because the latter's failure to do so may be a condition for the level or speed of long-run performance.[6]

---

[4] U. S. v. Trenton Potteries Co. et al. 273 U. S. 392.

[5] Cf. P. B. Frankel, *Essentials of Petroleum*, for an interesting discussion of the rôle of restriction and innovation in the rise of the great oil companies.

[6] The quotation is from *Capitalism, Socialism, and Democracy*, p. 83. It is cited in A. C. Pigou, *Lapses from Full Employment*, p. 71.

The condition of long-run effective performance is perpetual innovation — the "process of creative destruction" — and this condition is incompatible with those price-quantity relationships which, at any moment of time and assuming unchanging data, would be conducive to the most efficient use of resources. While applauding recent analysis in the field of monopoly and competition and of welfare economics which, among other things, has indicated how very restrictive are the conditions under which we are entitled to suppose that profit maximization is compatible with maximum output, Schumpeter was highly skeptical of any possibility of drawing from this analysis conclusions or principles useful in the field of public policy. "It is . . . . always important to remember that the ability to see things in their correct perspective may be, and often is, divorced from the ability to reason correctly and vice versa. That is why a man may be a very good theorist and yet talk absolute nonsense whenever confronted with the task of diagnosing a concrete historical pattern as a whole." [7]

The role of the large firm in the competitive process and the significance of business strategies and practices in relation to the monopoly problem were, for Schumpeter, very much matters of diagnosing a concrete historical pattern as a whole. The historical pattern was that unfolded in the development of capitalism and the essential fact about capitalism is the process of creative destruction. "It is what capitalism consists in and what every capitalist concern has got to live in. This fact bears upon our problem in two ways."

First, since we are dealing with a process that takes time, "we must judge its performance over time, as it unfolds through decades or centuries."

"Second, since we are dealing with an organic process, analysis of what happens in any particular part of it — say in an individual concern or industry — may indeed clarify details of mechanism but is inconclusive beyond that." [8]

This view of the proper approach to the problem of the large firm and monopoly takes the question pretty much out of the area of economic analysis and into one that Schumpeter was accustomed to call ideology. In fact, he once indicated to the author of this paper that he was anxious to clear existing work out of the way in order to undertake a study of the question whether anything could be said about the "monopoly problem" that was anything other than "sheer ideology."

Certainly Schumpeter had a well-developed "ideology" concerning capitalist development and the relation of the process of development to competition and monopoly. It was clearly opposed in his mind to what he thought of as anti-trust ideology which emphasized existing positions of market power and current business practices and strategies without considering the role these positions, practices, and strategies played in the process of economic development. But though his view of capitalist development might serve to cast doubts on the validity of particular anti-trust actions, and though he might demonstrate that anti-trust policy was, in general, "nothing but ideology," had he anything better to suggest? Were not all ideologies pretty much equal in the eyes of science?

This relation of "ideology" to science and logic was very much in the front of Schumpeter's thought in the late years of his life and formed the subject of his presidential address to the American Economic Association in 1948.[9] Here he argues that "ideology," giving this term a rather special meaning, viz., "the initial vision of the phenomenon we propose to subject to scientific treatment," [10] not only provides the impetus to new departures in scientific research but is not necessarily incompatible with objective research findings. The possession of an "ideology" is not necessarily incompatible with the drawing of objective conclusions from careful research but it may be, and it is clear that, in Schumpeter's view, the possession of a traditional anti-trust ideology was apt to be. The anti-trust vision, according to him, was of an economy of small enterprise capable, in the absence of growth of positions of monopoly power, of accomplish-

[7] *Capitalism, Socialism and Democracy*, p. 76, fn. 3.
[8] *Ibid.*, p. 83.

[9] "Science and Ideology," *American Economic Review*, March 1949, pp. 345–59.
[10] *Ibid.*, p. 351.

ing an efficient allocation and use of economic resources.

> Theirs is the ideology of a capitalist economy that would fill its social functions admirably by virtue of the magic wand of pure competition, were it not for the monster of monopoly or oligopoly that casts a shadow on an otherwise bright scene. No argument avails about the performance of largest-scale business, about the inevitability of its emergence, about the social costs involved in destroying existing structures, about the futility of the hallowed ideal of pure competition — or in fact ever elicits any response other than most obviously sincere indignation.[11]

This is not the place to analyze Schumpeter's conception of the relation of ideology to science. It is clear — and not too surprising — that he regarded his own ideology of the nature of the capitalism as being quite compatible with objective research. He obviously thought of the "process of creative destruction" as that "initial vision of the phenomenon" which had shaped and fructified his own scientific work and might fructify the work of others. However, whether his own or the opposing anti-trust view would prove to be the most useful ideological framework must depend, in his opinion, on the quality of the scientific work issuing therefrom. What is to be noted here is that Schumpeter recognized that his own views on the role of the large firm in the economy had a large ideological content, and that his opposition to anti-trust policy represented in part a clash of ideologies that might or might not be resolved by subsequent research.

III

Two further strands in Schumpeter's thought must be briefly mentioned to round out his total conception of the monopoly problem and of anti-monopoly policy. He had pronounced views on the scarcity of first-rate talent, including the ability to create and to organize new combinations of economic resources; he was also highly skeptical of the capacity of democratic government to devise and execute sensible policies concerning business organization and business practices.

Effective use of the limited supply of first-rate entrepreneurial ability requires opportunity to create and organize economic structures large enough to give full rein to excep-

tional talent. During the heyday of American capitalism, in fact — the late nineteenth and early twentieth centuries — a large percentage of the best brains in the United States were devoted to the formation of those huge combinations whose contribution to efficiency, he holds, is mainly responsible for the rapid growth in national output. Economic progress in the United States, according to Schumpeter, "is largely the result of work done within a number of concerns, at no time much greater than 300–400. . . ."[12]

As far as economic progress is the result of organized industrial research, current data indicate a much higher concentration than these figures would suggest. But innovation, as Schumpeter insisted, is something other than the discoveries of applied science. And whether in fact innovation in his sense has generally been the product of the largest firms, during the last few decades of American economic history, is seriously open to question.

During the nineteenth century innovation, according to Schumpeter, was typically the product of new firms. "The new processes do not, and generally cannot, evolve out of the old firms, but place themselves side by side with them and attack them."[13] In the twentieth century epoch of "trustified" capitalism, however, innovations issue from existing firms and, as indicated above, usually from large ones. Furthermore, although the creation of giant firms represents a high form of innovating ability that could not be expected to be brought to fruition except in a capitalism that gives full scope to exceptional talent, the process of concentration ends up by making innovation quasi-automatic.

> It meets with much less friction, as failure in any particular case loses its dangers, and tends to be carried out as a matter of course on the advice of specialists. . . . Progress becomes "automatized," increasingly impersonal and decreasingly a matter of leadership and individual initiative.[14]

---

[11] *Ibid.*, p. 358.

[12] *Business Cycles* (New York, 1939), II, p. 1044. Since the 300–400 largest firms in the United States control a high percentage of total business assets, this is not, perhaps, a very striking statement.

[13] "The Instability of Capitalism," *Economic Journal*, September 1928, p. 384.

[14] *Ibid.* Cf. also "Der Unternehmer in der Volkswirtschaft von heute," in *Struktur wandlungen der deutschen Volks-*

Thus although trustified capitalism could not be created without economic leadership of the highest quality, and although the large-scale organizations of a trustified capitalism function with the highest efficiency, the culmination of the process is a situation which makes exceptional entrepreneurial talent unnecessary. "Since capitalist enterprise, by its very achievements, tends to automatize progress, we conclude that it tends to make itself superfluous. . . ." [15]

This is a conclusion that can hardly be pleasing either to the defender of large-scale enterprise or to the exponent of aggressive antitrust policy. Nor is it a conclusion clearly substantiated by the facts. Schumpeter's analysis raises more questions than it answers. Did the huge concentrations put together during the first and second merger movements in fact promote efficiency and progress in efficiency? Is it true that during the last few decades innovation has come mainly from the very large firms? What is the evidence that, in an economy in which the large firm predominates, successful innovation becomes "quasi-automatic" and is no longer dependent on exceptional entrepreneurial ability?

We have partial answers to some of these questions; further research can throw further light on others, particularly on the question whether innovation comes principally from large firms. In the main, however, the Schumpeterian view represents an historical interpretation of the process of capitalist development — a sort of *histoire raisonnée* of capitalism — that is hardly subject to proof or disproof.

IV

Particularly serious difficulties are presented when the attempt is made to apply Schumpeter's analysis in the field of public policy. Here the problems presented are what to do about a specific agreement in restraint of trade, a particular combination of hitherto independent firms, or a concrete set of business practices. If one took at face value his admonition

that, since we are dealing with an organic process that takes time, a judgment on the consequences of any particular part of it — say a combination of hitherto independent firms — can only be an historical judgment, as these consequences "unfold over decades," and a partial judgment, since the repercussions reverberate throughout an economy which is in process of "organic development," informed public action would clearly be impossible. However, Schumpeter assures us that what he is opposed to is not every anti-monopoly policy but only certain kinds of monopoly policy.[16]

What a "sensible" as opposed to a "vindictive" anti-monopoly policy would presumably emphasize are mainly the possibility that various restrictive activities may be a necessary concomitant to innovation with its accompanying investment decisions, and that a firm producing new products and processes may be a more effective stimulant to efficient behavior on the part of others than a large number of routine competitors. What this appears to boil down to in terms of practicable application is a useful admonition that the existence of a large firm or a few large firms in a market is not necessarily incompatible with effective competition.

Schumpeter was highly doubtful, however, whether a sensible anti-monopoly policy, even within this attenuated interpretation, was possible for American democratic government. It is impossible within the space available to do more than suggest the color of his argument. Economic concentration, by diminishing the relative importance of individual business proprietors in society and thus weakening the position of the natural defenders of all business, contributes to an increasing political vulnerability of big business. Accompanying this decline in the strength of its natural defenders is an increase in the numbers and the organizational strength of those with an anti-business bias and particularly those with a bias against big business. Even the executive of the large corporation requires an employee mentality. "Whether a stockholder or not, his will to fight and to hold on is not and cannot be what it was with the man who knew ownership and

wirtschaft, 1 (1928), p. 303, where these ideas are worked out in greater detail.

[15] *Capitalism, Socialism and Democracy*, p. 134.

[16] *Ibid.*

its responsibilities in the full-blooded sense of those words." [17]

The growing hostility of the environment, furthermore, is immeasurably increased by the current activity of that "scribbling set," the intellectuals, "who wield the power of the spoken and the written word" but who assume no "direct responsibility for practical affairs." [18] Among the intellectuals responsible for fomenting hostility to big business are those economists both in and out of government who propound an anti-monopoly policy running in terms of standards derived from a static analysis of the conditions of pure competition.

Under these circumstances, "Even if the giant concerns were all managed so perfectly as to call forth applause from the angels in heaven, the political consequences of concentration would still be what they are." [19] One of the conclusions deriving from these political consequences is the improbability of shaping, through current democratic processes, a public policy toward the large firm in particular, and business practices in general, that will give due consideration to efficiency and to conditions conducive to progress in efficiency.

[17] *Capitalism, Socialism and Democracy*, p. 156.
[18] *Ibid.*, p. 147.
[19] *Ibid.*, p. 140.

Much more likely is a policy of vindictive harassment.

V

Schumpeter most certainly exaggerated the extent of the influence exerted on American business organization and business practices by anti-trust policy. Furthermore, he painted a picture of anti-trust objectives and of the ideological justification of these objectives that is in many respects distorted and out of focus. Nevertheless, his powerful attack on the limitations of static economic analysis as an intellectual foundation for a public anti-monopoly policy is highly salutary and profoundly correct. And his discussion of the political environment in which public policy toward business organization and business practices actually gets shaped is a useful corrective to the thinking of those colleagues who conceive that policy can be divorced from politics. Finally, although it is difficult to the point of impossibility to derive from Schumpeter's "process of creative destruction" an analytical framework on which applicable and effective anti-trust standards might be built, his analysis suggests lines of research and invokes considerations that must play a role in formulating an acceptable public policy in this area.

SCHUMPETER'S ECONOMIC METHODOLOGY

Fritz Machlup

THE very first article which Schumpeter published — in 1906 — was a plea for the use of the *mathematical* method in economic theory.[1] Two months before his death — in November 1949 — he delivered a paper pleading for the use of the *historical* method in business-cycle analysis.[2]

Can the fact that the 23-year-old Schumpeter stood up for mathematical economics and the 67-year-old Schumpeter for economic history be taken as indicative of a trend in his development? Such a trend would be typical of great minds in our field. Yet those who know Schumpeter's work well will know that his was not an evolution from the youthful keenness of a mathematical turn of mind to the mature perspective of a historical one. For they know that Schumpeter never lost the one and never lacked the other. They have seen how consistently throughout his 44 years of writing he worked for a "combination of historical, statistical, and theoretical analysis" and "their mutual peaceful penetration."[3] They have seen how Schumpeter from the very beginning insisted that there was "no contradiction between the historical and the abstract approaches, and that the only difference was in their interest for different problems."[4] They have seen how he would accompany a strong plea for econometric research and mathematical economics by the reassurance that "nothing is farther from our minds than any acrimonious belief in the exclusive excellence of mathematical methods."[5] Indeed, they have seen how he could acclaim "Léon Walras as the greatest of all economists"[6] and Walras and v. Wieser as "the two authors to whom [he] felt closest affinity,"[7] and then turn around and pay most reverent homage to Gustav v. Schmoller, the militant leader of the historical school.[8]

Schumpeter spoke sometimes of the sterility of methodological debates, and once he wrote: "Not the first, but the last chapter of a system should deal with its methodology."[9] Yet his very first article as well as his first book were on the methodology of economics; and indeed almost everything he ever wrote contained general methodological discussions or comments. What may have driven him constantly back to the theme which apparently he wished to avoid and which he regarded as neither very "meaningful nor fruitful"?[10]

I submit that, with his superior understanding of general epistemology and scientific method and his extensive learning and reading in many fields of knowledge, he could not stand the methodological nonsense that was continually advertised by the various "authorities" in the field. When others reiterated their bigoted patter, Schumpeter could not help coming back with his own message, which urged methodological tolerance and was intolerant only of illiteracy and intolerance itself.

Methodological Tolerance

At the time Schumpeter began to write, hoping to contribute "to the epistemology of our science,"[11] most Continental economists' blood was still boiling from the excitement of the *Methodenstreit*, and his own teachers had not

---

[1] "Über die mathematische Methode der theoretischen Ökonomie," *Zeitschrift für Volkswirtschaft, Sozialpolitik und Verwaltung*, 15 Band (1906), pp. 30–49.

[2] "The Historical Approach to the Analysis of Business Cycles," Universities-National Bureau Conference on Business Cycle Research, November 25–27, 1949.

[3] *Business Cycles: A Theoretical, Historical, and Statistical Analysis of the Capitalist Process* (New York, 1939), p. v.

[4] *Das Wesen und Hauptinhalt der theoretischen Nationalökonomie* (Leipzig, 1908), p. 7.

[5] "The Common Sense of Econometrics," *Econometrica*, I (1933), p. 5.

[6] *Ibid.*, p. 9.

[7] *Das Wesen*, p. ix.

[8] "Gustav v. Schmoller und die Probleme von heute," *Schmollers Jahrbuch für Gesetzgebung, Verwaltung und Volkswirtschaft im Deutschen Reich*, 50 Jahrg. (1926), pp. 337–88.

[9] *Das Wesen*, p. xv. Cf. Dr. Schneider's essay in this volume. — Ed.

[10] "Gustav v. Schmoller," p. 337. Elsewhere Schumpeter has said: "The armor of methodological commentaries I renounce completely." (*The Theory of Economic Development*, Cambridge, Mass., 1934, p. 4.)

[11] *Das Wesen*, pp. 117–18; also p. xii.

forgiven their foes. Schumpeter attempted rec-
onciliation between the warring schools by
emphasizing that no method can be universally
good or bad, and that we should abstain from
claiming "general validity" or superiority for
any method.[12]

"Each method has its areas of application,"
he said, and by way of example he added that
one could not use the historical method for developing the theory of prices, or the abstract
method for "the problem of the organization
of the economy."[13] He explained the existing
antagonism between theorists and historians by
the fact that "description and theory call for
different methods, and appeal to persons of
very different talents and natural turns of
mind."[14] But "unless one chooses to characterize all reflection as essentially antidescriptive
theory, and all observation as essentially anti-
theoretical description, one will have to admit
. . . that both 'methods' often converge and
become indistinguishable."[15]

The social sciences, said Schumpeter, suffer
from two deep-seated and pernicious ills: "first,
from that almost childish narrow-mindedness
which regards its own method of work as the
only possible one, wishes to make it the universal one, and considers that one's foremost
task is to annihilate all others in holy anger;
second, from that complete lack of even elementary knowledge of all branches of learning outside one's own."[16] Schumpeter made this diag-

nosis of the state of the social sciences in a spirit
of disgust over certain "positivist" criticisms of
economic theory and he asked impatiently:
"When at last will the day come when all will
realize . . . that the ocean of facts has innumerable different aspects which call for innumerable different modes of approach?"[17]

Economic Science

The rejection of absolutism in economic
methodology, and the equal respect for modes
of approach which had been presented as mutually exclusive — a conciliatoriness which
could be misjudged as weak eclecticism —
rested in Schumpeter's case on very strong convictions in matters of scientific procedure.
Speaking for the founders of the Econometric
Society he stated: ". . . we have no common
credo beyond holding: first, that economics is a
science, and secondly, that this science has one
very important quantitative aspect."[18]

From the very beginning Schumpeter had
held that, methodologically, economics was
more closely akin to the natural sciences than
to other social sciences.[19] Later he went beyond
this position when he stated: "There is . . .
one sense in which economics is the most quantitative, not only of 'social' or 'moral' sciences,
but of *all* sciences, physics not excluded. For
mass, velocity, current, and the like *can* undoubtedly be measured, but in order to do so
we must always invent a distinct process of
measurement. This must be done before we
can deal with these phenomena *numerically*.
Some of the most fundamental economic facts,
on the contrary, already present themselves to
our observation as quantities made numerical
by life itself. They carry meaning only by virtue of their numerical character. There would
be [physical] movement even if we were unable to turn it into measurable quantity, but
there cannot be prices independent of the numerical expression of every one of them, and of
definite numerical relations among all of
them."[20]

Schumpeter's emphasis on the character of

[12] "The method which we have found useful need not on
this account have general validity. Surely we shall *try* to
continue applying it, but the attempt may turn out good or
bad; and in the latter case our method would no more be
generally bad than it would be generally good in the first
case." *Ibid.*, p. xiv.

[13] *Ibid.*, p. 7.

[14] *Ibid.*, p. 42. Schumpeter lamented, however, that so
many believed they saw methodological contrasts where
none existed. For example, he denied that the methods of
Ricardo and Malthus were different. He denied especially
that Malthus' work was more historical and less theoretical
in nature than Ricardo's, although many who wrote about
them were convinced of it and even Ricardo and Malthus
themselves thought so. Said Schumpeter: "It is quite common for scholars in a controversy, when they make no
headway with concrete arguments, to blame each other for
using faulty methods. Ricardo lost his patience with his
clumsier opponent, and the latter called anything he could
not grasp 'too abstract'. That is all." "Epochen der
Dogmen- und Methodengeschichte," *Grundriss der Sozialökonomik*, i. Abteilung (Tübingen, 1914), p. 60.

[15] "Gustav v. Schmoller," p. 375.

[16] "Die 'positive' Methode in der Nationalökonomie,"
Deutsche Literaturzeitung, xxxv Jahrgang (1914), p. 2101.

[17] *Ibid.*, p. 2108.

[18] "The Common Sense," p. 5.

[19] "Über die mathematische Methode," p. 36; *Das Wesen*,
p. 533.

[20] "The Common Sense," pp. 5–6. (Italics in the original.)

economics as a quantitative science, as an equilibrium system whose elements are "quantities of goods," led him to regard it as unnecessary and, hence, as methodologically mistaken for economics to deal with "economic conduct" and with the "motives of human conduct." [21] He conceded that a relationship between the value functions which the economist must assume and certain psychological or physiological facts may well exist, but this relationship "is only of philosophical interest. For the economic *results* it is irrelevant and it can never be the task of the economist to go into these matters." [22]

His conclusion, a strict denial of any "methodological or material connection" between economics and psychology,[23] has long remained a contested issue. But Schumpeter himself was by no means obstinate or narrow in the matter. In his own analytical work he soon found it fruitful to discuss types of human motivation and conduct. This was particularly true when he came to elaborate his model of economic development, for which he needed the conduct model of the "dynamic entrepreneur," of the man filling the "leadership function" in the economic system.[24]

Functional versus Causal Relationships

In his earlier writings Schumpeter tried to discard "causality" as a conception relevant for economic theory. He wanted "to avoid the concepts 'cause' and 'effect' and to replace them by the more perfect concept of the function." [25] His reason for this preference was that the latter, "carefully developed by mathematics, has a content which is clear and unambiguous while the concept of causation has not." [26]

On this point Schumpeter changed his mind. The "epistemological indictment" of the concept of causation, he later held, need not extend to its common-sense meaning. And "our mind will never be at rest until all our measurements and descriptions of mechanisms and propositions about relations are linked to the causes indicated in such a way that they may be understood to follow from them or, to put the same thing in our language, until we have assembled in one model causes, mechanisms, and effects, and can show how it works. And in this sense, whatever we may object, the question of causation is the Fundamental Question, although it is neither the only one nor the first to be asked." [27]

But, be it functional or be it causal relationships that to him were fundamental, Schumpeter never changed his views regarding the proper way to establish them. Even if general, economic, and industrial *history* are "really the most important contributors to the understanding" of our problems,[28] and even if *statistical* research appears to be required by the quantitative and numerical nature of economic science, it is economic *theory* which in its "schemas" or "models" and in its "theorems" defines and describes (or constructs) the relevant relationships. The "raw facts are, as such, a meaningless jumble," [29] and "it is absurd to think that we can derive [even] the contour lines of our phenomena from our statistical material only." [30] No "statistical method, however refined" [31] will help us toward this goal. "We must put our trust in bold and unsafe mental experiments or else give up all hope." [32]

Assumptions, Models, Facts, and Verifications

The model or schema (as it was invariably called in Schumpeter's earlier work) rests entirely on assumptions and "is, thus, a creation of our discretion, just as any other exact science. . . . To be sure, neither our 'assumptions' nor our 'laws' lie in the real world of phenomena. . . . But this does not preclude them from *fitting* the facts. How can this be? Simply

[21] *Das Wesen*, pp. 28, 30, 154, 542, 568.
[22] *Ibid.*, p. 542. (Italics in the original.)
[23] *Ibid.*, p. 544.
[24] In the first edition of the *Theorie der wirtschaftlichen Entwicklung* (Leipzig, 1912) he distinguished a "hedonic-static" and a "dynamic-energetic" type of economic conduct (p. 128) and proceeded to offer a "psychological explanation" (p. 134).
[25] *Das Wesen*, p. xvi.
[26] *Ibid.*, p. 47.

[27] *Business Cycles*, p. 34. As early as 1911 Schumpeter had abandoned his dislike of the concept of causation; for example, when he stated: "When we succeed in finding a definite causal relation between two phenomena, our problem is solved if the one which plays the 'causal' rôle is non-economic." *The Theory of Economic Development*, pp. 4–5.
[28] *Business Cycles*, p. 13.
[29] *Ibid.*, p. 30.
[30] *Ibid.*, p. 13.
[31] *Ibid.*, p. 30.
[32] *Ibid.*, p. 13.

because in constructing our schema we proceeded, no doubt arbitrarily, but reasonably in that *we designed the schema with the facts in mind*." [33]

This is the "decisive point" in Schumpeter's epistemological position: "On the one hand, our theory is in essence *arbitrary*, and on this are based its system, its rigor, and its exactness; on the other hand, it *fits* the phenomena and is *conditioned* by them, and this alone gives it content and significance." [34]

That our hypotheses, "although just as arbitrary as our definitions" are conditioned by "facts," distinguishes them, in Schumpeter's view, from "aprioristic speculations." [35] He concedes that "some of our refinements upon common sense are logically anterior to the facts we wish to study and must be introduced first, because our factual discussions would be impossible without them." [36] But this must not be confused with the aprioristic position in economic theory. Schumpeter insists that the "basic assumptions" of pure theory rest on "observation of facts," only that most of them "are so simple and are so strikingly confirmed by everyday experience as well as historical experience that it would be a shame to waste paper printing any special compilations of facts to confirm them." [37]

If facts — the simple facts of our immediate everyday experience as well as "statistical and historical facts" — "induce the theoretical work and determine its pattern," can they also fill "the function that theorists usually assign to them — the function of verification?" [38] No, said Schumpeter, and he explained his answer with reference to statistical facts: "But no statistical finding can ever either prove or dis-

prove a proposition which we have reason to believe by virtue of simpler and more fundamental facts. It cannot prove such a proposition, because one and the same behavior of a time series can analytically be accounted for in an indefinite number of ways. It cannot disprove the proposition, because a very real relation may be so overlaid by other influences acting on the statistical material under study as to become entirely lost in the numerical picture, without thereby losing its importance for our understanding of the case. It follows that the claim usually made for statistical induction and verification must be qualified. Material exposed to so many disturbances as ours is, does not fulfill the logical requirements of the process of induction." [39]

Quantitative and Numerical Economics

The position that statistical research serves more to ask than to answer questions of the economic theorist is sometimes regarded as antagonistic to empirical research. This was surely not so in Schumpeter's case. Indeed, by correcting the inflated claims of statisticians of the purely inductive school, he did more to bring about the coalition of statistical and theoretical analysts than could have been done in any other way. And in taking a most active part, or lead, in the promotion of econometrics, he worked for that mutual penetration of quantitative economic theory and statistical observation which had been his program during his entire career.

In his 1906 article, in which he championed the use of the "mathematical method" in economics, he was careful to distinguish between quantitative and numerical relations. He contended that the establishment of quantitative relations need not wait for numerical data and, indeed, must precede them. [40] But that the

[33] *Das Wesen*, p. 527. (Italics in the original.) Schumpeter refers in this connection to the analogy of the tailor who uses his discretion in cutting the cloth and making the coat, which nonetheless is expected to fit.

[34] *Ibid.*, p. 533. (Italics are mine.) It is noteworthy how closely these formulations — published in 1908 — correspond to the most recent statements with respect to the methodology of physics.

[35] *Ibid.*, p. 46. Remarks such as "aprioristic, unscientific speculations, little better than scholasticism," can be found in many of Schumpeter's writings. See, e.g., *Vergangenheit und Zukunft der Sozialwissenschaften* (Leipzig, 1915), p. 74.

[36] *Business Cycles*, p. 31.

[37] "Die 'positive' Methode," p. 2104.

[38] *Business Cycles*, p. 32.

[39] *Ibid.*, p. 33.

[40] "The most important thing is, first, to find the existence of functional relations and, second, to know as many properties of these functions as possible. One can, then, establish algebraic expressions even if their numerical magnitudes cannot be found." "Über die mathematische Methode," p. 37. Quite apart from any numerical magnitudes, the mathematical method, according to Schumpeter, is "just *the* appropriate instrument" of exposition because the use of "systems of simultaneous equations for the representation of economic interrelationships affords a comprehension [*Überblick*] of them that cannot otherwise be attained with the same clarity." "Epochen," p. 110.

numerical data would eventually have to be supplied through statistical research was clear to him. In his 1908 book, he coined the expression *"rechnendes Verfahren"* for this necessary cooperation between economic theory and statistics. And he said: "I expect much from it; even the most modest result, no matter how much it will be ridiculed and criticized — as it surely will be, since nothing is easier than to criticize first attempts — will be a colossal step forward on the road of the development of our discipline." [41]

This econometric program he presented more than twenty years before the foundation of the Econometric Society.

Economic Dynamics

We have pointed out how tolerant Schumpeter was with regard to methodological rivalries; he was similarly tolerant in terminological questions. He had originally adopted the terms "Statics" and "Dynamics" as suitable for his purposes. His 1908 and 1911 books made ample use of the terms; indeed, he stated that his "exposition rests on the fundamental distinction between 'Statics' and 'Dynamics'." [42] By 1926, in the second edition of his *Theory of Economic Development*, he found that the terms had been used by others with "innumerable meanings" and, in order to avoid confusion, he used "theory of the circular flow" for what in 1911 he had called Statics, and "theory of development" for what he had called Dynamics. [43] By 1939, when he published his book on *Business Cycles*, he used the terms Statics and Dynamics, "in deference to Professor Frisch," to distinguish theorems which include "values of

variables which belong to different points of time" from others where all variables refer to the same point of time. [44]

After this digression on Schumpeter's willingness to give up his private meanings of the terms when he found that in the public domain, or rather at the hands of respected colleagues, they had acquired different but precise meanings, we may turn to a discussion of the ideas for which he had originally used them.

"Statics and Dynamics are completely different fields, dealing not only with different problems, but also with different methods and different material." [45] Statics is the equilibrium system operating with given basic assumptions, mechanisms, and data, to show the effects of small and continuous changes of these data. [46] Large and discontinuous changes call for the method of "Dynamics." But Schumpeter emphasized that neither "smallness" nor "continuity" need be taken literally, and that it would be against his principles to give "an absolute, inflexible rule" determining an "exact boundary line" between Statics and Dynamics. There are, on the one hand, many safe applications for static theory; on the other, there are problems for which it would be clearly inappropriate and dynamic theory is prescribed. "In-between, however, there is a range which is methodologically and epistemologically most interesting; the range, namely, where it is advisable to use our [static] method — although its presuppositions are strictly not fulfilled — because it in fact leads to usable results; but also . . . where . . . we may prefer . . . [Dynamics] because we do not get enough out of [Statics]. To proceed correctly here calls for tact and judgment, or almost 'instinct', and it is here that we are confronted with perhaps the most fascinating questions of epistemology." [47]

Some of the problems which J. B. Clark had regarded as essentially dynamic, such as increase in population or capital, are for Schumpeter mere changes of data, disturbances of the static equilibrium; and "these changes are small per annum and therefore do not stand in

[41] *Das Wesen*, p. 607. An interesting suggestion for statistical research designed to yield numerical values for quantitative relationships was made by Schumpeter in 1914, when he called for "more exact data on the propensity to save [*Intensität des Spartriebs*] in different social strata." ("Die 'positive' Methode," p. 2105.) Similar remarks, made in 1915, on the significance of statistical research for our "knowledge about the shape of the demand curve" and even for the evaluation of the benefits and costs of particular measures of economic policy can be found in *Vergangenheit und Zukunft*, p. 125.

[42] *Das Wesen*, p. xix. He stated, however, that the terms were not felicitous (p. 182) and subject to gross misuse (pp. 614–15).

[43] *The Theory of Economic Development*, pp. 60–64. The English edition was translated from the second German edition, which was published in 1926.

[44] *Business Cycles*, p. 48.
[45] *Das Wesen*, p. 182.
[46] *Ibid.*, pp. 183, 458–59, 464–65.
[47] *Ibid.*, p. 185.

the way of the applicability of the 'static' method." [48] Changes in technique and productive organization, however, are truly dynamic problems, because they represent discontinuous "revolutionary change." Dynamics (or "theory of development") is needed to deal with "such changes in economic life as are not forced upon it from without but arise by its own initiative, from within." Development in this sense is "a distinct phenomenon, entirely foreign to what may be observed in the circular flow or in the tendency toward equilibrium. It is spontaneous and discontinuous change in the channels of the flow. . . ." [49]

The really revolutionary change which Schumpeter proposed for the structure of economic theory was to banish some of the most important economic concepts, such as profit, entrepreneurship, and interest, from the realm of Statics and to deport them to Dynamics. This methodological revolution has not been fully successful even with those who thought in terms of Schumpeter's original terminology. Most of them have continued to find some useful work which these concepts can do in Statics, from which they were to be locked out.

Methodological Individualism

A Schumpeterian innovation which was fully successful in the sense that it has been explicitly accepted by some and implicitly by practically all modern economists is the distinction between political and methodological individualism. [50]

The distinction is essential because political and methodological individualism are often mistakenly considered to be the same, but in fact "have nothing in common. The former starts from general premises, such as that freedom contributes more than anything else to the progress of mankind and to the common welfare, and proceeds to a series of practical assertions; the latter does nothing of the sort, asserts nothing and has no particular premises. It means merely that in the description of certain economic processes one had better begin

with the actions of individuals." [51] Some people may, of course, endorse both political and methodological individualism; but it is equally possible that a socialist finds methodological individualism preferable for use in his analysis, or that a political individualist chooses to employ "social categories" [collectives] in his. The significance of the conceptual separation is, to Schumpeter, that economic theory may employ a sound individualistic or "atomistic" method without burdening itself with a political program such as *laissez faire*. [52]

Schumpeter rejects methodological collectivism — which he calls the "*soziale Betrachtungsweise*" or the "use of social categories" — simply because it "has no appreciable advantages, and thus is superfluous," in economic analysis. He does not deny strong social influences upon the conduct of the individual, the close ties between the members of the social group, or the importance which social entities may have for sociological analysis. But he is concerned with pure economic analysis, and for it methodological individualism — although not preferable on any *a priori* grounds — has proved most useful.

Again, "that social influences determine the conduct of the individual, and that the individual is a microscopically small factor, is all admitted but entirely irrelevant for our purposes. What matters for us is not how these things really are but how we must schematize or stylize them in order to serve best our purposes. . . ." [53]

Pure Science versus Practical Aims

"Our purposes" which are to be served by the methods in question are the development of a satisfactory economic theory — not the development of economic policies. Schumpeter was most emphatic on this point. He bitterly decried attempts to use "pure theory" in the solution of questions of practical politics. [54]

Even in his book on *Business Cycles*, a subject on which few writers refrain from making or discussing policy recommendations, Schum-

---

[48] *The Theory of Economic Development*, pp. 60, 63.
[49] *Ibid.*, pp. 63, 64.
[50] I assume Schumpeter was the first to make the distinction, or at least that he coined the words necessary to express it, because he said that he was "proposing the name 'methodological individualism'." (*Das Wesen*, p. 94.)

[51] *Ibid.*, p. 90.
[52] *Ibid.*, p. 91. See also *Business Cycles*, p. vi.
[53] *Das Wesen*, pp. 93–94. In lieu of "schematize and stylize" Schumpeter in later years would have used "model."
[54] *Ibid.*, p. 575.

peter wrote in the preface: "I recommend no policy and propose no plan. . . . But I do not admit that this convicts me of indifference to the social duty of science. . . . What our time needs most and lacks most is the understanding of the process which people are passionately resolved to control. To supply this understanding is to implement that resolve and to rationalize it. This is the only service the scientific worker is, as such, qualified to render." [55]

One frequently hears the old dictum that correct prediction is the best or only test of whether a science has achieved its purposes. What this saying naïvely overlooks is the difference between prediction in physical or mental experiments, or under circumstances where events can by and large be controlled, and prediction in the real world of uncontrolled phenomena. Economic forecasting has come in for a good deal of not quite undeserved disparagement. One can hardly picture the task of the economic forecaster better than Schumpeter has done in this sentence: "It is as unreasonable to expect the economist to forecast correctly what will actually happen as it would be to expect a doctor to prognosticate when his patient will be the victim of a railroad accident and how this will affect his state of health." [56]

Schumpeter was convinced that the advance of knowledge in our field was retarded because "economic problems have most of the time been approached in a practical spirit, either indifferent or hostile to the claims of scientific habits of thought. No science thrives, however, in the atmosphere of direct practical aim, and even practical results are but the by-products of disinterested work at the problem for the problem's sake. We should still be without most of the conveniences of modern life if physicists had been as eager for immediate 'application' as most economists are and always have been. . . . Nobody who craves for quick and short answers to burning questions of the day will care to entangle himself in difficulties which only patient labor can clear in the course of many years." [57]

[55] *Business Cycles*, p. vi.

[56] *Ibid.*, p. 13.
[57] "The Common Sense," p. 6.

REFLECTIONS ON SCHUMPETER'S WRITINGS

Wolfgang F. Stolper

IT seems that a really great man in our field is known chiefly by one contribution which may or may not be his main achievement. As Malthus suggests "population" and Ricardo "rent" or perhaps the "law of comparative advantage," so "economic development," "innovation," and "entrepreneur" are the catch words associated with Schumpeter.

Such associations may be correct and may even have a function. Yet in the case of every great name in economics they are at best a small part of what constitutes the greatness. At worst they are a caricature. For what matters is not merely the one or the other idea, however great, however significant. What matters is the place of the idea in the "vision" of the genius, the theory in the literal sense: the view of things as a whole.

Schumpeter, in his own writings, repeats this again and again: If a statement has logical flaws, it must be discarded. If it is free of logical mistakes, it receives its meaning only from its context. This viewpoint not only gives the clue to Schumpeter's open-mindedness and tolerance toward other men's ideas, his willingness and ability to see every point of view; it not only explains how he could understand everything and yet cling to his own view; it is essential to the real understanding of his theory.

II

A few references, taken almost at random and only from Schumpeter's early writings will make this clear. "What a theorist aims at with a theory is a question which is always decisive for its understanding. We do not tire of emphasizing that every theory is a creature of arbitrariness — artificially made for a definite purpose — and it is clear that it can be fully understood only from the standpoint of this purpose." [1]

Schumpeter himself has scrupulously adhered to his own advice. When writing about others — as diverse as J. B. Clark, Gustav v. Schmoller, and Werner Sombart — he has interpreted them with their own aims in mind; and his criticisms have come not so much from showing logical mistakes or internal inconsistencies, nor have they consisted merely in asserting the falsehood of some statements. They have been that the authors have used more principles of explanation than necessary; that the multiplication of explanatory principles not only detracts from the scientific elegance of their performance but may, so-to-speak, lead to an overdetermination of their system; and that, as a result, the whole scientific view becomes distorted.

For example, Schumpeter goes into great detail in his discussion of the disutility approach:

> What is the disutility theory intended to do? It is supposed to explain the shape of the supply curve. . . . Now it is immediately obvious that the supply curve is, formally, nothing but an inverted value curve. . . . No doubt the shape of the supply curve can also be explained differently. . . . But it is superfluous to bring up additional hypotheses. This is our *own* argument and we want to stress only it. Those hypotheses of economists are not simply "wrong." I refer to the "law of diminishing returns" and to disutility. Facts can be adduced in their support, and they perform on the whole what they are intended to perform. But if we can supplant them by the value function, we will consider this a progress and we shall enjoy the magnificent unity and purity which our system gains thereby. [2]

This example stresses the strong esthetic qualities in Schumpeter's scheme. On a different level, Schumpeter's willingness and ability to see what others are driving at finds a beautiful, and to us more significant, expression in his appreciation of J. B. Clark. Even before the appearance of his *Wesen und Hauptinhalt* in 1908, Schumpeter continuously drew the attention of his Austrian compatriots to the important work done by American economists. His American hero was J. B. Clark, on whose theory of distribution Schumpeter reported in 1906, critically but nevertheless in glowing

[1] *Das Wesen und Hauptinhalt der theoretischen Nationalökonomie* (Leipzig, 1908), pp. 221–22.

[2] *Ibid.*, pp. 225–28. Schumpeter's italics.

terms.[3] It is hardly surprising that Schumpeter felt that concepts such as producers' or consumers' rent were too formal to be useful and that the "very fact that such a limitless generalization of the concept of rent is possible . . . shows how little content it has."[4] Nor do we find nowadays anything unexpected in Schumpeter's objection "against the American school that it put the law of diminishing returns beside that of diminishing marginal utility without recognizing that they have only the formal element of diminishing continuously in common, and that the former is made superfluous by the latter."[5]

It is, however, very surprising to find a sympathetic interpretation of J. B. Clark's essentially static interest theory in the same book in which Schumpeter had already developed a detailed sketch of his own views on this matter. It is necessary to quote this passage at length:

> Originally I thought that because of Böhm-Bawerk's objections and my own reservations [Clark's productivity theory] had to be rejected together with all the others. However, repeated study has induced me to modify my opinion. We have already discussed Clark's concept of capital and admitted that this fiction has a certain justification and that it cannot be denied a certain usefulness. If one now assumed that this "fund of productive power" represents a continuous source of income exactly as labor and land, *without exhausting itself*, well, then one could speak of interest in a static economy. However, in such a case two things would have to be stressed. First, that all this is a fiction and no *explanation* of interest may therein be looked for, and secondly, that this fund has utterly nothing to do with "tools" — otherwise it would be *wrong*. All this sounds very adventurous, and we ask the reader for a considerable willingness to make theoretical sacrifices when we invite him to follow us here. However, we shall not be deterred easily, but ask whether such a fiction could not have a meaning. And it *has* a meaning. It provides the only way to speak of interest in a static state. If this is desired — and it certainly is — but if at the same time our own standpoint is correct, we can proceed as fol-

lows: One separates the problem of interest from statics and solves it somehow. Then, based on the fact of the great regularity and continuity of income from interest one assumes such a continuous source for it in the static state, and simply places it side by side with rent and wages, what may be for certain purposes, useful. One must merely be careful not to say anything which could collide with this solution, and particularly not to forget the fictitious character of the whole matter. From the standpoint of the static state this means that one furnishes economic subjects, which according to static laws have no income, nevertheless with such an income. . . . And though we do not wish to tread this path, we do not deny that it is not meaningless.[6]

Enough has been said to illustrate Schumpeter's approach to the ideas of his fellow economists. This tolerance combined with a keen critical insight explains his appreciation of Schmoller and of Sombart.[7] It explains his continual insistence that economics is not a philosophy, but a developing science, and it gives most of all the clue to Schumpeter's third *magnum opus*, his *Epochen der Dogmen- und Methodengeschichte* (1914). For the subject matter of this history is the development of economics as a science, and in particular the development of economic theory out of its internal logic, rather than out of external accidents. It becomes clear on reading this volume that the historical sequence in which both theory in general and particular theories have developed is not accidental or arbitrary and to be simply explained by the birth of this or that genius. Schumpeter indicates how one theory has grown out of the internal difficulties of another: a more recent example is furnished by the theories of monopolistic and imperfect competition which, at least with Pierro Sraffa, clearly have emerged from the difficulty of reconciling increasing cost with pure competition while at the same time increasing cost is needed to make the equilibrium size of a firm determinate. It follows as a corollary that, at any particular stage of development of economic theory, competent theorists have

[3] In his article, "Die neuere Wirtschaftstheorie in den Vereinigten Staaten" (Recent Economic Theory in the United States), published in *Schmollers Jahrbuch für Gesetzgebung, Verwaltung und Volkswirtschaft im Deutschen Reich*, 1910, Schumpeter must have been too enthusiastic for the editor. For the article has an editorial footnote to the effect that, while the editors had asked Schumpeter as one thoroughly familiar with American theory to report on it, they felt nevertheless that only the future could show whether Schumpeter had not been somewhat over-enthusiastic in his appraisal of Clark, Fetter, etc.

[4] *Das Wesen*, p. 380.

[5] *Ibid.*, pp. 379–80.

[6] *Ibid.*, pp. 403–5. Schumpeter adds: "Of course, Professor Clark has not meant it that way. As to his theory as it is, we can only say that he constructs an income which does not exist; but we can say also that this construction, interpreted in a slightly different manner, cannot simply be rejected."

[7] "Gustav v. Schmoller und die Probleme von heute," *Schmollers Jahrbuch*, 1926; "Sombart's Dritter Band," *Schmollers Jahrbuch*, 1927.

neither simply the choice of the kind of theory to accept nor the freedom to start a school of their own *ab ovo*.

Moreover, in this passage there is also one clue as to why Schumpeter always stayed aloof of the *Methodenstreit* of any day. In a sense the whole question of "deduction vs. induction," of mathematical vs. literal methods, is beside the point. There are, of course, illegitimate uses of any method: facts are not found merely by contemplating one's navel in a Buddha-like fashion. Yet "the science has gone beyond the *Methodenstreit*. Not by fighting out epistemological differences to the end and by converting the fighting parties to a common creed, but simply because the practical (scientific) labor, without bothering with the problem, continued on the paths which were shown it by the nature of the specific task. And gradually the recognition was emerging that there was no more point in fighting, that basically the fight never had had any meaning in the first place." [8] Not general considerations, but the nature of the specific scientific problem and the competence and tact (as Schumpeter put it in *Das Wesen*) decide on the method almost automatically.

Schumpeter's vision of the multiple aspects of reality, about which we will have more to say later on, dictates his procedure in every respect. "The historical school does not tell us anything new when it points out that every economic phenomenon is the result of manyfold influences, of complicated processes; but the demand to take all this into account means to do without economics. The attempt to avoid these difficulties does not imply a denial of their existence but merely a methodological operation." [9]

Thus Schumpeter discusses the general Walrasian equilibrium system, carries it to its limits, and is content with what it can do. It cannot only explain and describe that part of reality which is usually referred to as statics. With Schumpeter it clearly explains both *more* and *less* than what is usually included in this term: *more*, for his theory of money (following Walras and preceding Hicks) follows freely from general equilibrium theory:

Question . . . can it happen that the maximum utility which can be obtained under given circumstances can be reached only by such a detour, by such an *acquisition of goods exclusively for the purpose of further exchange? Certainly . . . In the great majority of cases there will and must be a demand for goods — one or several — which cannot be explained by "needs" in the narrow sense, but can be explained only by the technical requirements of the market. . . .* The fact that what has just been said has, to my knowledge, been discussed in price theory by only one theorist, Léon Walras, who by the way did not make the decisive application, explains quite a few weak spots in the economic system. . . .[10]

But also *less*: for be it observed again that Schumpeter discusses as the essence of monetary theory only those parts which follow, so to speak, by themselves from the intellectual starting point. "The function of a commodity as a means of exchange and its function as a measure of value must be *strictly separated*. . . . Only the function of means of exchange does money *necessarily* fulfill. . . ."[11] Schumpeter takes what can be taken and proceeds then to the solution of difficulties which lead outside the static system. Thus he agrees that it would be helpful, *"if this can be done,"* to take account of savings within the static system, since saving undoubtedly is an economic phenomenon. "But it need not be possible by any means. For nothing entitles us to assume *a priori* that our formal assumptions necessarily fit every economic phenomenon, that every one of them can be subsumed under our schema." [12]

In the particular context out of which the quotation just given is taken, Schumpeter discusses the theory of saving. But his method and his view are general. He does not throw out statics as a method just because it does not explain everything. It seems perfectly natural to him — as indeed it is from his view which I shall try to sketch below — that "statics does not by any means make up even all of economic theory." [13] Savings, credit phenomena, the theory of interest are not usefully described by the static schema — in spite of the fact, as Schumpeter himself pointed out, that this could be done by some intellectual *tour de force*.

It is, however, just as important to see that

---

[8] "Sombart's Dritter Band," *loc. cit.*, p. 2.
[9] *Das Wesen*, p. 125.

[10] *Ibid.*, pp. 274, 275. Italics by Schumpeter.
[11] *Ibid.*, pp. 289, 290. Italics by Schumpeter.
[12] *Ibid.*, pp. 290–91. Italics by Schumpeter.
[13] *Ibid.*, p. 291.

Schumpeter delimits statics not only vis-à-vis dynamics, but also vis-à-vis those phenomena which require an essentially historical explanation. In his earliest writings he was quite impatient with attempts to make static theory do more than it can possibly do, even with respect to phenomena which he recognized as being within the legitimate sphere of statics. Thus, right after stressing that wages were essentially a value phenomenon, Schumpeter adds, "Yet very many very interesting questions remain open." [14] And as the supply of labor cannot be explained by the value principle, it seems legitimate to Schumpeter to ask, perhaps somewhat (though certainly not entirely) rhetorically, "whether the application of the categories supply and demand is at all meaningful and valuable here." [15] But to throw out a perfectly good (static) theory simply because it has explanatory limits would have seemed to Schumpeter absurd. For if truth is not only static it is certainly also static, and to neglect it would be just as mistaken as to believe it all-embracing.

III

No doubt, many things became clearer to Schumpeter as he grew older. To be sure "Josef Schumpeter was never a beginner but, a precocious genius; he entered the scientific arena a full-fledged master." [16] Yet he continued to grow to the end. What is it then that Schumpeter was fundamentally interested in? How is it that he could always see what others were driving at, accept it without being eclectic, and end up with a thoroughly developed theory which is most definitely his own? How is it that he could insist that the final word in economic theory would never be spoken, and yet have nothing of the relativity and the cynicism of Pilate's query, "What is truth"?

In rereading Schumpeter's work, the reader gradually and at an accelerating pace becomes filled with the insight of an almost miraculous unity of thought. The bare skeleton of Schumpeter's economic thought has been so well pictured by Smithies that it is not necessary to repeat it here: Schumpeter's distinction be-

tween statics and dynamics which he learned from the elder Clark, but transformed into something which will be forever associated with his name; his distinction between economic and "outside" phenomena whose usefulness is questioned by many, particularly but not only by Marxist critics. I shall rather make a possibly insufficient attempt to suggest an answer to the question which Schumpeter always asked in the interpretation of other theories: What is the purpose of all these distinctions? What does Schumpeter want?

The answer can, as a first approximation, be summarized in one word: the truth. Not policies, not social usefulness, but the truth. This does not mean that Schumpeter was necessarily against policy application or that he despised social usefulness. If his active life and his journalistic essays in the *Deutsche Volkswirt* are not sufficient proof, his sympathetic interpretation of the aims of Schmoller ought to make this perfectly clear. Talking about ". . . the sense in which Schmoller has made value judgment and posited goals," Schumpeter continued:

He has done it only in those cases in which this was possible (at his time). Only that it was then an *art* what once will be a *technique*. This art can be put briefly thus: to state and to defend those measures which, if carried through, will appear to all members of the next generation as self-evident . . . elements of the social order. This task suited him so well and he succeeded in it so perfectly that it is hardly possible to find a parallel to it. And to create an economics which can do just that, to work on a technique which probably will achieve what he did intuitively — this was what he really wanted. . . . If actual situations of actual economies are to be understood and if, relevant statements about their actual problems are to be made, every thing that economic theory assumes as "given" . . . becomes the proper subject of investigation. To furnish facts becomes the fundamental task whose successful performance becomes the basis of everything else.[17]

What is truth? At the center of truth are, for Schumpeter, the historic fact and the his-

[14] *Das Wesen*, p. 331.
[15] *Ibid.*, p. 352.
[16] Arthur Spiethoff, "Josef Schumpeter in Memoriam," *Kyklos*, III (No. 4, 1949), p. 290.

[17] "Gustav v. Schmoller und die Probleme von heute," *loc. cit.*, pp. 352, 353. Schumpeter added the following footnote: "I have to state here . . . that my earlier characterization of the essence and the aims of the so-called 'neo-historic school' in my *Epochen der Volkswirtschaftslehre* appears to me unsatisfactory. Even more so Salin's sketch in his *Geschichte der Volkswirtschaftslehre*, pp. 36–37. His assertions, that Schmoller 'made the . . . beginning of historic investigations [i.e., detailed views] appear as their meaning'

toric process. This seems to me to be the conclusion to which the reader is forced by the cumulative effect of Schumpeter's work. The real question, to the discussion of which Schumpeter addressed himself during his entire life, is: What is the nature of this unique fact and the nature of the historic process?

It becomes clear from reading Schumpeter — certainly to those of us who had many years of personal and scientific contact with him — that he did know and, as it were, had a feeling of responsibility toward a reality which consisted of his wide knowledge of history. This meant that he was aware, first of all, of the tremendous universe of unique facts. But he also felt that they could not be understood except by their relations. And in seeing these relations he rejected any simple scheme but understood them, as far as we can see, intuitively and from the very beginning, both as static (that is, as timeless) and as dynamic (that is, as in-time-relations). Yet both these relations co-exist, that is, any historic fact, in itself unique, has to be understood as being simultaneously part of a static and of a dynamic system. In short, he saw the truth as an exceedingly complicated phenomenon yet as *one* rather than as a multiplicity.

Since there is only *one* reality, what one calls economic and what one calls extra-economic *does* become largely arbitrary — or perhaps better a matter of the scientific division of labor. Here is the clue to Schumpeter's deep interest in history: Schumpeter's theory is a historic theory, and he did come closer to achieving the goals of the historic school and its institutional cousin than these schools ever did themselves; it explains the deep respect he had for the contribution of other sciences. And he also was for the same reason impatient of commonplaces masquerading as science in the standard economic books of his time. Passage after passage in *Das Wesen* scornfully deals not with ethical or historic discussions themselves but with the bad ethics and pseudo-history offered in economics books in the place of economic analysis.

I believe that this interpretation also gives the clue to the statements he so frequently made that economic theory would never be formulated in a final form. Since reality is continuously developing, how could it be otherwise? Yet this never does excuse technical incompetence. It should now be clear that Schumpeter's tolerance toward other ideas was not mere pretense. Barring logical mistakes, these ideas would be bound to deal with aspects of reality and he could see them immediately as such.

Schumpeter's mention of "dynamic" or "static" phenomena should not be interpreted to mean that they existed, each in isolation. To be sure, there *are* phenomena which can be reasonably well understood merely by their static relationships. But essentially the meaning of either set of phenomena depends on their being seen in both contexts at once. For the "fundamental problem of all economic theory is always to show that economic life is not chaotic but proceeds according to certain rules which may be formulated in a general way, and that given conditions always lead to definite economic behavior and definite results whenever no extra-economic circumstances interfere. . . . To be sure such a static state never and nowhere exists. But its justification in the science lies in the fact that it gives scheme for actual existing processes." [18]

Note that Schumpeter does not say that the static state is somehow the best assumption that could be made, although he did state in *Das Wesen* that it does satisfactorily describe a large chunk of reality. Nor is there the slightest suggestion anywhere in Schumpeter that equilibrium or statics is somehow an "ideal" state of affairs. Even when he speaks of a "norm," as he frequently does, the term is used purely in a statistical sense without any ethical overtones.

Because of his ability to see the multiple aspects of reality simultaneously, Schumpeter's schema, even if only approximately grasped, is singularly helpful in understanding the complicated relations between individual facts, their relations in time, and those relationships which are independent of time; between what is unique

---

and that he 'denied completely the meaning of abstract theory' contradict not only the actions but also the literal expression of Schmoller's decisive statements." (*Ibid*, p. 355, note 1.)

[18] "Die neuere Wirtschaftstheorie in den Vereinigten Staaten," *loc. cit.*, pp. 921 and 923.

and yet repeats itself; between what necessarily happens and what may or may not happen.

Observe certain strategic aspects of Schumpeter's theory: in this context it is not necessary to stress that economic life has continuous and discontinuous aspects. Both the continuity and the discontinuity are related to statics and to dynamics: a boom cannot go on indefinitely because the economic system must from time to time adapt itself to its (changed) norm. But the function of the norm is that of a gyroscope: it prevents the economic system from going off in all directions. Note also that every equilibrium is different from every other one; it is always an rather than the equilibrium. But note also that if equilibrium is a tool of analysis, it is not merely a tool. Schumpeter always insisted that he could identify particular historical moments when the economic system was in the neighborhood of equilibrium. Even here, equilibrium is seen both as unique in history yet understandable in its generality.

The capitalist process is seen as one, and though the description of the process requires that its individual aspects are laid out one after the other, it remains undoubtedly true that Schumpeter himself did see it as a unity. The best we can do to point out this "one-ness" is to stress that the nature of the (dynamic) boom depends as much on the (static) equilibrium from which it starts, and on the nature of the (unique) historic innovation, as the new equilibrium itself depends on the dynamic process, the innovation, and the many unique historic events which occur during its course and which (such as "speculation") are "accidental" in the sense that they could be eliminated without changing the nature of the process. Moreover, what unique facts are possible in any given historic situation depends also on what occurred before.[19]

Let it be observed how the discontinuity is linked with the continuity. The innovation — and each one is unique, and is not repeated — cannot come except in the neighborhood of equilibrium. Moreover, it need not come. Booms do not follow from depressions, as depressions (or rather recessions) necessarily follow booms; the economic system is not a *perpetuum mobile*. Nevertheless, the process of change is quite general. If there is nothing deterministic in the scheme, yet neither is there anything accidental. And if individuals are not automata, neither can they act as if they were outside history or outside social contacts. Characteristically, Schumpeter prefers to say that "a belt of equations limits the economic sphere of influence of the individual."[20] "Economic development in our meaning of the term does not so much resemble organic growth. It does not obey *one* law but consists of parts which alone have their homogeneous law. It occurs as if in jerks and it carries different characteristics in these different periods of upswing. Each such period dies as it were to make room for a new one," Schumpeter wrote in 1910[21] in an article which was essentially a preview of the "Theory of Economic Development."

This view of reality is so penetrating that it lends itself automatically, as it were, to the interpretation of non-economic phenomena. I quote extensively only one such application of this general view to the historic and sociological phenomenon of social classes. In "The Social Classes in the Ethnically Homogeneous Milieu," Schumpeter sketches a theory of the origin of social classes, characteristically again by taking two specific historic phenomena — medieval German nobility and the industrial bourgeoisie of the 19th century — to make his points. Schumpeter takes a special problem — the exact nature of which does not matter here — and carries it through for both nobility and industrial bourgeoisie.

. . . the successful (noble) families settle down in the position they have gained by temporary success, as if such a state of affairs could maintain itself forever, exactly as the bourgeoisie of the first half of the 19th Century established itself in the positions gained by its

---

[19] It is remarkable how closely, say, Samuelson's analysis dovetails into the Schumpeterian view. When Samuelson says that the static equilibrium is a special case of a dynamic system, this is a mathematical way of speaking. For the equilibrium is not somehow inferior or less significant than the dynamic system, since it places restrictions on the dynamic systems: unstable dynamic systems are not permissible. Furthermore, the specific system depends on the specific values of the parameters, i.e., on historic and statistical facts.

[20] *Das Wesen*, p. 132.
[21] "Wirtschaftskrisen," *Zeitschrift für Volkswirtschaft, Sozialpolitik und Verwaltung*, 1910, p. 301.

success, created a legal framework to correspond to these successes, and considered individual domination over the means and the result of production self-evident, and this order permanent because "natural." Yet the analogy does not go all the way. It leaves us because the old lord-position did not require for its administration and maintenance the continuous repetition of the acts which had led to its conquest. The position of the industrialist, however, vanishes in short time if he does not continue to have the kind of success which created his position. This is the main reason why the analogy between feudalism and industrial power breaks down if one attempts to take it seriously in detail. There are, however, also other reasons for this of which the two most important may be hinted at: the class of feudal lords was at one time — and the bourgeoisie was never — the apex of a uniformly constructed social pyramid — the feudal nobility was once lord and leader in all areas of life — which makes a difference in prestige which can never be equalized. And the feudal nobility was at one time — and the bourgeoisie was never — not only the sole possessor of physical power, it was itself physical power incarnate. The mentioned main differences mean, on the one hand, that with the nobility the position of the class and the individual family is maintained better and longer than with the bourgeoisie. It means, on the other hand, that the objective social importance of the function of the latter as a class is not as easily destroyed by its own failure as that of the former one. . . . Put differently and stressing a slightly different point we can also say: the nobility has *conquered* the material complement of its position, the bourgeoisie has *created* it.[22]

It is perfectly easy, even in a quotation taken from the context of a sixty-page article, to see all the features of Schumpeter's vision. But although the article appeared as late as 1927, we are not justified in considering it simply an application of Schumpeter's theory of economic development — though this by itself would be interesting enough. Schumpeter, in the preliminary note to the article, states that the basic ideas of the article date from 1910, when he expounded them in Czernovitz, and that he expanded them in 1913 into lectures on "the theory of social classes" which he gave at Columbia University. It seems much more likely that both his theory of economic development and his non-economic writings are expressions (or, if you wish, applications) of the same fundamental vision of reality which I have tried to sketch.

The similarity of this fundamental vision to that of Marx has been mentioned frequently, even by Schumpeter himself. Of course this similarity exists, but it would be a serious mistake either not to see the differences or to believe that it was Marx's influence in particular which was important to Schumpeter. "The scientific vision in which theory and understanding of the historic process become one, does not come from Marx — it is basically and in fact already the property of the earliest thinkers in our field — but he pointed it up with unique consciousness."[23]

Marx cannot be too closely identified with Schumpeter, not only because he used a value theory that Schumpeter never ceased to consider obsolete. In fact, in the present context the use of the labor-cost theory of value would be hardly more than a minor flaw, a *Schönheitsfehler*. Marx's scheme is too rigid to leave room for the "accidents," the many uniquenesses essential to Schumpeter's view. Nor is Schumpeter's an economic interpretation of history in any exclusive sense. Rather, the economic interpretation is part of the larger vision of the historic process.

The real ancestors of Schumpeter's are not Marx but St. Thomas Aquinas, St. Augustine, Plato, and Thucydides. This sounds surprising and farfetched; therefore, to avoid any misunderstanding let me stress that I am referring neither to the religious nor the ethical nor for that matter to the economic content of the writings of these great intellects. My concern is exclusively with the *intellectual* content of their writings, specifically the belief that one could understand Being only by simultaneously understanding its Order and Motion. This particular view of the world as discussed in the doctrine of the Trinity is extremely well formulated by the late Professor Cochrane, stripped of its particular religious content which might be an "offense to the Jew and foolishness to the Greek":[24]

[22] "Die sozialen Klasses im ethnisch homogenen Milieu," *Archiv für Sozialwissenschaft*, 1927, pp. 51–52.

[23] "Sombarts Dritter Band," *loc. cit.*, p. 7.

[24] I hope that the statement will not offend those who believe perhaps correctly that the religious and ethical content of the writing of the great Saints is more important than the purely intellectual content. The doctrine of the Trinity means indeed much more to the believer than what has been stated in the text. However, it is *also* a statement about the nature of the real world, and as such a purely intellectual statement, it may be accepted without accepting also the religious connotations which, to repeat, to the believer are at least as important. This view of the

. . . the creative . . . principle is apprehended as a single essence, the nature of which is fully expressed in its order and activity; in the language of religion, as one God in three *hypostases* or *persons*. . . . In this formula the first *hypostasis*, *Being*, the creative principle properly so-called, is strictly speaking unknown or unknowable, except as it manifests itself in the second and third; the second *hypostasis*, the principle of intelligence, reveals itself as the *logos*, *ratio*, or order of the universe; while the third, the *hypostasis* of the spirit, is the principle of motion therein. To assert that these hypostases are uncreated is simply to assert their existence as principles. As such they are not to be "confused" in person; being is not to be resolved into order, nor is order to be resolved into process. At the same time, as a substantial unity or unity of substance, they do not admit of "separation," i.e. they are not mutually exclusive or antithetic. In other words the opposition between them is purely and simply one of internal, necessary relations.[25]

world which, of course, bears some relation to the Platonic views (which I feel hardly competent to discuss even if this were the place to do so) has undoubtedly entered Western thinking in general, and from this standpoint the Marxian view is heretical rather than plainly wrong.

The influence of this view on Schumpeter must be sought in the general picture of the world or in methodology. It is doubtful whether much more mention will be made in the forthcoming *History of Economic Analysis* than was made in the early *Dogmengeschichte*. Since what the Saints had to say on economic theory as we understand it is negligible, they have no extensive place in such a history. Consciously or not, Schumpeter's is probably the best application of this particular view of the historic process to economic theory.

[25] Charles Norris Cochrane, *Christianity and Classical Culture, A Study of Thought and Action from Augustus to Augustine* (Oxford University Press, 1944), p. 410.

It is this impressive uniform view of reality which makes Schumpeter's theory unique in its breadth of vision, its tolerance toward other ideas, its ability to appreciate and absorb other ideas without losing either their or its own individuality, its way of dealing with history theoretically and with theory historically. But it is also clear that for that very reason the Schumpeterian system [26] cannot lend itself to a very elegant brief formulation, and that it requires a greater degree of work and tact on the side of the student than any other theoretical framework I know.[27] For this reason too, Schumpeter's is an open system in the sense that it develops continuously as theory and historic knowledge progresses — something it shares with the work of all great theorists. Schumpeter's vision is truly part of Western tradition and an important contribution to Western thought.

[26] To avoid any possible misunderstanding, I would like to add that I am not referring to Clemence and Doody's *Schumpeterian System* which I have purposely refrained from reading for the time being.

[27] The only time that I can recall Schumpeter coming near to losing his temper toward his younger colleagues was during a discussion of his *Business Cycles* which had just appeared. After the usual simplifications had been made, Schumpeter said that he felt he had spent sufficient effort on the book to require from the students at least 150 hours intense work for its understanding.

JOSEPH A. SCHUMPETER AS A SOCIOLOGIST [1]

Herbert von Beckerath

IN appraising the work, it is fitting and often useful to begin with an appraisal of the man. Avoiding the laudatory cliché of the obituary article, we want to leave it to posterity to decide in its longer perspective whether Joseph Schumpeter belonged to the truly great, school-founding scholars in the social sciences. His claim to high eminence is already established beyond doubt. It rests on exceptional theoretical and analytical powers, an outstanding capacity to assimilate and master enormous masses of fact and thought, aided by a prodigious memory. It rests no less on the capacity for penetrating observation of life, of the forces that make it grow and change, and on a sense for directing his research towards theoretically and practically significant problems.

Whatever elements of greatness a man possesses, they are never a matter of intellectual endowment alone. Greatness is also a matter of character qualities. If dedication to and self-discipline in the service of the chosen and self-limited life task can be called a character basis for a great scholarly life work, it was certainly present in this case.

This might not have been apparent at first acquaintance. Easy, gracious and obliging ways and manners, an occasional tendency to the baroque and even the slightly eccentric were surface manifestations, cloaking a basic scholarly austerity and in part compensatory expression of a vital and lively nature.

An understanding of Schumpeter *the man* is of particular significance in understanding Schumpeter the sociologist. He was an Austrian, and, for all his reticence to show it, a devoted citizen of the Dual Monarchy. This fact, that his heart was most deeply attached to something of the past, irretrievably lost, may account in part for his remarkable and sometimes misunderstood capacity for detachment from current problems and aspirations. He learned to like Germany, where he spent what he called some of his happiest years. Yet he never felt entirely as a German. His relations to the United States seemed to be somewhat similar, where again he found much personal happiness.

Born to a fairly affluent industrial family of Moravia, with aristocratic connections, he had acquired an early understanding for the milieu and spirit of the industrial entrepreneur, as well as the knowledge of the aristocratic society of imperial Vienna. During his school years at the famous Theresianum, school of the political, social, and military elites of the Hapsburg Monarchy, he must have acquired from his teachers not only a great part of the wide range of general knowledge and culture which distinguished him, but also a sense for rigid methodical discipline.

So wide a social horizon, containing the diversified cultural and national landscape of old Austria, was bound to favor early maturity of an eminently observant, keen, and sensitive mind, and to form a definite type in which scholar and man of the world were blended. His wide and early academic experience as a student and teacher which had led him from Vienna [2] to England, where he met Edgeworth and Marshall, and then to Czernowitz, and Graz, and in 1914 to the United States (Columbia University), where he formed a close personal friendship with Frank Taussig, and later to Bonn and Harvard, interrupted only at various times by his activity as barrister (in Egypt) and as Austrian public servant, minister of finance, and banker, could only accentuate those traits.

Schumpeter at heart always was preeminently what Fritz Kern has described as *Herrenbürger* (gentlemen-bourgeois), whatever other *goûts de tête* his rational and realistic mind might have acquired.

---

[1] Reprinted with permission of the author and *Weltwirtschaftliches Archiv*.

[2] The young doctor and instructor was, as François Perroux reports, in Schumpeter's own words, the "enfant gâté et terrible" of the brilliant Vienna faculty of those days. Joseph Schumpeter, *Théorie de l'évolution économique, Recherches sur le profit, le crédit, l'intérêt et le cycle de la conjoncture*, Avec une introd. de François Perroux: "La pensée économique de Joseph Schumpeter," Trad. de Jean-Jacques Anstett sur la 2e ed., Collection scientifique d'économie politique, VI (Paris, 1935), p. 8.

Into this pattern fitted his minor defects, an occasional playful cynicism on the surface, too much yielding tolerance, largely a by-product of his Austrian urbanity, and a certain liking for ostentation, at least in his younger years. Into it fitted his great, more basic qualities, not only of the mind, but of the heart: urbane grace, wit and charm, punctilious old world courtesy, and underneath, a truly warm, sensitive heart, capable of a practical generosity that was all but ostentatious. This personality prevented him from developing the contentious, doctrinaire and self-satisfied traits which mar so many scholarly natures.

It made him, who was decidedly "university minded" rather than "college minded," an eminently effective teacher for qualified students, both young and old. Especially in the ease and informality of friendly, intimate, private conversation, it was a great experience to feel the force and wealth of his mind. The power of his intellect was at once a challenge and a compulsion to higher intellectual achievement, the generosity and considerateness of his nature a beneficence — gratefully to be remembered. On such occasions, he never spoke "with the voice of authority," even if he had all the right to claim it with regard to the subject under discussion. Indeed he possessed to a very high degree the gracious art of initiating an exchange of minds, most stimulating and inspiring to his partners in conversation.

In the intellectual temper of the scholar, rationalistic, positivistic, and, to a point, deterministic traits prevail. Early matured and early accomplished, he may well be characterized as the fruit of the intellectual and philosophical climate of the European continent of his youth.

The depth and scope of the scholarship of his early manhood was astounding. Two major economic treatises in the nature of comprehensive and often highly original and independent "economic systems" fall in his early and middle twenties. His brilliant, sensitive, and penetrating history of economic thought appears in his early thirties. With its characteristic stress on the sociological climate, from which the various schools of thought spring, and on their common and mutually complementary content rather than on their apparently or really irreconcilable traits, it is representative of a lifelong effort to bring out the common constructive content in the work of different economic thinkers. Most of his later thought is already present in his early publications, at least in preliminary form, and has been retained and developed with great constancy and consistency in his mature masterpieces, the *Business Cycles*[3] and *Capitalism, Socialism and Democracy*.[4]

These works, his studies in the field of econometrics and statistics, and a vast array of articles and essays in leading Austrian, German, English, American, and French scholarly magazines and other periodicals, his contribution to the *Handwörterbuch der Staatswissenschaften*,[5] his co-editorship of the *Archiv für Sozialwissenschaft und Sozialpolitik*, and the *Quarterly Journal of Economics* and other learned periodicals, and a great number of biographical sketches,[6] always with a characteristic emphasis on the sociological explanation of the mentality and character of his subject, have firmly established Schumpeter's rank among the foremost international social scientists of his time.

Obviously not from lack of talent for other scientific pursuits, nor from lack of preparation, which included legal, philosophical, and especially historical training, mostly of a wide international scope and range, and familiarity with the leading exponents of the Anglo-American and continental European schools of sociology, especially the Italian and French, Schumpeter confined himself *primarily* to the field of economics and especially theoretical economics.

He early understood the secret of mastery, which is limitation. Yet the scope of economics as understood and practiced by him might have been too vast for a less strong and clear mind

[3] Joseph A. Schumpeter, *Business Cycles: A Theoretical, Historical, and Statistical Analysis of the Capitalist Process* (New York and London, 1939, 2 vols.).

[4] *Idem, Capitalism, Socialism and Democracy*, with a new Preface, 3rd Ed. (London, 1950). German Ed.: "Kapitalismus, Sozialismus und Demokratie," Einl. von Edgar Salin, Übers. aus dem Engl. von Susanne Preiswerk, *Mensch und Gesellschaft*, Bd. 7 (Bern, 1946).

[5] *Idem*, "Angebot," *Handwörterbuch der Staatswissenschaften*, 4., gänzl. umgearb. Aufl., Bd. 1 (Jena, 1923), pp. 299 sqq. "Kapital," *ibid.*, Bd. 5 (1923), pp. 582 sqq. "Unternehmer," *ibid.*, Bd. 8 (1928), pp. 476 sqq.

[6] Among these the article on J. M. Keynes, written with a peculiarly intuitive understanding, due to an obvious congeniality of both men, was the last and one of the most brilliant. See Joseph A. Schumpeter's review of J. M. Keynes, *Essays in Biography*, in *The Economic Journal*, XLIII (London, 1933), pp. 652 sqq.

and might have caused a less indefatigable worker to fall exhausted before so enormous a task.

That self-imposed limitation makes it understandable why Schumpeter's purely sociological work, which is mostly confined to political sociology, is not more extensive, and why much of his sociological thought is incidental and subordinate to his thinking as an economic theorist.

Of his purely sociological essays his papers "Zur Soziologie der Imperialismen"[7] and "Die sozialen Klassen im ethnisch homogenen Milieu"[8] stand out and apparently are so considered by the author, as he lists them with his major works in the *International Who's Who*.

The main purpose of his economic work is not to replace, but to amend, the neoclassic theoretical system. In doing so he brings it closer to reality. All his economic theories deal with more than the mere functional and dynamic logic of the economic process. They deal with the life and growth of a civilization of which the industrial system with its production through applied science (industrialism) is the core. This is especially true for the theory of the entrepreneur, the spontaneously creative leader among business men, who with the aid of the credit-creating financier built that system, and who with the "innovations," which he creates or at least creatively applies, maintains drive and life in the capitalistic process, which without the profit chances resulting from innovation would run down like a clock that is not wound up time and again. It is true for the notions of the "perennial gale" of dynamic, "innovating" competition, which destroys what cannot keep pace with progress, especially in the largely, yet not entirely, static world of small business.

This view produces a deeper understanding of monopolistic attitudes and practices in economic life than is common among economists. It provides scientific support for the claim that such attitudes and practices sometimes can be justified, as too much "gale" would wreck the windmill that it is supposed to drive. Likewise, the explanation of the business cycle out of the spasmodic and uneven impact of innovation, just like the rest of his economic thought, is abstracted from a rich and full vision of the whole social process. Nevertheless, it is abstracted.

In Schumpeter's economic treatises, categories such as "entrepreneur" are economic abstractions in the sense that only the economically essential traits of their nature and activity are stressed and that they are taken as data for the economic argument, without trying to explain how this type of economic leader came into being.

While the economic treatises, especially *The Theory of Economic Development*,[9] which in the first edition contained an essentially sociological last chapter, and his *Business Cycles*, are full of brilliant sociological side glances into the folklore of big business, all this is incidental and subordinate to the economic argument.

Apart from his essays on the sociology of imperialisms and the social classes in an ethnically homogeneous milieu, Schumpeter the (political) *sociologist* is free from the self-imposed subordination to Schumpeter the *theoretical economist* only in his *Capitalism, Socialism and Democracy*. This is not to say that this book is not also an eminent, highly original economic treatise. It emphatically is. The scope of the work, however, is not confined to economic theory. With the latter, elements of philosophy, of history, sociology, and political science are artfully interwoven into a brilliant appraisal of the social forces behind the march of modern history.

This fact and the remarkable constancy and consistency of his sociological thought from his youth on may justify us in concentrating our further discussion mainly on that work.

Even in this book the author at least twice claims to speak as a "mere economist," however, only in an overly modest plea for the reader's tolerance with his noneconomic argument.

The initial chapters contain a sovereign appraisal of Karl Marx's political and economic thought and his messianic message, displaying

---

[7] Joseph Schumpeter, "Zur Soziologie der Imperialismen," *Archiv für Sozialwissenschaft und Sozialpolitik*, Bd. 46 (Tübingen, 1918–19), pp. 1 sqq., 275 sqq.

[8] *Idem*, "Die sozialen Klassen im ethnisch homogenen Milieu," *ibid.*, Bd. 57 (1927), pp. 1 sqq.

[9] Joseph Schumpeter, *Theorie der wirtschaftlichen Entwicklung* (Leipzig, 1912). English Ed.: *The Theory of Economic Development, An Inquiry into Profits, Capital, Credit, Interest, and the Business Cycle*, translated from the German by Redvers Opie, Harvard Economic Studies, XLVI (Cambridge, Massachusetts, 1934).

all of Schumpeter's powers of analytical acumen and intuitive understanding. Marx's work is understood as the fruit of "his time and environment" ("the zenith of bourgeois realization and the nadir of bourgeois civilization" [Kultur] [10]). With striking clarity and originality of exposition, Marx's doctrines are reformulated so as to bring out their intelligible meaning, especially for the surplus value theory.

Those pages allow the author, intentionally or otherwise, to reveal his own social philosophy and philosophy of science and scholarship. There is the laudatory comment: "Nowhere did he betray [sic!] positive science to metaphysics." [11] There is the remark: [12] "These facts [with which Marx illustrated his social vision] he embraced with a glance that *pierced through the random irregularities of the surface down to the grandiose logic of things historical.*"

Refuting some aspects of it, especially the purely economic and oversimplified conception of the rigid class structure which labor cannot transgress, Schumpeter accepts much of that philosophy. He does so in a broad interpretation, allowing for the interaction between material and ideational forces. The latter he tends to consider as at least decidedly molded by economic conditions, but possibly by economic conditions of the past, all of which is indeed no deviation from Marx. "Social structures, types and attitudes are coins that do not readily melt." [13] This tendency towards a *predominantly* materialistic, yet not exclusively economic, interpretation of the historical process shows also in other works of his; for instance, in his above mentioned article, "Unternehmer," where the advent of capitalism is traced to the gradual cumulative effect of economic innovations in the world of the medieval craftsman-entrepreneur and merchant-entrepreneur rather than to the advent of a new capitalistic spirit (*Geist*) (Sombart) or the influence of protestant ethics (Weber).

To call a philosophy of history such as that of Marx, and, to a point, such as his own, materialistic, is to him meaningless. It "is logically compatible with any metaphysical or religious belief." [14] It may be logically compatible, but it is hardly compatible with Marxist credo. In Schumpeter's work, the realization of the objective importance of spontaneously creative individual choice and action, of individual leadership in the economic and other social spheres of life, and the absence of any rigid dogmatic determinism, which is especially noticeable in his views of the future, redound to a social philosophy which for all family relationship is widely different from that of Karl Marx.

As to socialist policy, there is the revealing statement in a later chapter: [15] "For me, the fascinating thing . . . that gives it . . . a dignity all its own that is both intellectual and moral — is its clear and close relation to a doctrinal basis."

Certainly Schumpeter could claim companionship with Marx in a distinction which, strangely enough, many leading economists of our day do not share. They both knew that economic life and the social process in the last century, in their dynamic aspects, are determined, not only by their distributive aspects based on the institution of private (inheritable) property and private contract, but at least as much by the systematic application of natural science to production (industrialism); and both drew theoretical conclusions from that fact.

Perhaps Schumpeter's greatest contribution to sociology is his "moving picture" ("film") of industrial capitalism in action, growth and decline, the role of its controlling class and of the leading element in that class: the capitalist entrepreneur, as he grows and changes from the ingenious craftsman and venturesome merchant to the head of an industrial family and finally the executive of a big corporation, and promoter of industrial ventures.

The entrepreneur is not only — at least in vigorous, "unfettered," capitalistic society — the pivotal figure of the dynamic economic process, he is likewise the essential and the originating element in bourgeois civilization. Perhaps with some one-sided exaggeration, the rational spirit of modern science is shown to have been cradled in the double-entry book of the medieval merchant.

[10] Schumpeter, *Capitalism, loc. cit.*, p. 5.
[11] *Ibid.*, p. 10.
[12] *Ibid.* Italics mine.
[13] *Ibid.*, p. 12.

[14] *Ibid.*, p. 11.
[15] Schumpeter, *Capitalism, loc. cit.*, p. 305.

The best fruits of "Capitalism" with its entrepreneurship in a civilized life made infinitely healthier, safer, and more comfortable than that of any previous period, in a growing understanding and hence tolerance of the various forms of human life, in modern science, which, even if it has not grown out of capitalism, certainly could not grow without it and its material and technical facilities, and in rationalistic humanitarian ethics ("the golden rule") are duly entered to its credit.

That the best of entrepreneurs, far from being mere money-makers, generally are leaders and builders endowed with more social responsibility and more tolerance for divergent and even hostile views and interests than most, if not all, leading groups known to history, had to be said by a social scientist. Schumpeter, unlike other intellectuals, does not bite the hand that feeds and provides conditions for professional work so far unsurpassed in history. There is nothing of adulation in this. The religious, philosophical, and artistic sterility of the bourgeois century get their full due.

The picture of social forces in growth and at work which emerges on a few pages is as admirable in its parsimony and judicious balance as in its suggestive vividness, making the essentials stand out and using the work of historians and sociologists with an ingenious eclecticism.

No less striking is the demonstration in proof of the thesis that capitalism, which is of course to pass over the historical scene just like any other social phenomenon, need not owe its decline to the frictions and structural deficiencies of its economic system, nor to economic maturity, that is, to lack of outlets and investment opportunities, nor to an inevitable stagnation of the process of technological and other innovation that is its life elixir, but rather to its very success, which creates a political climate to which it will ultimately succumb.

In order to emphasize and dramatize this thesis, the *economic* difficulties in the way of continued operation are perhaps somewhat underplayed in *Capitalism, Socialism and Democracy*, especially so in comparison to the discussion in *Business Cycles*.

First the capitalist spirit of rational egalitarian utilitarianism undermines the precapitalistic spiritual and political sanctions for the authority of the bourgeois class over the dependent classes. The rationalistic criticism, which attacked the authorities of Throne and Church and of the whole feudal order, in order to emancipate the rising bourgeoisie, does not stop before the bourgeois institutions themselves, especially not before that of private property and inheritance, and incorporated business. This argument is not unlike that raised by Lorenz von Stein a hundred years ago. The growing institutionalization of innovation in systematic team research and schooling, the bureaucratization of industrial management and the replacement of the mill-owner, the *Fabrikherr*, interested in the prosperity of his family enterprise through the generations, by the corporation executive with his temporary stake in the enterprise, reduces in the entrepreneurial class the sense for the requirements of the maintenance of the social and economic foundations of private business, especially the resistance to policies which threaten capital formation. The typical ineptitude of a highly specialized rational and unheroic profession, devoid of social glamor, in the *political* defense of its position, makes attack on them easy.

In a class-conscious labor class, and also in the "salariat," the "private business system" creates its own political enemies. Egalitarian democracy, logical political concomitant of the rationalistic individualism of the capitalistic system, lends that enmity force. The bureaucracy, logical outcome of the mode of operation of modern business and government, emerges as a ready and willing tool for collective administration of the economic process, especially after the concentration characteristic of modern business has run its full course.

Meanwhile, the protective social layers remaining from an older economic society, the independent small businessmen and farmers with their conservative traditional ways, gradually melt away. At the same time, that other product of capitalistic society, the intellectual, often socially footloose and a professional critic and "debunker," frequently animated by an unsatisfied urge for more political power than the capitalistic system will allow him, becomes the professional spearhead of open and subversive attacks against the system.

It is difficult to say that this picture is not true to life. Its *components* are of course not original. Yet again the composite argument and the way these facts are turned to account for what is essentially a sociological rather than economic theory of the decline of capitalism is highly original and of convincing forcefulness.

That the logical outcome of this all points towards socialism is obvious. Capitalism withers away in a process that makes the economic and political system ripe for socialism. In this view Schumpeter is certainly and admittedly Marxian.

The serenity with which this is stated seems to have caused misunderstanding and disapproval in a time which is passionately engaged in a life and death struggle with undesirable and destructive forms of socialism. Yet Schumpeter is otherwise no Marxist, least of all the ardent kind. For the "scribes and pharisees" of the creed he has only contempt. He does not believe in a classless socialism of the proletariat, and he has neither the desire nor the power for messianic prophecy, nor obviously, too much patience with it. He confines himself to the task of understanding the drift of events in the light of established facts and historical and theoretical logic.

Nor does he foresee the necessary downfall of bourgeois capitalism for the near future. It may last for another fifty or hundred years, even in its present "fettered" form. But socialism is not only inevitable, it is also, as a rationally operating economic system, logically and factually possible. The pertinent argument, following lines familiar since Barone's classical deduction, will probably be accepted by most modern economists. Socialism need not mean the tyranny of a few rulers forcing through a "Gosplan" made to suit their fancy. Schumpeter grants to the humanitarian socialist (in a Machiavellian effort to break down doctrinaire imperviousness to rational argument?) that to do this is not a realization of Marx's concept. Socialism can (and apparently should) consider individual needs and desires, though the latter will be more subject to censorship and sifting by the rulers than in a liberal society.

There is a general admission, unsupported, however, by much elaborate argument, that on the road to socialism there are many opportunities for fatal error, failure, and ruin. One might wish that these possibilities, especially in the shadow-land of transition between what is vaguely called "fettered capitalism" and premature socialism, had been found worthy of the author's usual penetrating, analytical, and critical acumen. Perhaps, compelling considerations of discretion, in order not to disturb the official policies of a difficult period, may have been in the way of this. Nevertheless, one cannot help but feel that a very real *thema de nuestro tiempo* has not gotten its full due. The halfway houses between a liberal economy and a socialist one, where private business is supposed to do the bidding of socialist planners under the influence of persuasion and mostly indirect controls, while subject to crushing taxation, to inflation, "repressed" or otherwise, price controls, and subsidies, are clearly rejected as incapable of lasting existence and consistent operation.

For the current democratic welfare state schemes the author has no brief. In a recent article on "English Economists and the State-Managed Economy," [16] he marvels at the concessions which even liberalistic English economists like Robbins and Jewkes make to these views, and at the gradual growth of egalitarian and statist views among English economists during the last half century. This phenomenon indeed does not seem fully accounted for by the positivistic explanation which he prefers, as it may have much to do with the direct or indirect influence of Christian humanitarian notions on economic thinking.

Premature socialism, before the economic structure (concentration, incorporation) and the public mentality are ripe for it, to Schumpeter can only mean failure. Socialists had better bide their time and be satisfied with what steps they can take "piecemeal" in a still predominantly capitalistic society. He calls this "socialism before the event" (of the socialist *coup d'état*). England's rather obvious example is adduced with observations, which, in the light of later events, show a striking force

[16] Joseph A. Schumpeter, "English Economists and the State-Managed Economy," *Journal of Political Economy*, LVII (1949), pp. 371 sqq.

of penetration under the surface to the core of determining social forces.

Schumpeter believes in the possibility of "workable" socialism in the fullness of time, when public attitudes in all essential layers of society are adjusted to it and when concentration in private business has proceeded considerably further, an eventuality which he seems to consider certain, though recent statistical evidence does not seem clearly to support it. Even then, further conditions have to be fulfilled in a country in order to make its socialism a success. The existence of a "social stratum" capable of providing competent and responsible economic and political leaders whom the public vests with authority, and last but not least, the existence of a reliable civil service of high professional and ethical qualifications are specially stressed.

Only one kind of socialism seemed ultimately feasible to Schumpeter, one that recognizes classes — a sociologist of his historical grounding and realism could not possibly believe in the utopia of a classless society — and that operates under centralized government control of the economic process, carried out by a vast bureaucracy, though possibly leaving much of the peripheral details of production, distribution, and, of course, consumption to private initiative. This is indeed a very qualified forecast for the possibilities of a successful socialism. The positivistic scholar and trained historian does not seem too happy in the role of the long run forecaster.

His remarks about the "cultural indeterminedness" of socialism (in his sense) seem well taken in principle. It is, however, not obvious and not convincingly demonstrated how such a socialism, which apparently is not conceived as being static, could still produce "entrepreneurs," and how they could still function as such. Also one might doubt that farmers (peasants) could be left by such a socialist state to their traditional private conduct of agricultural production and to the concomitant traditional way of life, after farming tends more and more to become a mechanized industry deeply enmeshed in the credit nexus. Whether, after capitalism and socialism have continued their disenchanting and leveling work for many more decades, an "authoritative stratum" in a democratic socialist society is still possible might also be questioned. It is not quite clear whether "stratum" means historically grown class in this context. Lastly, there remains the (unexplored) problem, whether isolated national societies on the socialist plane could sustain themselves economically and what the pattern of a socialist international world could be.

In his earlier discussion of the sociology of imperialism,[17] imperialism is defined as warlike aggressiveness for aggression's sake and explained through an atavistic attitude of the aristocratic elites controlling foreign policy in the nineteenth century, maintaining the ways of their ancestors, who had been warriors by status and profession. It is claimed that neither capitalistic bourgeois strata nor labor share this attitude. The theory, which was abandoned in *Business Cycles* in favor of Karl Renner's theory of "social imperialism," seems corroborated through the political fate which England's great, noble, and universally revered war leader suffered at the hands of the British electorate after the war, and through the pacifist tendencies in American public opinion. It would point to a pacific socialist world.

Yet, socialism apparently does not exclude an intolerant nationalism. Conflicting socialistic national planning schemes and ideologies in an internationally interdependent world might well give *real* cause for war. War for real cause in a postfeudal society was not excluded by Schumpeter's theory of imperialism.

After the manuscript for this article had already been completed, Schumpeter's last contribution to social science, his paper "The March into Socialism,"[18] appeared in print.

In the main it corroborates the previous analysis of his views on socialism and on philosophy of science and his theory of sociology in general. They did not undergo any fundamental change in his last years, exception being taken for some modification of his opinion on socialism and the socialistic future.

His aversion to "prophecy" as "unscientific" is here made explicit.[19] A determinism which

[17] Schumpeter, "Zur Soziologie der Imperialismen," *loc. cit.*

[18] Joseph A. Schumpeter, "The March into Socialism," *American Economic Review*, XL (1950), pp. 466 sqq.

[19] *Ibid.*, p. 447.

considers certain events, such as the advent of bolshevism in Russia, as the *inevitable* outcome of *economic* forces, is likewise refuted as unscientific. In the Stolypin era nothing of the sort was in the cards in Russia, and it was the lost war which produced bolshevism.

As far as the socialist future is concerned, he admits now the possibility that some halfway house, perhaps in the nature of a "laboristic" capitalism with some concessions to the "subsidized independence" of the farmer and to the small businessman, might show some durability. Also for countries under predominantly catholic control, a solidaristic economy of the "Quadragesimo Anno" type is not entirely ruled out. Among socialist forms of economy a guild socialism is considered remotely possible.

In one respect, which is the sociologically decisive one, the previous argument is fully maintained and clarified. Capitalism, not as an economic system, but as a civilization based on its specific values (he seems to refer to the values of individual initiative and self-reliance and a life centered on the individual family and home) is rapidly disappearing. This he claims is true even in those countries which are not aware yet that they have left the age of capitalistic liberal civilization behind.

Yet even in a purely economic sense, socialism remains "the likely heir apparent." One of the strongest forces undermining the moral order and stamina of a liberal society is the inflationary bias inseparable from the high-level employment policies of laboristic economies, politically devoted to the idea of social security through permanent prosperity at all cost.

With arguments in which the sober, incorruptible realism of the master economist shines, it is shown that in the political and social climate of modern society, the classical remedies against inflationary pressure, credit restriction and higher taxes, would likely be applied in such a manner as to make them ineffective and even counterproductive. Direct controls, such as price-fixing, rationing, allocation, subsidies, and the like would merely mean the surrender of private enterprise to public authority. Obviously the fundamental vision of the future has not changed, except perhaps that the doubts concerning the continued high productivity and dynamic character of socialism are more pronounced.[20]

Granting the usual decelerations and temporary reverses of the process, socialism is still considered to be on the march. Under the spur of inflationary pressures, it might even march too fast for its own good, not allowing time for the development of the social values necessary to the stabilization of a socialist society which would be worthy of the title of "civilization."

While the discussion on the future socialism seems inevitably more tentative and less conclusive than that of the liberal capitalist era, Schumpeter the political sociologist appears at his best in the concluding discussion on democracy. This is true, whether or not we accept his argument that socialism, as he defines it and which he considers as the only workable one, is compatible with democracy. This argument rests on a definition of democracy which one might consider not quite germane to this problem, as many contemporaries see and feel it. There is a characteristic positive appraisal of the disciplinary possibilities of a socialist state, which he hopes (perhaps, for his type of socialism, rather optimistically) will not have to cope with the subversive hostility of the intellectuals, to educate for social discipline and, if necessary, to impose a reasonable amount of it. This points to a society of a somewhat fascist type, stripped of course of the sadistic atrocities and stupid tyranny of German fascism, which he loathed. It is indeed difficult to see how otherwise the execution of a national economic plan in the future socialist society would be guaranteed.

Socialism, given its "cultural indeterminedness," is not considered either as a supreme expression of democracy or as *necessarily* combined with it, yet a *possible* coexistence and compatibility is claimed.

The Marxian contention that only the rule of labor is true democracy is refuted, because of the inadequacy of its foundation in the theory of exploitation and in a purely economic concept of class power and class interest. The classic bourgeois doctrine of democratic government as establishing and carrying out the will of the people (the *volonté générale* in the

[20] Schumpeter, "The March into Socialism," *loc. cit.*, p. 448.

sense of the common will of all informed and sensible people) fares no better. Its criticism on logical and factual grounds, the elaboration of its real significance as an outgrowth of a specific historic situation, of its survival as official doctrine, in the face of its lethal defects, through its historical alliance to religious or pseudoreligious (humanitarian) aspirations, carries much conviction. The explanation of the interests and ideas of the bourgeoisie of the seventeenth and eighteenth centuries shows at their best the qualities of intellectual acumen, power of logic, independence of view and realism which distinguished Schumpeter. In our days it is certainly not superfluous to fight the ideological contention which vests democratic government, as such, with a dignity which it only derives from the social values of which, in a special historical situation, it was the most successful vessel and vehicle, but not the cause. It is strikingly and judiciously demonstrated, with examples imaginatively drawn from a rich and ever present store of historical knowledge, that the most wanton and barbaric deeds just as well as the most useful and noble can be and actually have been democratically determined and carried out.

There is certainly nothing wrong scientifically with Schumpeter's positive definition of democracy as an institutional arrangement by which candidates for government competitively present themselves to the electorate for selection as members of the governing agency, and his description of modern democracy as rule by politicians. However, it may be less certain than Schumpeter wants us to believe, that democracy even in this rather technical sense is compatible with socialism of the type which he is willing to take seriously. In this socialism, where it is coupled with democracy, he wants the essentials of the economic process under the competent and consistent control of the bureaucracy, and therefore exempt from the impact of the parliamentary-democratic process with its incalculable irrationalities. This raises the question, even assuming that the people have at one time freely agreed to make such an arrangement, as to how this taboo is to be maintained and respected by ambitious politicians, who, in their play for power and competition for votes and backing interests, seem to be bound to violate it. They and their voters, if democratically free, could hardly stay satisfied with such a limited scope for their freedom.

Such a scheme, even if workable, would be democracy only in a technical, formal, and politically not exclusively relevant sense. What in the current political debate is meant by "democracy" — and imperfect terminology does not destroy vital issues — and what is often confused and wrongly identified with specific governmental arrangements is, after all, something else than what Schumpeter defines. However correct and valuable for a theory of government, his definition is not suited to produce an answer to the question whether democracy as a way of life, aiming at the fulfillment of Christian and humanitarian ideals of free brotherly cooperation of all men under equal rights, is compatible with socialism in general and with socialism as he prefers it.

There is, in spite of Schumpeter's sense and admiration for creative individual performance, much of the positivist and rational scholar's tendency in his thinking, a tendency which loves consistent execution of logical plans, even with some compulsion, and is not unwilling, at least at times, to pay the price for this in terms of individual creative initiative, which might easily, even in purely economic terms, be too high a price for it.

This may be in part a counsel of desperation. Schumpeter the positivist scholar may underrate the possibility for a revival of the spiritual forces and ideals which in the past have given sanction and protection to individual rights and initiative as well as direction, cohesion, and discipline to the social process.

He was, as we all are, conscious of the unquestioned, at least temporary, confusion and decline which they have suffered, indeed largely under the impact of scientism and industrialism. He considered, probably rightly, the future development of such forces and their social impact as unpredictable in detail, though he believed in the ultimate advent of socialism due to the immanent logic of dynamic industrial developments. Being no messianic prophet and not aspiring to that role, he built his model of a possible, workable type of a socialist society from the material which he had at hand in a reasonably reliable way.

SCHUMPETER ON "IMPERIALISM AND SOCIAL CLASSES"[1]

Paul M. Sweezy

THE two papers, "The Sociology of Imperialisms" and "Social Classes in an Ethnically Homogeneous Environment," were recognized in pre-Hitler Germany as being among the most important works on their respective subjects. Moreover, Schumpeter himself counted them among his major scientific writings. After his death, Mrs. Schumpeter found in his desk a note in his own handwriting listing a half dozen titles. The note had apparently been jotted down in response to a request that he name his most important works — probably the information was wanted for advance publicity announcing a series of lectures. He listed his four full-length books [2] and the two papers which appear in this volume.

Nevertheless, Schumpeter's work on imperialism and social classes has not only not been translated into English until now; it has apparently been almost totally ignored by Anglo-American social scientists. It is, of course, difficult to speak with complete assurance about such matters, but at any rate a reasonably careful survey of the relevant literature has not revealed any evidence of serious attention to Schumpeter's theories.[3] One could no doubt give many reasons for this neglect. For one thing, until recently neither imperialism nor social class has been a major concern of Anglo-

American social science,[4] and continental work on these subjects has been rather generally neglected. For another, in the present highly compartmentalized state of the social sciences, Schumpeter has been looked upon as an economist who could hardly be expected to have anything very profound or important to say about subjects which are located in the preserves of the political scientist and the sociologist. Nor should Schumpeter himself be held blameless. He rarely mentioned his own writings on imperialism and social classes, and it is likely that the vast majority even of the students who came under his direct influence were unfamiliar with this work.[5]

But whatever reasons may have explained the neglect of Schumpeter's work on imperialism and social classes in the past, there would certainly be no excuse for the continuation of such neglect in the future. Even Anglo-American social science is now coming to recognize the importance of these problems; and the realization that Schumpeter was a social scientist in the broadest meaning of the term, and not merely an economist in the traditional sense, has spread in the years since 1942 — that is to say, since the publication of *Capitalism, Socialism and Democracy*. It can hardly be questioned that the time is ripe for an English trans-

[1] This is the editor's introduction to the English translation of Schumpeter's famous essays on imperialism and social classes. The translation, made by Heinz Norden, entitled *Imperialism and Social Classes*, was published in January 1951 by Augustus M. Kelley, Inc., New York. The introduction is reproduced here by permission of the publisher and the author.

[2] *Das Wesen und der Hauptinhalt der theoretischen Nationalökonomie* (1908); *The Theory of Economic Development* (first German edition 1912, revised edition 1926, English translation 1934); *Business Cycles* (1939); and *Capitalism, Socialism and Democracy* (first edition 1942, revised second edition 1947, enlarged third edition 1950).

[3] An exception should perhaps be made in the case of Earle Winslow's work on imperialism: "Marxian, Liberal and Sociological Theories of Imperialism," *Journal of Political Economy*, December 1931; and *The Pattern of Imperialism* (1948). But Winslow's treatment of Schumpeter's theory of imperialism is quite superficial.

[4] Strictly speaking, this is inaccurate. The founders of American sociology — men like Ward, Cooley, and Sumner — were very much concerned with the problem of classes. Later sociologists, however, tended to ignore or deny the importance of the problem. See C. H. Page, *Class and American Sociology* (1940).

[5] This reticence about his own work was, of course, by no means confined to the cases under discussion. Haberler quite rightly says that all his courses "suffered from one defect: by listening to Schumpeter's lectures and studying his reading assignments and suggestions, students could never have found out that he himself had ever written anything on those subjects." (See above, p. 39.) I remember, when I was his assistant in the first-year graduate course in economic theory in the mid-thirties, arguing with him about this. I tried to convince him that students often came to Harvard to study under him and that he owed it to them to give an exposition and elaboration of his own theories. He listened sympathetically but never did anything about it.

lation of two works which, I am confident, will long be regarded as among the classics of the literature dealing with their respective subjects.

The history of these essays can be briefly told. The essay on imperialism first appeared under the title, "Zur Soziologie der Imperialismen," in the *Archiv für Sozialwissenschaft und Sozialpolitik* in 1919 (Vol. 46, pp. 1–39, 275–310), and it was issued in book form in the same year by J.C.B. Mohr (Paul Siebeck) of Tübingen, the firm which also published the *Archiv*. It is clear from internal evidence that the work was written during the war years; and, as Haberler points out, it reveals more plainly than any other writings of Schumpeter the "pacifist, pro-Western (especially pro-British) and anti-German attitude" which he held throughout World War I.[6] I think it is probably safe to assume — though I know of no direct evidence on the matter — that Schumpeter's interest in imperialism was first aroused by what he called the Neo-Marxist theory, the chief authors of which (Otto Bauer and Rudolf Hilferding) he had known since the days when they were all students together in Vienna. But the actual stimulus to a deep study of the problems of imperialism no doubt came from the war itself. The purpose of the essay could therefore be said to be twofold: on the one hand to elaborate a critique of the Bauer-Hilferding theory,[7] and on the other hand to offer an alternative theoretical framework into which the war and its antecedents could be appropriately fitted.

The essay on social classes (German title: "Die sozialen Klassen im ethnisch homogenen Milieu") likewise appeared in the *Archiv für Sozialwissenschaft und Sozialpolitik* (Vol. 57 [1927], pp. 1–67) of which Schumpeter himself was by this time one of the editors. At the outset the author describes the evolution of the ideas to which the essay gives expression:

The basic idea here briefly set forth dates back to the year 1910 and was first presented in a lecture course

---

[6] See p. 30, above.

[7] Schumpeter was at the time almost certainly unacquainted with Lenin's writings on imperialism. Lenin's major work on this subject, *Imperialism, the Highest Stage of Capitalism*, was written in 1916 and published in Russian before the end of the war. But German and French editions did not appear until 1920.

for laymen on the subject of "State and Society" which I delivered at the University of Czernowitz (Cernauti) in the winter of 1910–1911. Subsequently, at Columbia University in the winter of 1913–1914, I presented it at length in a course entitled "The Theory of Social Classes." Since that time I have never altogether stopped developing my thoughts and analyzing the material on the subject, but after 1916 the topic took second place to other interests. Hence I am glad to seize upon the occasion of a lecture, delivered on November 19, 1926, at the University of Heidelberg, under the title "Leadership and Class Formation," to formulate once again and to publish for the first time a line of reasoning which, according to my present plan of work, I shall be able to work out fully only years from now, if at all.

Actually, the subject of social classes retained a place in his plan of work throughout the rest of his life — I have on several occasions heard him voice the intention to return to it some day — but, like many other subjects, it remained in the category of unfinished business at the time of his death.

Economists who conceive of their science in traditional and rather narrowly restricted terms — and that means most of the economics profession in this country today — will naturally be inclined to treat Schumpeter's essays on imperialism and social classes as forays into other fields, brilliant, perhaps, but essentially unrelated to his main work on business cycles and the theory of economic development. Thus, for example, R. V. Clemence and F. S. Doody have written a (very useful) book entitled *The Schumpeterian System* (1950) without even mentioning either of these essays; and both Haberler and Smithies set them apart as representing Schumpeter's "sociological" views.[8] No doubt there is much to be said for this position, and I am sure that it would be possible to find support for it in Schumpeter's own writings and still more in his oral teachings: no one made a sharper distinction between economic and noneconomic phenomena than Schumpeter when it suited his purpose to do so. But at the same time I think it would be possible to construct a broader "Schumpeterian system" — comparable in its scope to Marxian social science, though not to Marxism as a whole — into which these essays fit as integral parts. I cannot undertake so ambitious a task in a mere editor's introduc-

---

[8] See above, pp. 28–29, 12–13.

tion, but I think it may be useful in "placing" these works to indicate "in desperate brevity" (to use a favorite expression of Schumpeter's) the main lines which such an attempt might take.

Schumpeter's central concern throughout his entire scientific career is best described by the subtitle to *Business Cycles*, his largest and in many ways his most ambitious work: "A Theoretical, Historical, and Statistical Analysis of the Capitalist Process." The core of this analysis, the body of organizing principles which informs all the rest, is set forth in his *Theory of Economic Development*. But there are many observable aspects of capitalist reality which are not explained by this theory. Some of these, of course, are of relatively minor significance. But at least one such aspect, comprising the phenomena of imperialism and war, is obviously of crucial importance. Any theory of capitalism which leaves it out of account is unquestionably incomplete. More, it is *prima facie* inadequate and even wrong. Now Schumpeter's theory of economic development not only does not explain imperialism and war; it leads to the expectation that the advance of capitalism will push them further and further into the background and eventually relegate them to the scrapheap of history. It is perfectly clear, then, that unless this contradiction between theory and reality is resolved, Schumpeter's whole system would be, to say the least, suspect. The essential point of the essay on imperialism is precisely to resolve this contradiction, and in this sense it forms a crucial part of his entire structure. To use an analogy of which he was very fond, his theory of imperialism is not one of the stones out of which the edifice is built but it is one of the flying buttresses which keeps the structure standing.

The theory of social classes occupies a different position in the grand design of Schumpeter's thought. To Schumpeter — and in this respect, as in others, he was undoubtedly deeply influenced by Marx — capitalism is, like all social systems, a transitory phenomenon. It had a birth, it is now living its life, and sooner or later it will die. A complete theory of capitalism, from this point of view, would have to consist of three parts: the theory of origins, the theory of functioning and growth, and the theory of de-cline. Most of Schumpeter's work concerns the theory of functioning and growth, but he was perfectly conscious that this is not the whole story. Origins are important not only for their own sake but also because they explain much that does not belong to the pure logic of the system; and decline is — at least at a certain stage of development — the heart of the problem of diagnosis (and prognosis). At the risk of being somewhat overschematic, I would say that the essay on social classes is Schumpeter's central work on the theory of origins, while *Capitalism, Socialism and Democracy* occupies the same position with respect to the theory of decline.[9]

This estimate of the essay on social classes will certainly not impose itself upon the reader as self-evident, and he may decide to reject it as untenable. The essay certainly has the form of a general theory of social classes, and its conclusions are relevant to all of recorded history. But the substance of the theory is based upon an analysis of two classes, the (western European) feudal nobility and the modern bourgeoisie. Now it is clear that the origins of capitalism can be treated in terms of the decline of the nobility and the rise of the bourgeoisie. These problems are in fact aspects of the transition from feudalism to capitalism and cannot even be intelligently considered in abstraction from that process. Schumpeter does not deal with the transition systematically — more's the pity, since it undoubtedly presents a whole series of fascinating and difficult problems [10] — but the broad contours of his thought can, I think, be clearly discerned, certainly more clearly here than in his other major works. No more need be claimed, it seems to me, to substantiate the view that the essay on social classes occupies an important place in the over-all structure of Schumpeter's thought and is not a mere excursion into the "foreign" realm of sociology. One

[9] Though here his writings are much more varied and voluminous, the decline of capitalism playing some part in almost everything he wrote after World War I.

[10] I refer the reader to a recent interchange of views between myself and Maurice Dobb on this subject, not because I think he will find the solution to all, or even any, of the problems involved, but because I do think the interchange has the merit of explaining more or less clearly what some of the most important of these problems are. See "The Transition from Feudalism to Capitalism" in *Science & Society*, Spring 1950.

more point should be added in this connection. The decline of the feudal nobility was, in Schumpeter's view, a protracted process which extended far into the capitalist period, and he traced many important aspects of capitalist reality to this fact. The essay on social classes gives his analysis of the reasons for the slow decline of the nobility, and hence in this respect too forms a part of his general theory of capitalism.[11]

Since these essays were written a quarter of a century or more ago it is reasonable to ask whether they represent Schumpeter's final thoughts on the subjects with which they deal. In one sense, of course, the answer is definitely "No." An active, restless intelligence like Schumpeter's had few absolutely final thoughts. He was always absorbing new material and deriving new views and insights from it, and it is clear that on such vast subjects as imperialism and social classes his ideas must in any case have gone through a process of development in a period of two or three decades. But there is another sense in which the question can be put: did Schumpeter in later years change his mind about any of the essential arguments of these earlier essays?

In the case of social classes, I think not. There is a good deal of comment in *Capitalism, Socialism and Democracy* — some of it of substantive importance, some merely incidental — bearing on the problem of classes, and I think it all runs in terms of the theories of the earlier essay. Moreover, I have discussed social classes with him and never heard him express an opinion which would in any way conflict with these theories.

It is different, however, in the case of imperialism. Here there is clear evidence that Schumpeter did change his mind, though how extensively and radically it is impossible to tell. In a footnote in *Business Cycles* (Vol. 2, p. 696) Schumpeter has the following to say about imperialism:

The Marxist theory of imperialism (Bauer, Hilferding) . . . made the attempt to construe prewar imperialism as an outgrowth of the conditions of trustified

capitalism. This explanation, which conserves unity of principle, has, of course, great attractions for every mind that has an analytical bent, and could be generalized to include postwar fascism. It is not possible here to expound the reasons why it is inadequate.[12] A glimpse of a view that now seems to the writer to be nearer the truth than either the Marxist or his own theory [i.e. the theory expounded in the 1919 essay] is embodied in Karl Renner's concept of Social Imperialism.

I have not been able to reach any definite conclusion as to the significance which ought to be attached to this remark. Schumpeter does not refer to any specific work of Renner, and I suppose Winslow is probably right to cite in this connection Renner's 1917 work, *Marximus, Krieg und Internationale*. I can find the term *Sozialimperialismus* only once in this book — in the title of a subsection which can be translated: "The Overwhelming Counter-Interest. The Error of Social Imperialism."[13] Renner argues *against* those who maintain that on balance the working class gains from an imperialist policy, and in the text he uses the phrase "socialist imperialism" rather than "social imperialism." I can hardly imagine that Schumpeter would have been impressed with the crude theory of immediate economic benefits to the working class from imperialist expansion which Renner sketches. In fact, Schumpeter could have thought up many more objections to such a theory than Renner did.

It seems to me more likely that Schumpeter saw a "glimpse" of the truth in the bare concept of "social imperialism" rather than in the content which Renner ascribed to it. Schumpeter would doubtless have elaborated the concept along lines suggested by Winslow on the basis of personal correspondence with Schumpeter:

Without committing himself definitely, Schumpeter feels that the problem must be approached . . . by recognizing that so-called rational ends are not what motivate human behavior, but rather that the fundamental volition arises from impulses which appear from the economic (rational) viewpoint to be nonrational or irrational. If this is a common characteristic of practically all human behavior outside the economic sphere, the conclusion is unavoidable that the will to fight and to conquer may be found elsewhere than solely in the

[11] Note also that at this point the essay on social classes and the essay on imperialism touch on the same range of problems.

[12] Schumpeter devoted several pages to expounding his reasons for rejecting the Bauer-Hilferding theory in *Capitalism, Socialism and Democracy* (pp. 51–55). He had also, of course, analyzed this theory in the 1919 essay.

[13] 1918 edition, p. 336.

old professional military class. Thus, the way is opened to the recognition of a true imperialism of a people as a whole, that is, a *Volksimperialismus* similar to that which Schumpeter had assumed existed only among ancient peoples.[14]

It must be emphasized, however, that mere acknowledgment of irrational or nonrational motives, while it may "open the way to" recognition of "a true imperialism of a people," is still a long way from a theory of "social imperialism." Whatever others have made of this concept,[15] it is certain that if Schumpeter had elaborated and defended his own interpretation of it, he would have done so with his customary ingenuity and dialectical skill. Since he did not, it is perhaps as well for others not to try to do the job for him.

To this I would add just one more point. Actually, the theory of imperialism contained in the 1919 essay is a good deal less monolithic than its critics seem to have assumed. A careful reader can easily find several theories of imperialism — note, for example, the very different explanation of ancient Roman imperialism as compared to, say, ancient Assyrian imperialism — and I think Schumpeter could easily have added another theory without actually repudiating much that he had already written. All he would have had to say was that one or more of his earlier theories had less general validity than he had once been inclined to assume.

Haberler says of Schumpeter's style: "It is characterized by long sentences, numerous qualifying phrases, qualifications of qualifications, casuistic distinctions of meaning. These qualities of his style are especially pronounced, as one would expect, in his German writings, because the German language offers more freedom for complicated constructions."[16] The essays in this volume are good examples of Schumpeter's style at its most complicated (this is even more true of Social Classes than of Im-

perialism). Let me give a sample sentence, by no means unrepresentative of others of its kind:

Der Prozess des Aufgebens der Grundfunktion unserer Klasse durch diese Klasse selbst — worunter nach dem Gesagten nicht bloss initiatives Aufgeben durch bewusstes Nichtwollen zu verstehen, sondern auch der Druck der objektiven sozialen Tatsachen mitbegriffen ist, welche eine Entwöhnung bewirkten und das Nichtwollen, wo es auftritt, begründeten, so wie auch der Umstand, dass, nachdem einmal das *Aufgeben* im Gange war, stellenweise ein *Wegnehemen* hinzutrat — setzte also die Persönlichkeit des adeligen Herrn frei und ermöglichte es dem Adel als Klasse, auch die übrigen Bindungen des Lehensverhältnisses zu lockern, die ja damit ohnehin an Sinn verloren und ganz von selbst atrophisch wurden, — was wir eben unter unserem Ausdruck "Patrimonialisierung der Persönlichkeit" im Falle des Adels verstehen.

In translation this sentence is broken up into no less than four sentences:

The process by which our class relinquished its basic class function implies not merely voluntary surrender and failure of will power, but also the pressure of the objective social situation which resulted in inactivity and flagging will. It implies not only *giving up* but also, once that had begun, *taking away*. For the nobles this process was at the same time a process of individual emancipation, and it enabled the nobility as a class to loosen all the other feudal bonds — bonds which had already begun to lose meaning and to enter into a state of atrophy. This is just what we mean, in the case of the nobility, by "patrimonialization of the individual."[17]

An editor's introduction is not a book review, and I have neither the intention nor the desire to evaluate or criticize the substance of these essays. But I could not reconcile myself to closing this introduction without paying my respects to their distinguished author.

I first met Schumpeter in the fall of 1933. I had just returned from a year of study abroad, and he was starting his second year of teaching at Harvard. From then until I left Harvard to enter the army at the end of 1942 it was my privilege to be with him often, first as a student, later as his assistant and junior colleague, always as a friend.

It is not easy for me — as I am sure it would not be easy for most of those who studied under him — to express my intellectual debt to Schumpeter. He made no attempt whatever to form a group of disciples around him, and yet I have

---

[14] *The Pattern of Imperialism*, pp. 235–236. I fail to see, however, why Winslow attributes such ideas to Renner. For the most part Renner's theory of imperialism is pure Hilferding, and for the rest he stresses immediate (real or supposed) economic interest.

[15] See Franz Neumann, *Behemoth: The Structure and Practice of National Socialism* (1942), Part I, Ch. 6.

[16] Haberler, *op. cit.*, pp. 369–370.

[17] *Imperialism and Social Classes*, translated by Heinz Norden, pp. 197–198.

never known a teacher who took a more personal and painstaking interest in his students. He was convinced that the third decade of life is the period of genuine creativity — in his obituary essay on Menger he had called it "that period of sacred fertility" — and he saw it as his function, one might even say duty, to help those who were living through that period to bring every bit of talent in them to fruitful expression. For this, what they needed was encouragement, sometimes advice, but above all an atmosphere of intellectual clash and excitement which would sharpen their interest and challenge their ambition. And throughout the thirties, when his physical vigor still matched his mental vigor, Schumpeter spared no pains to see that just such an atmosphere existed for the best graduate students in economics at Harvard.

He corresponded with economists all over the world and drew them to Cambridge for lectures, seminars, or just visits. He was faculty adviser to the Graduate Economics Club and always helped to shape its program. He organized private seminars and discussion groups, and entertained them with good food and wine to bring the students, often of many nationalities, into intimate relationship with one another. He read and criticized manuscripts and was almost always able to find some idea worth developing even in the weaker efforts. He was ready to meet students individually — most frequently at lunch which was always "on him" — to discuss whatever problems might be on their minds. And he would go to gay parties, not as a sedate professor doing his duty but as one of the liveliest and, in spirit, youngest of the participants.

We all got ideas from him, of course. His range of knowledge and interests was encyclopedic, and his ability to express himself was rare and scintillating. But he never sought acquiescence to his own point of view. Quite the contrary, he usually sought to stir up disagreement, to shock his hearers out of their complacency, and he was never averse to playing the role of *advocatus diaboli*. I do not mean to suggest that he had no strong opinions of his own. He had plenty of them, as anyone who reads at all attentively in his writings will quickly recognize. But he never tried to impose them on others and — rarest of all quali-

ties in a teacher — he never showed the slightest inclination to judge students or colleagues by the extent to which they agreed with him. Keynesians (regularly in a substantial majority after 1936) and Marxists (often in a minority of one as long as I was in Cambridge) were equally welcome in his circle. He didn't care *what* we thought as long as we *did* think. And anyone who met his standards in this respect could count on his loyal support, regardless of personal or intellectual differences. Schumpeter's gift to all of us was not a "system" or a set of doctrines — it was only an education, and intellectually the most stimulating years of our lives.

He is gone now, and neither Harvard nor the economics profession will ever be the same again. But I like to think that those who feel his absence most deeply are the students who, flocking to Harvard from all over the world, sat at his feet during the thirties when we were young and he was at the peak of his mature powers. My brother, Alan Sweezy, who first studied with Schumpeter when the latter was a visiting professor at Harvard in the academic year 1930–31 and remained a member of the "Schumpeter circle" until he left Cambridge nearly ten years later, wrote me the day after Schumpeter's death:

As I was going into my 10 o'clock class this morning, one of the younger instructors here [at California Institute of Technology] stopped me and said: "I see we've lost Schumpeter." At first I didn't quite take it in; and then suddenly, as I realized what he meant, a whole flood of memories rushed in on me and for a few minutes I had a hard time holding on to myself. It seemed just as though I were hearing about the death of part of my own life. I didn't really think of the Schumpeter of recent years, whom I had grown away from and had rarely seen, but was living over again those years at Harvard when Schumpeter was the center in our group of graduate students and young instructors. That they were such good years — so lively and interesting and enjoyable — was largely the result of Schumpeter's personality and influence. Whatever my later disagreements with him, I'm tremendously grateful for all he did for us in that enormously important formative period of our lives. And I feel terribly sad to think that he, genius and symbol of that period, is gone.

There must be a good many others all over the world who felt that way when they heard the news.

HISTORICAL IMPLICATIONS OF THE THEORY
OF ECONOMIC DEVELOPMENT

A. P. Usher

THE theory of economic development is rich in historical implications, and as it stands in Schumpeter's *Business Cycles* many of the more important historical implications are explicitly incorporated in the exposition. It was Schumpeter's deliberate intention to combine historical, statistical, and theoretical analysis in a comprehensive exposition, but he was too modest when he said, "nor do I think that there is anything novel in my combination of historical, statistical, and theoretical analysis — as far as that goes I have merely moved with the general tendency toward their mutual peaceful penetration." [1]

His combination of the different techniques of analysis was in fact highly original. He broke new ground at many important points, in particular fields of analysis, as well as in the combination of the techniques. Few writers in any of the three fields made any serious effort to use more than a single technique of analysis. At no time during Schumpeter's career was there any established technique for the interpenetrating use of the different techniques outside the scope of the Marxian literature. This body of Marxian literature stands in a somewhat special class, because the principles of historical interpretation do not meet the requirements of empirical analysis and documentary verification. The doctrines mesh more adequately with theory than much of the work of the other historical schools because they are in effect sociological theories with historical elements. History and theory are brought together in what purports to be a unified system, but only by the sacrifice of many principles of criticism and interpretation that are essential to genuine analysis of the total array of historical events. The non-Marxian schools sacrificed theory to history, the Marxians sacrificed history to theory.

These historical sociologies were useful in the preliminary classification and interpreta-

tion of historical materials, but there was no adequate concept of process, and historical analysis cannot rise above the level of wholly subjective narrative until there is some defensible and workable concept of process. The vital question for history is: "How do things happen?" The theory of economic development is addressed specifically to this question, and it offers the highly significant answer. The events of history find their movement and their meaning in the process of cumulative innovation. The processes of history are neither transcendental and unknowable, nor mechanical and foreordained.

Such a concept of process affords a basis for the comprehensive analysis of events in terms of history, statistics, and theory. The underlying principles of Schumpeter's thought were thus far in advance of the historical sociologies of his contemporaries. The full compass of his vision is to be found in the introduction to the historical material in *Business Cycles* (Vol. I, p. 220):

. . . Since what we are trying to understand is economic change in historic time, there is little exaggeration in saying that the ultimate goal is simply a reasoned (= conceptually clarified) history, not of crises only, nor of cycles or waves, but of the economic process in all its aspects and bearings to which theory merely supplies some tools and schemata, and statistics merely part of the material. It is obvious that only detailed historic knowledge can definitively answer most of the questions of individual causation and mechanism and that without it the study of time series must remain inconclusive, and theoretical analysis empty. It should be equally clear that contemporaneous facts or even historic facts covering the last quarter or half of a century are perfectly inadequate. For no phenomenon of an essentially historic nature can be expected to reveal itself unless it is studied over a long interval. An intensive study of the process in the last quarter of the seventeenth and in the eighteenth century is hence a most urgent task, for a quantitative and carefully dated account of a period of 250 years may be called the minimum of existence of the student of *Business Cycles*.

The full achievement of these aims is still somewhat beyond the scope of currently established techniques of analysis in all three com-

[1] Joseph A. Schumpeter, *Business Cycles* (New York, 1939), Vol. I, p. v.

partments of the general field. History still suffers from the dominance of sociological points of view that are directed toward a mere classification of material. Economic theory is concentrated upon problems of category formation in the field of income analysis and income management, and upon static formulations of general equilibrium theory in which space and time are largely if not entirely ignored. Many current interests obstruct rather than stimulate the development of the program for the comprehensive interweaving of all techniques of economic analysis.

In his own thought, it seems evident that Schumpeter assumed that an adequate method could be based on some formulation of the dialectic process, combined with the recognition that history and theory were complementary rather than alternative techniques. Occasional passages[2] suggest an acceptance of Rickert's concept of the relations between historical analysis and the natural sciences, so that we may assume that the general postulates of Kantian idealism were qualified by the Hegelian and Marxian concepts of dialectic process.

Such a formulation of the underlying problems of method and epistemology would carry one far, but the concepts of innovation, leadership, and entrepreneurship carry one beyond any achievements that could be logically derived from the dialectic processes even when revised. Notable as they were, the achievements of both Hegel and Marx were limited, and failed to resolve the issues to which Kant had given a sharp formulation. The appraisals of the dialectic processes by F. S. C. Northrup and Otis Lee reveal very clearly the place of both Hegel and Marx in the development of philosophy and epistemology.[3] Karl Pribram's recent book, *Conflicting Patterns of Thought*, affords an even more commanding basis for the revision of our judgments about the relation of intuitive idealism to the problems of analysis in the social sciences.

The development of the philosophical bases of empirical analysis within the last twenty

years makes it possible to deal more consistently with the analysis of innovation and affords a comprehensive resolution of the difficulties that have hampered us in dealing with the concepts of time and the related problems of the analysis and interpretation of historical events. A concept of emergent novelty cannot be developed consistently without abandoning the spatialized concepts of time which have dominated all the idealistic philosophies and the Newtonian formulations of the physical sciences. The theory of economic development, therefore, involved a greater break with nineteenth century techniques of analysis than even its author was prepared to recognize. His vision carried him to the primary conclusions, but the techniques of his time were an obstacle to complete exposition. For these reasons, no doubt, he wrote in the preface to *Business Cycles*, "The house is certainly not a finished and furnished one — there are too many glaring lacunae and too many unfulfilled desiderata. . . . The younger generation of economists should look on this book merely as something to shoot at and to start from." (p. v.)

II

The idealistic philosophies explain social change as the result of unconditional acts of great men, to whom underlying truths are directly revealed. Religious leaders, poets, and social reformers can easily be accepted as vehicles of the Divine Purpose. Statesmen, military leaders, and businessmen present different problems. Logical difficulties increase as the number of great men becomes larger, but if the nature of the process of change is ignored, the difficulties are not insuperable. These concepts of change are consistent with the ideal culture types of the various descriptive sociologies of the later nineteenth century. But these positions rest upon two postulates; the changes must be infrequent and of large magnitude. As long as one is satisfied with a description of what happens, the idealistic interpretation is plausible and, to many, completely satisfying.

The theory of economic development advances beyond the limits of the idealistic position both in terms of the number of innovators and in terms of the explicit interest in the proc-

---

[2] Cf. *The Theory of Economic Development*, p. 58.

[3] F. S. C. Northrup, *The Meeting of East and West* (1946), pp. 212–21; Otis Lee, *Existence and Inquiry* (1949), pp. 150–59.

ess of change as such. It moves into positions that subject the idealistic categories to severe strains, and really require a complete abandonment of the idealist position. Even in the first edition of *The Theory of Economic Development*, innovation is conceived as a massive social process closely related to the process of learning by an individual of techniques already significantly established in the traditions of the group. But the application of a concept of innovation to cyclical fluctuation involved a truly final break with earlier interpretations of social change. The romantic idealists and the various historical sociologies identified change with the transitions from one stage to another. The discontinuities of history were, thus, restricted to long-term movements dated in terms of centuries. In *The Theory of Economic Development*, change became a completely pervasive feature of social life. It was presented as a fundamental internal phenomenon in addition to the purely external factors which would in some measure account for many of the cyclical phenomena.

Even in its most abstract formulation, *The Theory of Economic Development* opened new vistas in the interpretation of economic history. When expanded in *Business Cycles*, all these features of the theory became explicit. Nothing less is at stake than a massive revision of the interpretation of the economic history of Europe since the age of discovery. Many of most important new judgments are presented in the 30 pages at the beginning of the historical section, but there is much important historical material scattered all through *Business Cycles* and through the later volume, *Capitalism, Socialism, and Democracy*. Full documentation of all these revisions of economic history will occupy many historians for many years.

The implications of these new views could not be fully developed by Schumpeter because the elaboration of the criticism of the intuitive philosophy was proceeding slowly throughout the period and is only now emerging as a comprehensive presentation. We now have basic elements of a new epistemology, a revised and extended discussion of logical theory, and a new analysis of behavior.

The modern effort to resolve the dilemma between idealism and materialism reaches far back into the past. It is in fact a revision of the empiricism of Berkeley and Hume. The basic achievements in the modern period, however, first emerge explicitly in the pluralism of William James, and the sociological writing of Gabriel Tarde. These new attitudes were an important factor in the interval from 1895 to 1910. At that time, new work was undertaken by younger men. In philosophy and logic, the outstanding personalities are Bertrand Russell, A. N. Whitehead, Wittgenstein, Carnap, and Clarence I. Lewis. In the field of Gestalt psychology, Wertheimer, Kohler, and Kafka dominated the development of the new points of view. These men were contemporaries of Schumpeter, and their work developed at about the same time as his.

Much important work on the empirical philosophy was coming out during the late stages of the composition of *Business Cycles*, but even now there is little literature dealing explicitly with the impact of these new views upon the social sciences. Schumpeter was obliged to work with the old tools of analysis, though each new problem he encountered revealed vividly the inadequacy of the idealistic categories and techniques of analysis.

III

The ever widening gap between his objectives and the techniques available to him was not without consequences. It was impossible to deal with some of the problems without new categories and new techniques. Within the limits of space available here, it will be impossible to do more than describe briefly two cases in which fundamental technical difficulties arise. There is a sharp antithesis drawn between the functions of management and the functions of the entrepreneur. There is also a problem in the description and analysis of the secular trend.

Once innovation is conceived as a social process, differences and changes that seem to involve qualitative differences are actually resolved into quantitative differences. The theory of innovation is therefore inconsistent with a qualitative differentiation between routine and novel action. Even when action has been stylized and stabilized by habits and policies, much novelty still emerges. Some forms of novel action are ignored by Schumpeter, and the pervasiveness of novelty is certainly underestimated. It is not possible to refer to any single description of the types of novel behavior that is either comprehensive or adapted to the present problem, but the analysis in Kafka can be summarized roughly in four major classes of activity. Novel behavior emerges on the lowest level as acts of skill, in all forms of activity, economic, artistic, military, hunting, and sport. Invention and discovery develop without clear hierarchical rank in the related fields of material instruments and abstract concepts. Synthetic or concrete value judgments stand at a higher level because they require purposive use of the categories of abstract thought in conjunction with various techniques and skills. The formulation of patterns of action in the form of policies involves a higher degree of synthesis and rests upon materials elaborated at lower levels.

Even at the lowest level, novelty emerges in the execution of acts of skill. The performance of instrumental music affords, perhaps, the greatest possible opportunity for the control of underlying conditions, but even under the best conditions and the highest degree of proficiency each performance has unique elements. The virtuoso is distinguished by his capacity to rise above the level of a routine or perfunctory performance. In golf, conditions are never subject to complete control, so that the individuality of each stroke and each match is explicit. The higher levels of achievement in business life similarly rest upon a capacity for taking pains that rises clearly above the level of perfunctory performance of routine duty. Routine performance is mediocre performance. Innovation in the economic world does not cease to be important at the level of primary policy formulation and the creation of new production functions.

Schumpeter is skeptical of the existence and significance of real trends. "The effects of growth in our sense afford an instance. Their presence undoubtedly accounts for a real trend which, however, is so much overlaid by the effects of other and more important external and internal factors that it cannot be found by any process of curve fitting." [4] In an earlier passage, growth (changes in the population and total savings) is held to be "incapable of producing those fluctuations in industry and trade which interest us here." [5] There are qualifications, but the general conclusion stands: the effects of growth as such are currently absorbed.

The importance of these postulates is revealed more explicitly in another passage: "Increase in productive resources might at first sight appear to be the obvious prime mover in the process of internal change. Physical environment being taken as a constant — that increase resolves itself into increase of population and increase in the stock of producers' goods." [6] The concept of the physical environment suggested here is common, but for these purposes it is certainly inadequate. Productive resources consist of the portion of the total geographic environment made available for economic activity by existing techniques of utilization. For purposes of analysis it is necessary to recognize several types of environment: the total geographical environment, the potential economic environment, the actual economic environment, the immediate economic environment. Potential resources imply probable changes in technology and in market demand. Actual resources are presumably available without appreciable change in either technology or market demand, though many such resources are not now in use. Immediate resources are, of course, resources currently exploited. The total sum of productive resources is, therefore, an explicit function of technology, and is very sensitive to innovation, because potential resources are increased by inventions and discoveries that are not of economic significance at cost levels realizable at that time.

The phenomena of growth are thus closely associated with innovation, and cannot safely be treated as an essentially external factor. A real trend can develop as a result of the factors that are the essential cause of fluctuation. The concepts of "growth" and "development" are defined as qualitative differences,[7] and are represented as dominated respectively by external

[4] *Business Cycles*, Vol. I, p. 204.
[5] *Ibid.*, p. 83.
[6] *Ibid.*, p. 74.
[7] *The Theory of Economic Development*, p. 63.

and internal factors. These interpretations can be defended only in terms of a rather rigid application of the qualitative analysis of the idealistic philosophies. It is peculiarly unfortunate in this connection because it makes it difficult to apply the concept of innovation to major changes over long periods of time.

Schumpeter's treatment of capitalism involves many interesting problems. The conventional outlines of the concept are substantially qualified, and many of the naïve oversimplifications are sharply criticized. But despite all these changes the primary features of the concept as an ideal culture type remain. It can be shown that the retention of these features of the idealistic philosophy makes the tasks of historical analysis more difficult. The modern empirical positions offer alternatives that are certainly more convenient for the historian, and ultimately these newer positions should be more satisfactory as a basis for economic analysis. Adequate discussion of these problems would require much space, and would be out of place in this connection.

The theory of economic development is thus singularly rich in implications. The postulates which seem to be the basis of the analysis are in many respects inconsistent with a fully developed theory of invention. The fundamental thesis carries us far beyond the general conceptual framework of analysis. It is a vivid index of the vision that inspired all of Schumpeter's work — more evident in oral instruction and conversation than in the formal writing. Many economists have been so preoccupied with narrow immediate issues that their work was dated and soon lost all vital significance. Schumpeter's interests were too broad to be dominated even by the engrossing problems of the wars and the inter-war period. He addressed himself to the most difficult tasks in the field and worked on them in what we may legitimately describe as the grand manner. His mind was too eager, too alert, to be limited either by the materials or by the techniques he found ready to his hand. The full realization of the vision, however, will be accomplished in due course. Others will carry the work to its logical conclusions, and fill in the incomplete portions of the design.

SCHUMPETER'S POLITICAL PHILOSOPHY

David McCord Wright

IN this paper we will attempt a review and an evaluation of some of Schumpeter's major ideas on democracy. I wish, however, to disclaim from the first any special private knowledge of Schumpeter's personal views. Curiously enough, in all our years of correspondence and conversation, the question of political *theory* hardly ever obtruded itself. We corresponded and talked at length on economics and sociology but, perhaps because he knew I disagreed with him on some rather fundamental points, he seldom mentioned political ideas. Nevertheless, it is impossible to know a man well without catching something of the flavor of his views on things generally. I did know Schumpeter well, and I hope that what I will have to say will not be wholly misleading.

II

In order to understand Schumpeter's ideas concerning political theory — as expressed, for example, in *Capitalism, Socialism, and Democracy* — and in order to translate them into American context, it is necessary to bear in mind one vital distinction. Schumpeter's concept of democracy was a mechanistic one. The word, he felt, should refer only to a particular *machinery* of government. But I believe that any close student of American constitutional law and ideas will realize that the dominant American democratic tradition has been not merely a mechanistic but an *ethical* one.

In other words, it is impossible, I submit, to read the "founding fathers" — for example, the infinitely revealing pages of the Jefferson-Adams correspondence — without seeing that for them democracy is ultimately the rule of "tolerance," "justice," and "brotherhood," and that mere electoral government is regarded as only a means toward that end and a means concerning which they were always somewhat skeptical.[1]

[1] Cf. *Jefferson and Adams*, Paul Wilstach, ed. (Indianapolis, 1925).

I find it hard to believe, indeed, that Schumpeter ever read the American constitutionalists. His discussion of eighteenth-century democracy is almost wholly in terms of the Continental European tradition stemming from Rousseau.[2] Even Montesquieu is disregarded. Surely Schumpeter had little understanding of Jefferson. For Jefferson emphatically did *not* believe in the unqualified "right" or "wisdom" of the majority.[3] Still more, of course, was this the case with the Federalists. *Both* Jefferson and the Federalists wanted to protect minorities. Of course, each school had a special minority in which it was particularly interested. The Federalists feared the plunder of the rich and drew up the original constitution with that fear very much in mind. Jefferson also saw that danger, but still more he was concerned with the protection of the political dissenter (for whom the Federalists' concern was scarcely red hot), and insisted upon the addition of the "bill of rights" amendments to the constitution.

The basic American political tradition has, therefore, nearly always been skeptical of the unrestrained majority. Jackson, in this connection, differs from Jefferson merely in degree. I doubt if *any* of the hard things Schumpeter has to say about mob rule and the public will would have been "news" to the framers of the American republic (unhappily, however, a good deal of it is news to many modern specialized technicians). My guess would be that Jefferson would say — regarding extreme cases where Schumpeter "lays it on" a bit thickly — that, of course, such irrationalities, hysteria, etc., were exactly what he prophesied when he spoke of the danger of our being "piled upon ourselves in the cities" like the mobs of Europe.

[2] J. A. Schumpeter, *Capitalism, Socialism, and Democracy* (New York, 1947), Chap. XXI, "The Classical Doctrine of Democracy."

[3] Cf. *Jefferson and Adams, op. cit.*; Bernard Mayo, *Jefferson Himself* (Boston, 1942).

III

But I doubt if Schumpeter would have changed his definition even if he had gone in for a detailed analysis of the American tradition. In my *Democracy and Progress* I distinguished between "ethical" and "ballot box" democracy.[4] Yet, in one of the few conversations we ever had on political theory, Schumpeter expressed himself quite unfavorably (and forcibly) concerning such a distinction. It seemed to him "unscientific."

The truth is we should never forget that Schumpeter was profoundly influenced by positivist philosophy. He tended, that is, to lay stress wherever possible on the "objectively" observable and measurable. To be sure, he was not always consistent about this. The increasing emphasis upon ideology which distinguishes his later years is not wholly to be reconciled with naïve positivism. Also he said "facts as facts are a mere meaningless jumble."[5] Yet his bias is always to avoid the emotional and qualitative if one can. He spoke of himself as a "positive" scientist.

Now the trouble with talking about "ethical" democracy is that it equates "true" democracy simply with a "good" society. And thus one cannot talk about "democracy" without landing oneself plump in the middle of the problem of the "good, the true, and the beautiful," which — at least the first and last parts — the scientific mind flees as the devil is said to flee Holy Water.

Schumpeter, however, did not really succeed in avoiding the value problem. And here I must stop to defend the memory of a man who was one of the kindest and most generous of individuals. Schumpeter was *not* the mere cynic many people considered him. He did feel and feel deeply.[6] He had values, and his values were those common to all sharers of the Western Christian tradition. He believed in mercy, tolerance, and loyalty. He believed in keeping compulsion at a minimum, in kindliness and friendship. If his economics looks "hard-boiled" to us, we must remember that he never advocated or tolerated "coercion," "aggression," or "conflict" for its own sake. He only felt, on the basis of a profound historical knowledge, that the vestiges of those forces which we find in Capitalism were probably the "least worst" forms of them which he knew. All societies, he felt (I think rightly, and so would such liberals as Reinhold Niebuhr), are bound to contain some element of coercive evil. Thus Schumpeter was not a Utopian. But even when a man disagrees with him in his estimate of the dangers of removing particular social strains, or concerning their relative importance, he ought to realize that the most ardent liberal socialist and Schumpeter are nevertheless common bearers of much the same ethical tradition.

IV

Thus, thinking it over, one comes to realize that what annoyed Schumpeter was not so much the references to "values" as the attempt to equate the "good" society, in an ethical sense, with a particular political mechanism. In the "mental experiment" section of his chapter on democracy he does in fact develop, though in different terms, precisely the same ethical-versus-ballot box distinction which he criticized to me.[7] But he does so in order to maintain that the one standard does not necessarily imply the other. And what man of experience can deny that the two *do* sometimes diverge? As I have put it: "If democracy were only majority rule, what would be more

[4] Cf. David McCord Wright, *Democracy and Progress* (New York, 1948), Chap. III: "Modern thinking is perpetually confused by a tendency to consider democratic government as an automatic cure for our problems rather than an additional problem in itself."

[5] J. A. Schumpeter, *Business Cycles* (New York, 1939), p. 30.

[6] It should of course be realized that since Schumpeter, for the most part, did not object to dictators *qua* dictators, but only to *bad* dictators he naturally would appear cynical to many.

The other charge often made against Schumpeter was that he "permitted" the Austrian inflation and should have

resigned rather than continue in office. This criticism is easier to make than to evaluate. I have no doubt that he fought the inflationary measures within the cabinet and did all he could to restrain "that untamed wild beast the politician." Nearly every man at some point in his career has to make the choice as to whether he will do more good by "going along" with an organization and arguing behind closed doors, or by frontal opposition. Only the individual directly concerned can really know — and then only years later — which policy was best.

[7] Schumpeter, *Capitalism . . . op. cit.*, pp. 240–43.

democratic than a lynching?" And it should be remembered that we can, in effect, lynch with full ballot and legal formality. Complete and explicit recognition of this point constitutes one of the most unique and most valuable aspects of the American constitutional tradition. I am sorry that Schumpeter should have left this aspect of American thought so much to one side.

But although Schumpeter would have approved Jefferson's realism concerning the majority, Jefferson's tirades concerning the "race of kings" would have struck him as absurd — or perhaps as naïve.[8] The idea that an absolute ruler must always be "unjust" or stupid, and the mass mind relatively fair and tolerant, seemed to him ridiculous. And when one considers the circumstances of his life, this is not surprising. The empire of Franz Joseph, under which he spent his youth, may have imprisoned some radicals and some nationalists. But compare it with Hitler's gas chambers! Yet it is undeniable that Hitler during a considerable period did have the support of the majority.

Thus I believe that Schumpeter felt that the rule of a dynasty or oligarchy, even of quite an absolutist nature, but with strong family traditions of kindness, tolerance, and public service would be likely to give just as good results as many political democracies, and much better results than sheer mob rule. Dr. Arthur Schlesinger, Jr.'s *The Vital Center* shows, I believe, that even some modern American liberals can find a degree of sense in rather similar propositions.[9] But, however that may be, one must always consider Schumpeter's views in the light of his European background and of European history. The businessman, he said, "needs a master" and has "no political sense."[10] Was he not thinking of the sort of "partnership" that existed between the Imperial governments and the businessmen of the

Central Powers before the first world war, or between the British aristocracy and the British businessman of the nineteenth century?[11]

V

The foregoing sketch gives the essentials, I believe, of Schumpeter's political outlook. It remains, first, to apply these views to his dicta on socialist democracy, and, second, to evaluate them generally.

From what I have said about Schumpeter's mechanistic concept of democracy, and from any reading of his work, it should be clear that his statement that there was a "chance" (he conceded no more than that) that socialism would be "democratic" does not mean very much in terms of American ideals of democracy. By democracy he meant merely "that institutional arrangement for arriving at political decisions in which *individuals* acquire the power to *decide* by means of a competitive struggle for the people's votes" (italics added) or "free competition for a free vote"[12] — in other words, some form of popular or parliamentary government in which there is relative freedom to compete for leadership.

So he thought, in effect, that there was an off chance that a socialist society could continue to have parliamentary government and "free" competition for leadership. This did *not* mean, however, that such a government, even if it managed to exist, would necessarily be tolerant, or that it would necessarily be "just," or that it would realize any of the various ideals of worker "participation" or "industrial democracy" which the intellectuals of the labor movement like to talk of, or even that it would be administratively efficient. *All* that was meant is that the naked political mechanism of ruler selection might possibly hang on, if, among other things, the vast majority of the people were such convinced socialists, *and* so agreed on fundamentals that they could allow a great deal of competition for the job of administering the system. "In any case that democracy will not mean increased personal freedom. And, once more, it will mean no closer

---

[8] Cf. *Jefferson Himself*, op. cit.

[9] A. M. Schlesinger, Jr., *The Vital Center* (Boston, 1949). I do not wish to misrepresent Dr. Schlesinger's views. All that I mean is that his chapter on the "Failure of the Right" shows an appreciation of the good element in paternal aristocracy which has been rare in this country since the downfall of the Confederacy. One can, however, appreciate the good parts of such a system without adopting it. See the text below.

[10] Schumpeter, *Capitalism . . .*, op. cit., pp. 137–38.

[11] *Ibid.*, p. 136.

[12] *Ibid.*, pp. 269, 271.

approximation to the ideals enshrined in the classical doctrine." [13]

VI

The writer is even less optimistic than Schumpeter concerning the survival, over the long pull, of socialist "democracy" even if the word is given as barren a meaning as he gave it. My reasons for skepticism are, however, rooted in the evaluation of his general political philosophy, and it will help to treat the two together. Since space is limited, I must content myself with a few notes.

I have said that the problem of the "good, and the beautiful" probably has no "scientific" solution.[14] This does not mean, however, that it need have no democratic solution or that science cannot help in solving it. The basic problem involved in evaluating economic (and cultural) systems lies in the fact that one type of culture will stress and implement one ideal of the "good" life and "good" achievement, and another another. Now *if* we accept the basic ideals of tolerance and persuasion — and there is no use talking about democracy at all if we do not — then the way to choose among social systems and their concomitant "culture-concepts" is by presenting to the people *full* statements of the implications of each alternative ideal, and then letting *them* choose. Schumpeter is right, in this connection, that the people *per se* seldom *originate* such ideals, especially new ones, but he slurs over the very real negative veto function that they do have.[15]

Now while "science" alone cannot make the final choice among culture-concepts (those who think otherwise will always be found to have smuggled some culture-concept in through the back door), it does have a tremendous amount to contribute in the way of information useful *toward* making the choice. For example, the proposition, "security is better than growth," is both non-scientific and non-economic. As economists, we must simply take it or leave it. But the proposition, "*absolute* individual security cannot be combined with continuing growth in output per head," is a straightforwardly scientific and economic statement.[16] Furthermore, it is obvious that the knowledge that there will always be some degree of conflict between the standards of growth and of security helps a lot in making decisions. It becomes no longer possible validly to reject a system solely on the ground that it involves *some* insecurity. If we want growth, we are forced — where security is concerned — to deal in terms of "least worsts."

VII

This prologue brings me to the basic issue of evaluating Schumpeter's ideas and political philosophy. Intellectually speaking, I am quite willing to concede to him almost everything he has to say about possible benevolent rulers — provided that the concept is restricted to special groups of people with special ideals of life. It seems to me that we cannot scientifically deny that there have been tribes of people who enjoyed routine and were content to live under benevolent, "kindly," paternal absolutism. If I were forced to make so terrible a choice, I would, like Schumpeter, rather live under a tolerant absolutism of aristocratic *noblesse oblige* than a rabid, prejudiced, lynching majority of the Hitler type. But since we are not yet faced with such a choice of evils — and surely do not need to be — let us talk of something a bit more relevant.

Among the values which have hitherto shaped the American culture concept have been belief in independent opportunity, rising living standards, tolerance, satisfaction through activity. These are not the only possible values, but they happen to have been "our" values. My

[13] *Ibid.*, p. 302.

[14] There are numerous pseudo-scientific solutions, especially the Thomistic one. But most of them — especially the latter — will be found to be in the last analysis an elaborate manipulation of *ad hoc* definitions.

[15] To me the role of the populace in our democracy very closely resembles that of a jury before whom the leaders (lawyers) argue. But I would go further than Schumpeter and say that there can sometimes be more or less spontaneous upsurges or popular feeling — though even these must be implemented as to detailed policy by the leaders. Cf. J. A. Rosenfarb, *Freedom and the Administrative State* (New York, 1947). Of course, the effectiveness of the democratic solution outlined here may fail, as Schumpeter suggests, where the people are deeply split on *qualitative* values.

[16] Even so "liberal" a writer as Dr. Alfred Lauterbach in his *Freedom and Security: Can We Have Both?* (Ithaca, N. Y., 1948) reaches, albeit with some semantic circumlocution, precisely this conclusion.

thesis, for years, has been that such standards are linked together in a very close and special way, and that they are also very closely associated with the problems of democratic government and economic growth. The trouble with the "tolerant" absolutisms is that they are "kindly" only as long as their basic power and culture assumptions are not seriously challenged. Start "stirring things up" and the change is almost instantaneous.

Now in a stationary socialism with no technical change and none generally desired there would, indeed, be very little to disagree about, and it would be possible to confine election decisions to very broad general questions, etc., etc. I refer the reader to Schumpeter's list of requirements.[17] However, there still remain two questions to be considered:

First of all, such a stationary state — any stationary state — must have some means of keeping itself stationary. But I believe that in every generation of every culture there will be found at the least a few people who speculate about other possibilities of doing things — both technologically and socially — and who are not content to rest at mere speculation. Such men must be quietly eliminated or forced into line if the static culture is to remain undisturbed. They cannot be allowed "freely" to compete for leadership, on any dangerous scale, or to upset the industrial routine by new methods. But our mores do not, in theory anyhow, as yet approve of such authoritarian smothering of novelty. Thus we have a dilemma which I have summed up elsewhere as follows: "If we make men 'free' they become creative (questioning), and if they become creative they create trouble, and also, in many cases, growth."[18] Thus the emergence of unstabilizing novelty is an almost inevitable concomitant of what in this country has been considered "freedom."

VIII

The final question to be considered concerns the problem of growth. If the chances of socialist "democracy" (i.e., under Schumpeter's terminology, the survival of electoral government) depend, as he says, upon the avoidance

[17] Schumpeter, *Capitalism . . ., op. cit.*, pp. 289–96.
[18] Wright, *Democracy and Progress, op. cit.*, p. 197.

of important conflicts between groups, then it is vital that we consider what the introduction of the factor of growth will do to pressure group problems under socialism. But just here we find two tremendously important omissions from *Capitalism, Socialism, and Democracy.* First of all, nearly always in the book Schumpeter compares what is tacitly a *stationary* socialism with a developing capitalism.[19] Next, the analysis of motivation — especially in connection with the socialist chapters — is very narrowly "economic."

But it is not enough to ask whether socialism can effect a single massive redirection of industry and resources. The real question is: Can it *continue* to do so — as must be done if output per head is to rise, or creativity be implemented?[20] Again it is not enough to say that everybody will have a guaranteed income from the state, and then conclude that because this is the case, the great psychological insecurities relating to power, prestige, the instinct of work-

[19] To be sure Schumpeter does mention the bare bones of the problem, pp. 178–79, but he does not, I submit, ever really incorporate the problem of large scale *continuing* change into his socialist model. A "once-over" change (in Harrod's terminology) and a continuing change require very different institutional environments.

It is notable that where Schumpeter really does glance at the problem, as in his capitalism section, he is much less jaunty. For example (*Capitalism . . .*, p. 98): "Even the most patient of comrades would revolt if a socialist management were so foolish as to follow the advice of the theorist and to keep on scrapping plant and equipment every year."

I have discussed the Schumpeterian growth model in more detail in my obituary article "Schumpeter and Keynes," *Weltwirtschaftliches Archiv* (University of Kiel, 1950).

[20] Cf. Schumpeter, *Capitalism . . ., op. cit.*, pp. 131 ff. In this section Schumpeter's narrowly economic scheme of human motivation is particularly apparent. He overlooks the non-economic sources of pressure groups. Cf. David McCord Wright, *The Economics of Disturbance* (New York, 1947), Chap. III; also *Capitalism* (New York, 1950), Chap. I. Schumpeter highly praised the *Disturbance* chapter.

It seems to me that in his "obsolescence" doctrine Schumpeter showed a lack of experience with the inside workings of big business and big government. Though people may in general expect change and though its discovery may be sometimes automatic, the writer's experience in business and government has been that always the *introduction* of a large-scale departure from routine has required the "personality and will power" of some *individual* who "spark plugs" the group. Such an individual need not, of course, be very prominent externally or possessed of much *legal* power.

manship, friendship, and love of familiar things will not still present great barriers to technical change. I almost wholly dissent from Schumpeter's doctrine of the obsolescence of the entrepreneurial function.

Thus, to conclude, the pressure group problems raised by growth plus the emphasis on security will be likely to create, under socialism, or other regimes of *comprehensive, centralized* planning a general industrial and political stalemate.[21] Those who wish to introduce novelty — be it sociological or technical — will be forced to challenge this stalemate. But the group in power can scarcely permit such an unstabilizing development, and they will have readily at hand an important weapon: economic coercion. For holding the whip hand over the economic prospects of every region, industry, and even every large periodical in the country, the opposition can nearly always be choked off or driven underground — sometimes subtly, sometimes harshly. The possible survival of a shell of elective government under such circumstances hardly seems worth bothering about. And it could scarcely permit even Schumpeter's minimum degree of "freedom" of competition for leadership.

[21] Cf. the distinction in my *Democracy and Progress, op. cit.*, between planning and centralized planning; also *Capitalism, op. cit.*, Chap. v.

IX

The analysis given here is only a desperately compressed version of ideas enlarged upon in my books.[22] Only three more things remain to be said. First of all, I sometimes think the best way to hide one's thoughts is to print them in a book and publish them. It passes my comprehension how anyone who really reads my books can confuse my suggestion that there are possible limitations to the desirability of planning with suggestions of an advocacy of unmitigated *laissez faire*, or the hundred per cent eternally-balanced budget, or anything of that sort.

Next, and much more important, if I have pointed out some errors or rather, in most cases, some omissions in Schumpeter's analysis, this is not to minimize the wealth and keenness of his insight. If I think I can go further than he, I know that that is, in most cases, only because of the pioneer scouting which he had already done.

And finally, to paraphrase a well-known novel, "If I have not cast this epistle in terms of affection it is because I feared that if I did, I would lack the eyes to finish it."

[22] Wright, *Democracy and Progress, op. cit.; The Economics of Disturbance, op. cit.*, Chap. VII; *Capitalism, op. cit.*

SCHUMPETER AND KEYNES

Arthur Smithies

WHAT a misfortune it is that twentieth century economics is not enriched by a Schumpeter-Keynes correspondence. Despite an acquaintanceship of over twenty years, those two eminent figures apparently remained at arm's length intellectually. There is no reference to Schumpeter in the *General Theory*, and references to him in the *Treatise on Money* consist of hardly more than a quotation from Mitchell summarizing Schumpeter's view of innovation. There is no hint that Keynes was aware that Schumpeter was the creator of a system. On Schumpeter's side there is equally little evidence of intellectual indebtedness to Keynes. There are a few scattered references to his work in *Business Cycles*; and in *Capitalism, Socialism, and Democracy* the references are uniformly hostile to the Keynesian point of view. Even in his memorial article [1] Schumpeter did not credit Keynes with a single major improvement in the technique of economic analysis. His admiration was confined to the skill with which Keynes constructed a vehicle to convey his ideology — an ideology that, in Schumpeter's view, rivals Marx in undermining the pillars of capitalism. There was no compromise, no hint of a concession that Keynes might have prepared the way toward an enlightened conservatism.

Schumpeter's objections to Keynesian doctrine went far deeper than those of many other anti-Keynesians, which were largely concerned with trivia, such as the definition of saving. It is therefore important that they be understood and assessed. It is also of interest to consider what Schumpeter's fear of Greek gifts deprived him of in the way of tools of analysis that he could have used to improve his own system. I shall discuss the latter question first.

II

Viewed purely as explanatory systems the theories of Keynes and Schumpeter can serve as complements to each other. Keynes dealt

[1] *American Economic Review*, 1946, p. 495.

formally with phenomena whose range is limited by his assumption that techniques of production remain unchanged. Schumpeter's main strength was in his analysis of the process of capitalistic development, where changing technique is of the essence of the matter. His lack of precision and definiteness lay precisely in his treatment of those phenomena with which the Keynesian theory is expressly designed to deal. In my opinion he could have incorporated the whole of it, or an improved version of it, into his own theory without prejudice to any of the essentials of his point of view. Three examples will illustrate what I mean:

(1) Schumpeter could have supplied some important missing links to his theory of interest by incorporating Keynes' theory with his own. He devoted most of his argument to his contention that the demand for loanable funds depends on the prospect of entrepreneurial profit, but he is quite inconclusive on the subject of the supply of funds. This depends upon conditions in the money market, but it is by no means clear how conditions in the money market are related to the behavior of the rest of the economic system. Keynes' theory, on the other hand, shows how the rate of interest depends, not only on monetary factors, but on saving and the profitability of investment as well. Of course, Keynes' theory as it stands in the *General Theory* is rudimentary: price changes, for instance, are only implicitly taken into account, and he does not even discuss the banking system. But he did point out the way in which Schumpeter could have completed his theory. Further, the Keynesian relation of liquidity preference to uncertainty and the tendency for interest to fall as stationary state is approached should have been particularly congenial to Schumpeter.

(2) Keynesian and neo-Keynesian techniques could have improved Schumpeter's explanation of the secondary wave in his business-cycle model. They might have been used to provide a complete explanation of the short cycles where the explanation in terms of inno-

vation seems unconvincing. Had Schumpeter made these phenomena the subject of a dynamic analysis on the lines of the familiar Keynesian models, e.g., that of Hicks and Goodwin,[2] the essential rôle of the innovating entrepreneur in the capitalist process would have been clarified rather than obscured. But to this suggestion Schumpeter might well have retorted that he had no patience with the spurious precision that can be achieved by making highly artificial assumptions.

(3) Schumpeter of course denied that there can be any chronic tendency toward oversaving or overinvestment, but asserted that at the completion of every cycle the economy achieves a state of Walrasian equilibrium. This is one of his most heroic and least necessary assumptions. With modern rigidities and, especially, with modern fiscal policies, it is impossible to ignore the possibility of chronic imbalance. And whether the economy has a persistent inflationary bias or a persistent deflationary bias may have an important bearing on Schumpeter's main concern — the process of capitalistic development.

A synthesis on the lines I have suggested will undoubtedly be made, but it will do nothing to remove the real antagonism between the Schumpeterian and the Keynesian points of view.

III

Keynes' indifference to Schumpeter and Schumpeter's hostility to Keynes stem largely from the fact that Keynes was a lineal descendant of the English Utilitarians [3] while Schumpeter had no Utilitarian blood in his veins. Keynes regarded worth-while theory as a basis for programs of action. Schumpeter's theory led him to look with foreboding upon all action to which such theories and programs might lead.

Keynes' intellectual history parallels that of John Stuart Mill. Mill was brought up on the Benthamite creed that if Government made fair rules to govern the general relations of individuals, the best individuals could be relied on to win in open competition, and that legislative reform efforts should be mainly directed to that end. While Mill adhered to that creed with respect to production, he abandoned much of it with respect to the distribution of income. He came to recognize that the distribution of wealth depends on the laws of society, and to achieve equity went much further than Bentham or James Mill in his advocacy of state intervention. His land reform proposals, for instance, almost amounted to nationalization.[4]

Keynes, confronted with twentieth century issues, carried Mill heterodoxy into the area of production itself. While he agreed that with a given total demand and distribution of income, individualism, subject to proper regulations, could achieve an optimum allocation of resources, he believed that both the distribution of income and the level of effective demand should be subject to the control of the state.

Both Mill and Keynes believed that Utilitarian principles could and should be applied not only to the regulations made by the state but to positive programs executed by the state. They believed that representative governments would control the production and distribution of wealth, according to rational principles that advanced the general well-being.

To Schumpeter, the product of an entirely different tradition, all that made little sense. Let him speak for himself:

There is no scientific sense whatever in creating for one's self some metaphysical entity to be called "The Common Good" and a not less metaphysical "State," that, sailing high in the clouds and exempt from and above human struggles and group interests, worships at the shrine of that Common Good. But the economists of all times have done precisely this. While perfectly aware, of course, of the fact that the business process must be understood from the businessman's interest, most of them have been blind to the no less obvious fact that the political process and hence political meas-

[2] J. R. Hicks, *The Trade Cycle* (Oxford, 1950); R. M. Goodwin, Chap. 22 in Alvin H. Hansen, *Business Cycles and National Income* (New York, 1951).

[3] I make this statement despite Keynes' emphatic rejection of hedonism as an ethical principle and "benthamism" as an economic principle. (See "My Early Beliefs" in *Two Memoirs* by J. M. Keynes, New York, 1951.) I have discussed Keynes more elaborately in a forthcoming article in the *Quarterly Journal of Economics*.

[4] Professor Viner, who read the first draft of this paper, probably still thinks I have drawn too sharp a distinction between Mill and his predecessors. On this compare his admirable article on Mill and Bentham (*American Economic Review*, March 1949, p. 360) and Leslie Stephen, *The English Utilitarians*, Vol. III.

ures that affect economic life must be understood from the politician's interest. . . .

And political science itself was in general as little concerned about the facts of its subject matter and as prone to philosophize on this very same common good and popular will. It was, therefore, a major scientific merit of Marx that he hauled down the state from the clouds and into the sphere of realistic analysis.[5]

If production and distribution were exposed to government action, it would be inevitable, in Schumpeter's view, that the politician's interest would lead him to support, in the main, anti-capitalist measures, such as highly progressive taxation and heavy death duties. This would be especially true in modern societies where the social and political position of the business class had already been largely undermined. If only capitalism is permitted by governments to do its work, the meek shall inherit the earth. The factory girl shall have her silk stockings and the queens shall be dispossessed.

IV

The main burden of Schumpeter's charge against Keynes is not that he pursued the will-o'-the-wisp of state action for the common good, but that he made it intellectually respectable for other non-socialists to go further in an anti-capitalist direction than he had any inclination to go himself. He tore down the barriers, imposed by the classical economics and the Benthamite tradition, that had restrained the advocates of intervention in the past and that had provided the basis for an effective intellectual opposition.

In Schumpeter's words, Keynes destroyed "the last pillar of the bourgeois argument," private saving,[6] and, during the thirties made it possible for his followers to justify almost any policy provided it increased the propensity to consume. I do not believe that Keynes intended or desired to bring about this result, but I agree that he may have done so. While he probably admired abstinence and thrift no more than Schumpeter did himself, he had no desire to hasten the advent of the proletarian state. He and Schumpeter viewed "laborism" with the same distaste. The result came about because many Keynesians, under Keynes' influence, were prepared to use the short-run analysis of the *General Theory* to settle long-run issues.

As we have noted, Keynes based the *General Theory* on the assumption that productive capacity and productive techniques remained unchanged. Schumpeter therefore says, "the phenomena that dominate the capitalistic process, are thus excluded from consideration." [7] But this is by no means the interpretation that has been given to the *General Theory* by most Keynesians. Their view has rather been that if the state looks after the short run, the long run will look after itself. Keynes himself, would, I believe, have subscribed to the weaker proposition that if the state does not look after the short run, the long run will not look after itself. This is a position that, in different circumstances and with proper qualifications, Schumpeter might well have been persuaded to accept.

If the entire economic problem is merely one of maintaining full employment in the short run, the main arguments that have been advanced in the past for private saving do indeed disappear. The demand for commodities is the demand for labor, and the classical dogma that it is not becomes an absurdity. Measures to increase the propensity to consume stand on an equal footing with those designed to increase investment. Government consumption is as good as private consumption, and, from an economic point of view, it does not matter in whose political interest it is undertaken. Full employment, economic growth, and redistribution of income are all compatible. The slogan "recovery *versus* reform" embodies no economic truth but only political reaction.

No wonder Schumpeter protested. Even if short-run policies were based on some notion of the common good rather than on the flow of the political tides, they would be anti-capitalistic in his view. The rich entrepreneurial rewards that he held essential for capitalistic success emphatically do not conform to Utilitarian standards of equity in the short run. Short-run inequity is the price that must be paid by the masses for the rising living standards that capitalism can achieve.

[5] Joseph A. Schumpeter, "The Communist Manifesto," *Journal of Political Economy*, June 1949, p. 199.
[6] *American Economic Review*, 1946, p. 517.
[7] *Ibid.*, p. 512.

Whether Schumpeter or the Keynesians are correct will probably be settled only long after the practical issue has ceased to be relevant. So far the result is indecisive. Productivity in American industry has increased with obstinate insistence throughout the Old Deal, the New Deal, and the Fair Deal. Schumpeter contended that anti-capitalist attitudes and policies held down private investment in the thirties. With the experience of the forties to support them, Keynesians can argue that whatever depressing effects such attitudes may have had, they can be offset by a sufficient governmental stimulus to effective demand.

On the other hand, Schumpeter could and did insist that it was contradictory to treat the entrepreneur as a social outcast and at the same time to rely on him as the mainspring of economic growth. But Schumpeter would also argue, with wry satisfaction, that Keynesian attitudes and policies have destroyed the immunity of the capitalist world to the Keynesian malady. He would reject with scorn political advice that called for a return to the conditions of capitalistic success. Had he set out to devise a program rather than to emphasize a point of view that seemed to him to be in serious degree of neglect, he would have included Keynesian safeguards as well as safeguards against Keynesian excess.

V

Keynes' influence not only encouraged governments to take a short-run point of view, but it helped to free them from the major traditional restraints on short-run action. Keynes' efforts can fairly be described as a general attempt to free governments from all obstacles to action; and the wisdom of that effort depends on the extent to which governments are capable of rational action for the common good. Support for the international gold standard, a "free" money market, and the balanced budget succumbed to his attack. And at a time when ancient practices and traditional beliefs seemed to obstruct all efforts to rescue the world from its economic misery, which of us, brought up in the Utilitarian tradition, could fail to applaud?

Schumpeter must have felt all this to be exceedingly naïve. He must also have thought it naïve to regard Keynesianism as a reversible process. Mechanically the *General Theory* provided the cure for inflation as well as deflation. But whether it provided the political remedy is more doubtful. No country was prepared to follow Keynes very far on *How to Pay for the War;* and it remains to be seen how far any country will follow his teaching in a state of partial mobilization. The political line of least resistance is to suppress inflation rather than to cure it.

Credit control could stop the wage-price spiral in its tracks — at the cost of some unemployment until labor and management realized that the government was serious. But when the president of one of the country's largest corporations publicly states that a little more inflation is better than a strike, what political support is there for credit restriction on a scale that would be effective?

Some observers reconcile themselves to the idea that the way out of the dilemma is to resort to compulsory controls of wages and prices. But is this a way out or is it merely a transfer of the dilemma to a different sphere? If governments will not take rational action in the monetary sphere, are they more likely to be rational in the field of direct controls? Control systems worked during the war to the extent that countries were dominated by an overwhelming political objective and were therefore prepared to surrender economic powers to executive authorities who could act in pursuance of that objective. Wartime experience thus furnishes no reliable guide to the requirements of a permanent policy. A satisfactory resolution of our present dilemma is unlikely unless it is recognized that Schumpeter was partially right about the impossibility of rational government action. It is also unlikely if everyone accepts the view that he was wholly right.

VI

So far I have taken as correct Schumpeter's opinion that Keynes' influence exacerbated anti-capitalist attitudes and fostered anti-capitalist policies. Another view, which I have always held myself, is that not only Keynes' intention but to some extent his achievement was to rescue as much of capitalism as the strong political currents of the time would permit. With respect to the United States, is it unreasonable to argue that the short-run view was inevitable in the thirties and that unbalanced budgets came about through the force of necessity rather than the weight of argument? Was not the monetary system destined to come under political control with the establishment of the Federal Reserve System in 1914? England did not leave the gold standard in 1931 from choice, and the systems of exchange control and trade discrimination that now hamper world trade find general support in Keynes' writings. May he not have introduced some degree of rationality into a situation that was inevitably chaotic?

Schumpeter criticizes Keynes because he refused to "bend the full force of his mind to the individual problems of coal, textiles, steel, shipbuilding, and instead supported resolution of England's difficulties through 'monetary management.'"[8] But are not the aggregative fiscal and monetary policies that Keynes did recommend less anti-capitalistic in their import than any governmental policy that attempts to deal with a general economic problem on a specific industry basis? The policies of the early New Deal were far more radical than the fiscal program in 1938 which was more directly influenced by Keynes. During the early period, recovery and reform were commingled and to some extent in conflict. In 1938 policy was more directly aimed at recovery.

I find it difficult to agree with Schumpeter's contention that "practical Keynesianism is a seedling which cannot be transplanted into foreign soil: it dies there and becomes poisonous before it dies."[9] On the contrary, it seems to me that aggregative policies are the only kind of policies that can be consistent with private enterprise in the vastly complex U. S. economy. In England, on the other hand, it may be possible, and indeed necessary, to solve some of the most difficult problems by programs specifically related to the country's major industries.

It may be significant that conservative organizations in the United States — such as the Committee for Economic Development — advocate economic stabilization through the Keynesian monetary and fiscal devices. Schumpeter, however, might have retorted that this was just another instance of the propensity of the bourgeoisie to destroy itself. In fact, he did just that when he charged that, in their advocacy of Keynesian stabilization policies, the English economists, Pigou, Robbins, Tewkes, and others, had accepted laborism.[10]

Whether or not Keynes' own influence was, on balance, conservative or radical would hardly be a worth-while subject for argument were it not for the tendency, encouraged by Schumpeter, to reject, in the name of conservatism, everything connected with his name. Whatever the situation might have been without him, Pandora's box is now open, and Keynesian theory can contribute to a conservative solution of some of the problems its author may have helped to create. Historians may decide that Keynes' work as a whole can be described as "an attempt to use what we have learnt from modern experience and modern analysis, not to defeat, but to implement the wisdom of Adam Smith."[11] This Schumpeter refused to admit.

VII

Keynes' last published work was his posthumous article on "The U. S. Balance of Payments."[12] At about the same time, Schumpeter included in the second edition of *Capitalism, Socialism, and Democracy* a long final chapter on economic prospects in the postwar world.

Keynes' article was a plea to allow the "classical medicine" to do its work in removing the alleged chronic dollar shortage and a vehement protest against "modernist stuff, gone wrong and turned sour and silly." One can conjecture that, had he lived, he might have given similar advice on some aspects of domestic policy. Had he come to realize that the economic system, like the human psyche, works best when it is imperfectly understood? The classical medicine did work when its operation was a mystery, understood if at all by

[8] *American Economic Review*, 1946, pp. 505–6.
[9] *Ibid.*, p. 506.
[10] *Journal of Political Economy*, 1949, p. 371.
[11] This was Keynes' own characterization of Bretton Woods and the Anglo-American Loan Agreement; see *Economic Journal*, 1946, p. 186.
[12] *Ibid.*

the high priests of finance under whose aegis it was administered. Is it reasonable to expect that governments will employ the classical remedy when they know that the cure will be painful? Or can they be expected to surrender their newly-won power in favor of some automatic mechanism that will remove important economic adjustments from the sphere of political influence? Schumpeter's arguments would lead to the conclusion that such expectations were exceedingly naïve: it was as unlikely that governments would surrender their power as that they would act rationally. It is hardly necessary to add that Keynes' last words of advice have received scant official attention on either side of the Atlantic.

Schumpeter's last practical testament has become almost a commonplace since he wrote it, but it was novel in 1946 and still more novel when he presented the same point of view in his first edition in 1942. But no other economist that I know of perceived as clearly and as early as he did the critical importance of the rate of increase of total output. As he said, if output did increase in the future at the rate it has increased in the past all the dreams of the social reformers could come true. But if policy was directed to immediate redistribution, neither the aims of reformers nor the increase of output would be realized. While there are of course shades of opinion, hardly any modern observer of the national or the international scene would reject his contention in its entirety. His argument has gained importance from the fact that it is now national security rather than social betterment that depends on the rate of increase of output.

To attain the rate of increase of output that would permit social programs to be undertaken without strain to the economy, Schumpeter believed that several essential conditions must be met. First, the tax system should be revised to create conditions favorable to entrepreneurship — through the elimination of double taxation of corporate profits, increased reliance on sales taxes, and reduction of death duties. Second, efficiency must be achieved in government expenditure programs, and unemployment compensation rates must be held well below current wage rates. Third, prices, interest, and wage rates must be taken out of politics. Fourth, inflation must be avoided by "highly unpopular" but unspecified measures.

While he had no optimism that such a program would be undertaken, he did present it as the possible program for a postwar American government that by no means represented the entrepreneurial interest exclusively. Such a program would differ materially from a Keynesian program — though perhaps not radically from one constructed by Keynes himself — but it would involve greater political difficulties. A government that adopted it would not only have to deny itself the right of action in important fields, but would have to resist the strongest political currents. I do not suggest that Schumpeter became a Utilitarian, but he evidently did come to believe that state action for a common purpose was possible and desirable.

Difficult though it might be to make capitalism work, Schumpeter's diagnosis showed that the achievement of a *democratic* socialism would give rise to the same difficulties in more acute form. His solution was to surrender most of the economic management of the country to its bureaucracy, and he agreed that governments would be unwilling to forego political action on economic issues until a state of economic maturity had been reached — that is, until no major economic issues remained to be settled. His conclusion was that "socialist democracy may turn out to be more of a sham than capitalist democracy ever was." [13]

Schumpeter's contribution to political economy was not to prove that Keynes was wrong in his conception of the functions of the state, but to show that the way to effective state action was more tortuous and difficult than Keynes was wont to assume. On the other hand, he failed to realize that "that refractory wild beast, the politician," had to be tamed not only by the gentle arts of the bureaucrat but also by intellectuals who believed that there was such a thing as "The Common Good."

VIII

The theme for this paper was suggested to me by Schumpeter's review, in 1933, of Keynes'

[13] *Capitalism, Socialism and Democracy* (New York, 1947, 2nd edition), p. 302.

Essays in Biography.[14] He concluded with these sentences:

A pleasant hour might be passed in piecing together the author's sociology, social philosophy and politics from the abundant material scattered over these pages. In fact, the present writer added another one to his unpublished essays. The resulting picture was strongly suggestive of John Stuart Mill's views. Not indeed in every particular. Mill might have disliked some of the implications of the essay on the Villiers connection.

[14] *Economic Journal*, 1933, p. 652.

But he would have forgiven them on finding, in the essay on Lord Oxford, the term "stupidity" in the neighborhood of the term "conservative." He might have been saddened by evidence of disbelief in the fundamentals of Utilitarianism, but he would surely have been reconciled by still stronger evidence of firm adherence to its spirit and to some of its most important practical consequences. Philosophical radicalism is obviously not dead as yet — spreading among us as it does its generous hopes for humanity and its stout refusal to see in life but a little intermezzo of irritating nonsense between eternities of death.